Aliens in the Backyard

Aliens in the Backyard

Plant and Animal Imports into America

John Leland

University of South Carolina Press

© 2005 University of South Carolina

Published in Columbia, South Carolina,
by the University of South Carolina Press

Manufactured in the United States of America

09 08 07 06 05   5 4 3 2 1

Library of Congress Cataloging-in-Publication Data

Leland, John, 1950–
    Aliens in the backyard : plant and animal imports into America / John Leland.
        p. cm.
    Includes bibliographical references and index.
    ISBN 1-57003-582-2 (cloth : alk. paper)
    1. Biological invasions—United States. 2. Alien plants—United States.
  3. Introduced animals—United States. I. Title.
    QH353.L49 2005
    578.6'2—dc22

                                                                2005000544

Contents

Illustrations

Acknowledgments

This book could not have been written without the help of others. I wish to thank the Virginia Military Institute for encouraging me to pursue a topic only tangentially related to my professional interests and the Jackson-Hope Committee for the generous support and confidence in giving me my first-ever sabbatical. The late Elizabeth Hostetter of the VMI Preston Library was both a helpful colleague, by attaining interlibrary loan materials, and a joy to visit. Diane Jacob and Mary Laura Kludy of the VMI Archives helped me obtain the illustrations that appear in the text. My copy editor, Monica McGee, has been invaluable: her professional and perceptive edits have refined my text and improved the book.

My sisters, Cheves and Elizabeth, kindly read a rough draft of this book, their comments and suggestions improving it greatly; any remaining mistakes or infelicities are mine. My son, Edward, continues to inspire me to discover the stories behind the plants and animals we see on our walks together, and I enjoy revealing to Isabella *les plantes et les animeaux qui sont, comme elle, moitie europeane et moitie americaine.*

Aliens in the Backyard

As American as Apple Pie

An Introduction to Weeds

No Native American ever ate an apple pie before 1492. It couldn't have happened. While there was water aplenty and salt enough, there were no apples for filling, no lemons for juice, no cinnamon or cloves for spice, no sugar (other than maple) for sweetening, no wheat for flour, and no butter for pastry. Nor did any North American Indian before Columbus graze a horse on Kentucky bluegrass, eat an Idaho potato, see Boston ivy growing, get stung by a honeybee, or use a night crawler to catch a brown trout—because none of these was here back then.

Of course, the very notion of an America to be a native of is post-Columbian. The year 1492 is arbitrarily picked as the cutoff for things that came here "naturally." But a "natural" America is a cultural fiction. Not only did the Native Americans bring with them an "un-American" flora and fauna, they also reshaped what they found here, with the result that the forest primeval greeting the first Europeans was less primeval than it was man-made. Our "native" plants and animals themselves were—and still are—on the move. We tend to forget that a mere ten thousand years ago, a continental ice sheet covered everything north of Pennsylvania and boreal forests grew in Florida. What biologists a hundred years ago assumed were age-old forest or prairie communities that would, without human interference, perpetuate themselves as climax communities are thought by some today to have been catch-as-catch-can assemblages of opportunistic plants and animals scrambling northward to colonize land liberated from the Ice Age. Like participants in Mother Nature's version of the Oklahoma Land Rush, plants and animals, independently of each other, pushed farther north each year, light-seeded maples outpacing heavier chestnuts, nimble squirrels leaving slower possums behind, and winged mosquitoes trouncing earthbound worms. Nor did this progression stop with Columbus. Possums plodded into New England only after the colonists had arrived;

armadillos reached the East Coast five hundred years after the Spanish; and we only just managed to kill off the chestnut before it crossed the Great Lakes.

Nevertheless, the European "discovery" of America set off an immense biotic exchange. Tens of thousands (nobody knows the exact number) of alien plants and animals are thought to inhabit North America, and nearly 50 percent of America's threatened or endangered natives are victims of introduced biota. Some places are worse off than others. Exotics have overwhelmed Hawaii, an isolated island that is home to a highly indigenous flora and fauna. Many of its native species are extinct or threatened with extinction. Florida and the Gulf Coast have been inundated with aliens. The distinctive flora of California and the Pacific Northwest is under siege. The Great Lakes are under attack, and the headwaters of the New and Tennessee rivers are in peril.

It's now fashionable to decry the threat aliens pose to our native environments. In some cases, concern is warranted. Who doesn't wish that someone had stopped the chestnut blight, Dutch elm disease, and gypsy moth before they devastated our eastern forests? But the vast majority of alien plants and animals, like the vast majority of human immigrants, are quietly going about their business without really threatening anyone or anything. Like their human analogues, these immigrants often have fascinating stories of how they came to be here, stories that are as much a part of our history as the wars and presidents we studied in school.

Often cited as the "bible" of the environmental costs of nonnative species, the Congressional Office of Technology and Assessment's (OTA) 1993 report, *Harmful Non-Indigenous Species in the United States,* guesstimated that more than four thousand such species call America home. The OTA admitted that this was wildly underestimated, since half of all insects in the United States have yet to be classified, for example, and because it takes into account only the last one hundred years, ignoring the previous ten thousand years of tinkering that began when the first nonindigenous human walked into Alaska with a dog. Not that all nonnatives are bad. Our food is almost entirely un-American. Only the sunflower seeds and Jerusalem artichokes in our groceries can boast American roots. The chickens and their eggs, the cattle, and the pigs we eat are from the Old World. While the rainbow trout or bass that was either just caught or ordered did originate in North America, odds are that the fish was stocked in a river its ancestors could never have reached or in a lake that didn't exist a hundred years ago. The night crawler used to catch the fish came from elsewhere, as did the bamboo pole. Our gardens' lilacs, roses, peonies, lawns, and apple and cherry trees are as nonnative as the animals in our zoos. Even our forests are suspect, with 30 percent of all plants in many of our states originating from other lands. Even those forests sporting made-in-America trees, like southern pine plantations, are probably growing where no such trees grew before commercial forestry took hold.

The OTA had to decide what to call all these plants and animals from elsewhere. They decided that nonindigenous was the least loaded word they could pick. The words *alien* and *foreign* have obvious negative connotations, and *exotic* has equally positive ones. *Nonnative* ignores that many natives are growing where nature never intended them. So nonindigenous it was, meaning "the condition of a species being beyond its natural range or natural zone of potential dispersal." The OTA then had to define "natural range," which means "the geographic area a species inhabits or would inhabit in the absence of significant human influence."[1] All of this seems clear enough until you examine individual cases. I live near a Buffalo Creek and a Buffalo Gap, named after the bison herds that early settlers found grazing in the grassy Shenandoah Valley. But that grassy valley depended on fires set by Native Americans; suppress the fires, and you get cedar trees and forests and few, if any, buffalo. Since the valley was not the bison's natural range, it must have been a nonindigenous species. Was its presence there beneficial, a nuisance, costly, dangerous, or disruptive of ecosystems—all terms the OTA considered in evaluating nonindigenous species? It seems obvious that large herds of bison would have disturbed the natural, forested ecosystem, leading to the odd conclusion that we shouldn't try to restore what the first white explorers in the valley saw—if we want it natural. Since the OTA doesn't go back more than a hundred years, it neatly dodges such issues, which, however, can serve to liven up a moribund environmental discussion.

Are things getting better or worse? Doomsters see a proliferation of unwanted species in a world that feels increasingly smaller. Globalization means more permeable borders. Jet travel means quicker communication between disparate places. Larger ships mean more ballast water jettisoned into harbors and rivers. That's how the zebra mussel first made it into the Great Lakes, from the hold of some lightly loaded ship carrying ballast water taken from the Black Sea or one of its tributaries. Its 1988 discovery was too late. Now it is widely distributed throughout our eastern fresh waters and spreading rapidly, carried hither and yon by both commercial and pleasure craft. "Airport" or "baggage malaria," which is the accidental transport of and infection by malarial mosquitoes trapped in aircraft or luggage, is rare but increasing. Victims sometimes die because doctors in temperate zones are unlikely to test ailing patients for malaria.

Eradicating a nonindigenous species is generally expensive and sometimes impossible. By the time it is discovered, the species may be too safely ensconced to be removed. Such is the case with the zebra mussel and was the case with the gypsy moth, fire ant, killer bee, and other species. Sometimes, the introduction can even be well intended. In 1966 a kid returning from vacation in Hawaii smuggled three giant African snails into Miami, which his grandmother made him let turn loose in the yard. Ten years, eighteen thousand snails, and one million dollars later, Florida officials think they got all of the eight-inch-long snails—voracious devourers of anything green, prodigious baby makers, and disease vectors. In 2002 fish officials in Crofton, Maryland, poisoned a pond in order to eradicate a population of northern snakehead fish. A Hong Kong native had ordered two live fish from New York City to make soup for his sick sister. By the time they arrived, she was well and the man released the fish into the pond, where they multiplied into hundreds, each a saw-toothed, top-of-the-food-chain predator with no enemies, save people, and capable of surviving snowy winters and wiggling overland into other ponds and rivers.

If just what is and isn't native seems problematic, so too does the nature of "invasiveness." Since 30 percent of all the plant species in my home area in Virginia are nonindigenous, odds are that many of the plants I walk by every day are as unnatural inhabitants of the area as am I. Yet, I notice only some of these, the ones that appear to me to be weedy in some way. The most general definition of a weed is "a plant out of place." But this needs amending because we must include animals and because what I think out of place you might not. Field daisies are an example. I like them, and my neighbor farmer does not. He tries to eradicate them; I dig them up and plant them in my garden. While most gardeners might tolerate this poor kin to the Shasta daisy, they probably would draw the line at my Queen Anne's lace, a leggy invasive that even I must extirpate every two or three years.

In addition to being hardy survivalists, weeds also tend to have too many children. One way that ecologists have divided species is into r and K reproductive strategists. The r strategists have many offspring and spend little time and few resources taking care of them. K strategists have few offspring but invest more time and resources in their development. Humans, even the most prodigious of us, have relatively few, precious progeny. Weeds—be they dandelions or cockroaches—have dozens that are left to fend pretty much for themselves. Not only do weedy species have lots of kids, they have them earlier than better-behaved species, being as sexually precocious as some of the people we remember from high school. They also have these offspring in areas that appear inhospitable by most standards, which is often the lot for pioneer species that colonize recently opened land, whether sand dunes, avalanche slopes, volcanoes, or vacant lots. The term for such rude upstarts is *ruderal*, from the Latin for a pile of rubble.

If much of this strikes you as less than hard science, it does me too. Weediness is like Supreme Court Justice Potter Stewart's pornography, difficult to define, but you know it when you see it. What you think of as a weed has implications you never dreamed of. For weeds can be a stand-in for unwanted immigrants: both can be seen as promiscuous, having too many kids, debasing property values, living anywhere, and outcompeting established flora, fauna, and first families. Some letter writers to the *New York Times* declared themselves "Know-Nothings" in their intolerance of the ailanthus tree at the time when the Know-Nothing Party, or American Party, was in bloom in the 1850s. The anti-Catholic, anti-immigration Know-Nothings (so called from their assertion that they knew nothing of the originally secret party) sought to preserve what we now call WASP hegemony. The party's influence foundered on the issue of slavery. The socially prominent landscape architect Andrew Jackson Downing, though not himself a Know-Nothing, declared the ailanthus an usurper. When not confusing weeds with people, we confuse people with weeds. The *New York Times* reported in 1882 of "The Terrible Chinee," warning against allowing these "weeds" into the country. Currently, anti-Arab terrorist Web sites discuss "the wild weeds" of disaffected Arab youths. In what may have been serendipity, but probably wasn't, the fear some white Americans have for everyone and everything unfamiliar coalesced in the 1980s with the advent of Africanized killer bees, whose northward progression from Mexico into Texas provided an insect allegory both of black and white race relations and of the rising tide of Hispanic immigrants. In *Bowling for Columbine*, Michael Moore scores points in a hilarious but revealing look at the pervasive national culture of fear when he shows a news story on Africanized killer bees that are "more aggressive" and have "bigger body parts" than their European rivals.

We are paranoid of things foreign. Even before 9/11 gave support to our fears, they were there, a suspicion that the rest of the world had it out for us. Maybe they do. But this paranoia leaks into areas other than the political and is hard at work in our environmental circles. In the green equivalent of putting a flag decal on an SUV, we are increasingly concerned with exotic, alien, non-native species that threaten our fields and forests. Ignoring the fact that we're alien ourselves and that that SUV is a greater threat than, and at least as unnatural as, any purple loosestrife plant, why is it that now even the nongardeners among us know that there's a biological invasion in the offing? Not that this is anything new. Slurring the enemy as having bioterrorist intentions dates to 1492. The Indians called plantain the white man's plant and the honeybee the white man's fly. American revolutionaries called a European gnat the Hessian fly; Dakotans called tumbleweed Russian weed. Long Island fishermen in the 1950s labeled a newly arrived seaweed, "Sputnik weed," half-convinced that the Soviet spacecraft had spread the pest. Out West, ranchers likewise thought that the Soviets spread the newly invasive killer weed halogeton.

You can't be too careful in what you plant; you may be an unwitting dupe, if not a fellow traveler, of nefarious evildoers. Bedeviled by Poe's "imp of the perverse," part of me wants to plant a worst-ten garden: annoy my green friends with beds of purple loosestrife, groves of mimosa, and fields of halogeton. Another, more evil part of me wants to pack up some gypsy moth egg sacks, a few dozen Japanese beetle grubs, a vial of medflies, a bag of Formosan termites, and a jar of poison ivy berries and visit certain people's residences. But I'll probably keep to more mainstream gardening and walks in the woods, marveling to myself at the incredibly complicated stories lying behind many of the species I see.

I have organized the chapters in this book thematically. "Out of Africa" explains that many of our warmer weather grasses arrived here as bedding in slave ships, while some of the staples of southern cooking—cowpeas, okra, sesame, and watermelon—are also African. "Cowboys" investigates the role this figure played in distributing such alien life forms as the cow, horse, anthrax, and tumbleweed throughout America; ". . . and Indians" investigates the often-unexpected role Native Americans played in reshaping our natural environment and in eliminating old species and introducing new species to the continent. "A Green Nightmare" looks at the species involved in the almost entirely nonindigenous American lawn, while "Psychedelic Gardens" examines the unsuspected drugs many of us have growing in our backyards, and "An Entangled Bank" explores the stories of roadside weeds. "Bioterror" traces the history of this weapon of war back to colonial days, and "Bad Air and Worse Science" explains how a number of species arrived here as pre–germ theory attempts to eliminate malaria. "A Sow's Ear from a Silk Purse" tells of the ecological mishaps that resulted from various attempts to establish sericulture on our shores. "It Seemed a Good Idea at the Time" exposes the role individual people had in spreading carp, starlings, and kudzu around the country. "House Pests" explains how some of the many animals we share our quarters with arrived here with our ancestors, and "Misplaced Americans" shares the tales of animals we think of as native, but which have, for the most part, less claim than we do to being American. "Gone Fishin'" reveals the as often as not exotic origins of everything to do with going fishing.

Out of Africa

How Slavery Transformed the American Landscape and Diet

Two hundred and fifty years of slavery left an indelible mark on America. Twenty-six million of us descend from the one-half million men, women, and children brought to the New World on the infamous Middle Passage. American jazz, blues, rock and roll, and gospel music have deep African roots. African words—*okra, gumbo, juke*—enrich our language, and soul food graces many of our tables. Material traces of slavery are far fewer. Slave marts and cabins have decayed and disappeared. What few leg irons remain are in museums, as are the hoes, shovels, and rakes wielded by generations of black Americans.

Unnoticed by many of us, however, are the varied African flora and fauna naturalized in the New World. Perhaps the most ubiquitous African plant now naturalized in America is the misnamed Bermuda grass, the preferred species for many southern lawns and golf courses. *Cynodon dactylon* grows well in pastures, fields, and waste places coast to coast and, while most common to the south, is found as far north as Massachusetts, Michigan, and Oregon. Only heavy freezes limit its spread. It is probably the worst weedy grass in over eighty countries.[1] So cosmopolitan is Bermuda grass that regions other than Africa have been suggested as its original home. But modern researchers seem satisfied that *C. dactylon* was born in East Africa; and it is to Africa that they have gone in search of subspecies with which to breed superior strains. Although originating in Africa, Bermuda grass has long grown elsewhere. In India, for example, references to Bermuda grass appear in the sacred *Vedas*, Hindu texts that date back before 500 B.C.E. Various African tribes use it for both medical and religious purposes.[2] *Cynodon dactylon*'s earliest known American mention is in the diary of a Georgia planter, who credits British royal governor Henry Ellis with introducing the grass as a crop to Savannah in 1751.[3] Popular in the antebellum South as forage and pasturage, Bermuda grass was widespread by the early nineteenth century. It probably arrived in America along with African slaves, having been laid in the bottom of slave ships as bedding for their human cargo. Cargo and bedding were then unloaded in the slave ports of the New World, where both were fruitful and multiplied.

Although the widespread use of Bermuda grass obscures its accidental introduction into America, the origin of introduction for a fellow African grass, *Paspalum vaginatum*, was recently discovered from an examination of historic American slave ports. Seeking useful new species of grasses, grass expert Ron R. Duncan was puzzled by *P. vaginatum*'s erratic distribution in the New World. It grew on Carolina and Georgia sea islands, but not on the Gulf Coast, and while it was found on Caribbean islands, it was not at St. Augustine, Florida, or New Orleans. Wondering if the grass's distribution might have been an accidental byproduct of slavery, Duncan went looking for it. "In Charleston, I asked where they offloaded the slaves and they referred me to Sullivan's Island. In twenty minutes, I found the grass while I was just walking on the beach," he said. "In Savannah, they told me the ships came to Fort Pulaski. The grass was all through the marshes. I feel totally confident that's how these fine-textured grasses came to the United States."[4] Touted as America's new miracle grass, *Paspalum*'s roots reach further back in American history than do those of many Americans.

Seeking the perfect grass for southern golf courses, grass experts have toyed with *Paspalum*'s fellow passenger, Bermuda grass, since the first decades of the twentieth century, developing several varieties popular with both homeowners and country clubs. Not everyone, however, loves *C. dactylon*, which spreads readily by rhizome, stolon, and seed. Its invasive nature has given rise to several metaphors. In Virginia, where Kentucky bluegrass is the preferred lawn grass, Bermuda grass is cursed as "devil" or "wire grass" for its tenacity, ubiquity, and profligacy.

Even more roundly cursed is another African plant, Johnson grass, so close a cousin of the cultivated grain sorghum that the two cross-fertilize. Johnson grass, *Sorghum halepense*, originated in Africa but now grows throughout the warmer regions of the world. By the nineteenth century, it was so widespread that its American promoters obtained supplies, not from Africa, but from Turkey. Its species name, *halepense*, refers to Aleppo, Syria, where Europeans first noted it. Johnson grass also grows throughout the continental United States, although it is most common in the South, where it was first grown. But the question of who first planted it is controversial. Its common name recalls Alabama planter William Johnson, who grew it on his plantation near Selma, Alabama, in 1840, from where it spread by self-propagation while retaining the Johnson name. But Johnson had obtained the grass from John Means, who is said to have imported it from Turkey to South Carolina in 1835, where it became known as Means grass. In all probability, *S. halepense* had already established itself in the South, coming over as a contaminant of hay and bedding.[5]

Means actually called his grass "guinea grass," suggesting that, although his supplies came from Turkey, he associated it with slaves. The Guinea coast of Africa provided many slaves for the Middle Passage, and Americans came to use "guinea" as a synonym for "African," to which practice we owe terms such as *guinea corn, guinea grass, guinea hen, guinea melon, guinea men,* and *guinea squash.* A widely used grain crop in Africa, cultivated sorghum, or guinea corn, fed the slaves on their ocean crossing and became a staple of their kitchen gardens. John Lawson noticed Carolina colonists in 1700 feeding it to their hogs and poultry, and Catesby, calling it "bunched guinea corn," remarked in 1743, "But little of this grain is propagated, and that chiefly by negros [*sic*], who make bread of it, and boil it like manner of firmety. Its chief use is for feeding fowls for which the smallness of the grain adapts it. It was first introduced from Africa by the negros."[6]

Catesby's guinea corn is *Sorghum vulgare,* the cultivated form of sorghum with heavy masses of seeds superficially resembling corn, while Means's guinea grass is *Sorghum halepense,* whose splayed out seed head betrays its grassy nature. Just to confuse things all the more, a fellow look-alike from Africa, *Panicum maximum,* is also called guinea grass. It is sometimes difficult to know to which writers are referring. *Panicum maximum* came to our shores with the slaves, as bedding and as bird seed. Legend has it that a local planter imported both *P. maximum* and some exotic birds into Jamaica. The birds died, but the grass flourished, and many now mistakenly consider it a native species. Several times in the nineteenth century, Americans imported the Jamaican seed. In 1873 the American consul in Jamaica obtained seed that congressmen then used for a massive free mailing of seed samples, thus spreading both goodwill and bad seeds throughout their constituencies. Extremely sensitive to frost, guinea grass is largely limited to the warmer regions of the South.[7]

Panicum maximum is one of a number of alien grasses implicated in what some have called "the Africanization of American grasslands." Especially problematical in South America, the takeover of native grasslands by aggressive African grasses has a head start of five hundred years on nativists, or those interested in preserving native ecosystems, and is abetted by the continued clearing of forests by fire and deforestation. Adapted to heavy grazing and droughtlike conditions, African grasses not only outcompete native grasses when grown together, but they are also more likely to be planted than are native species. The first generation of invaders, introduced centuries ago, with the exception of *P. maximum,* usually is restricted to warmer regions. Hawaii is the only U.S.

state reporting problems, but African grasses are serious weeds in many tropical nations. The second generation of invaders comprises those deliberately introduced in the last one hundred years. Attitudes toward those depend upon whether you think the American Southwest should remain "undisturbed." For example, cattlemen in Texas tout buffelgrass (*Pennisetum ciliare*) as a range crop, but nativists in Arizona excoriate it as an invasive weed, likewise for kleingrass (*Panicum coloratum*).[8]

Africans were instrumental in importing a number of plants into the New World. At least four of these, okra, sesame, watermelon, and cowpeas, have been naturalized in the United States. Okra, both the vegetable and the name, are African, as is the dish most often associated with okra, gumbo. Okra eaters, a curiosity to many Americans, remain concentrated in the South, the region first populated by large numbers of Africans. Cooked okra is famously slimy—mucilaginous to the finicky. While this turns off many would-be gourmets, it is also the basis for its use as a thickener in gumbos. Gumbo, a souplike dish whose mandatory ingredients include okra, tomato, and meat, is today popularly associated with New Orleans Creole cooking, but early-nineteenth-century cookbooks, such as Mary Randolph's 1824 *The Virginia House-wife*, thought it West Indian. Fried okra, now available in some fast-food restaurants, is the only okra recipe with any claim to being part of our national palate. Although Americans use only the pods, okra leaves and flowers are also edible, and Africans and Asians cook the leaves like spinach.

Okra is one of a number of crops that have an Abyssinian center of origin, which encompasses Ethiopia, Eritrea, and part of Sudan. Wild ancestors of our cultivated okra still grow in the region, providing a gene pool for agriculturalists interested in developing new varieties. Other cultivated plants from this area include barley, sorghum, millet, cowpeas, flax, sesame, castor beans, coffee, myrrh, and indigo. By the time the transatlantic slave trade developed, many of these plants grew throughout Africa and elsewhere. West African slaves brought them to the New World, where they became staples in American soul food.[9]

Texas, Florida, Georgia, and California produce most of America's domestic okra crop, sixty-seven million pounds of which is frozen. Imports come from Guatemala, Mexico, and El Salvador. Much of this okra winds up breaded and fried, which is the way most Americans like their okra. Harvesting is still by hand, a job that required gloves before today's spineless varieties were developed. Left to mature, okra pods become woody and inedible, so only immature pods are used, and these must be harvested every two or three days during the growing season. While most people think of okra as green, the pods also come in red, gold, and white.[10]

Okra (*Hibiscus esculentus*) is a member of the mallow family and hence a relative of the hibiscus, rose of Sharon, mallow, hollyhock, and cotton. Being a close relative, requiring similar growing conditions, and looking somewhat like cotton, okra has managed to tag along with this more widely grown staple. It is now one of the more pernicious weeds of American cotton fields. First noticed in Louisiana and Mississippi in 1980, wild okra apparently descended from cultivated okra that sharecroppers planted alternately with cotton. The latter's seeds remain dormant in the ground until cotton cultivation encourages their growth. American farmers spend millions on herbicides to rid their fields of wild okra, while the Sudanese in Africa harvest the indigenous wild okra that grows in their cotton fields.

While herbicide companies make millions killing okra, no one seems to want to kill off the wild descendants of another African plant, the watermelon. Native to southern Africa, *Citrullus lanatus* is a staple of the Kalahari, where both natives and early explorers relied on its reserves of water to survive. Cultivated in ancient Egypt and buried with the boy pharaoh Tutankhamen thirty-five hundred years ago, watermelon reached India by 800 C.E., Spain by 1000, and China by 1100. So widespread was it that plant historians quarreled over its country of origin until the explorer David Livingston settled the matter for westerners when he wrote in 1857 of watermelons growing wild in the Kalahari:

> But the most surprising plant of the Desert is the "Kengwe or Keme" ("Cucumis caffer"), the watermelon. In years when more than the usual quantity of rain falls, vast tracts of the country are literally covered with these melons; this was the case annually when the fall of rain was greater than it is now, and the Bakwains sent trading parties every year to the lake. It happens commonly once every ten or eleven years, and for the last three times its occurrence has coincided with an extraordinarily wet season. Then animals of every sort and name, including humans, rejoice in the rich supply. The elephant, true lord of the forest, revels in this fruit, and so do the different species of rhinoceros, although naturally so diverse in their choice of pasture. The various kinds of antelopes feed on them with equal avidity, and lions, hyaenas, jackals, and mice, all seem to know and appreciate the common blessing. These melons are not, however, all of them eatable; some are sweet, and others so bitter that the whole are named by the Boers the "bitter watermelon." The natives select them by striking one melon after another with a hatchet, and applying the tongue to the gashes. They thus readily distinguish between the bitter and sweet. The bitter are deleterious, but the sweet are quite wholesome.[11]

Requiring long, hot summers to mature, watermelons did poorly in Europe but after the Spanish brought them to the New World, they flourished. Popular with the Indians, watermelons spread rapidly, and reached the Colorado River before the Spanish. Today different Indian groups grow different varieties, at least six of which are available online. Feral varieties have been located in states as varied as Connecticut, Michigan, Florida, Kentucky, Louisiana, and Texas, as well as in Puerto Rico and the Virgin Islands.[12]

While Captain John Smith did not notice watermelon growing in Indian villages in Virginia, English explorer William Hilton found them in Florida in 1664, and the French explorer Père Marquette thought that those he ate along the Mississippi River in 1673 were "excellent." Europeans were growing watermelon in Massachusetts by 1629. Popular with all who grow it, in America watermelon became associated especially with blacks. No one is quite sure why. Africans, no doubt, brought watermelon seeds to the New World, but so did Europeans. While sesame and okra are equally African, it is watermelon that became totemic. Practical-minded explanations suppose that watermelons were a good source of water and sugar for overworked slaves. Whatever the reason, minstrel shows popularized the association, and advertisers and Hollywood made it a staple of twentieth-century racist stereotypes. So demeaning did many blacks find the association that some refused to eat watermelon.

While southern blacks were characterized as inordinately fond of sliced watermelon, maiden aunts of all colors were enamored with watermelon rind pickle, which no right-minded southern feast would be without. Many Americans reserve the seeds for spitting contests (with Guinness claiming the world record to be 68 feet, 9.125 inches), while Asians roast and eat them. Our government farms have bred seedless, giant, miniature, red, yellow, and white watermelons. But the Japanese take the prize with their square watermelons, grown in boxlike glass cases so that they'll fit nicely into a refrigerator.

Hamburger buns, *Sesame Street*, and Aladdin may be what most Americans think of when they hear sesame. But *Sesamum indicum*, the world's oldest oilseed crop, is another African crop brought to America by slaves and one whose current popularity as a bread topping is the direct result of one woman's special pie recipe.

Sesame spread throughout the Old World so early and so widely that plant historians long debated its origins, some tracing it to Indonesia, some to India, and some to Africa. Today the consensus is that it originated in the Ethiopian highlands and spread via trade routes. Ancient Babylonians and Sumerians used sesame to flavor their wine and, like we do today, flavored their bread with the roasted seed, while Egyptians treated various diseases with sesame thirty-five hundred years ago. The Hindu use it in their religious rituals; all Indians use it extensively in cooking. The Chinese, Japanese, and Koreans use the oil both medicinally and in cooking. The Middle East consumes large quantities of sesame butter, or tahini, which when mixed with ground chickpeas is called hummus. The English word *sesame* comes, via Latin, from the Greek *sesame*, which is itself Semitic and kin to the Akkadian *samassamu*. In a sense, we are speaking ancient Mesopotamian when we utter the magic formula "Open sesame," which is the last legacy of sesame's once potent magical powers.[13]

Africans, however, called sesame *bene* or *benne*, which is what it is still called in places in the American South. A Civil War–era chronicler of indigenous plant uses, Francis Porcher records that "*bené* make[s] rich and nutritious soup, and act[s] as substitutes for meat. They are often parched, and beaten up with sugar, and served as a condiment or dessert."[14] Thomas Jefferson claimed sesame "is among the most valuable acquisitions our country has ever made. . . . I do not believe before that there existed so perfect a substitute for olive oil." This happy resemblance has led many a dishonest purveyor to adulterate his 100 percent pure olive oil with sesame oil. All accounts agree that Africans introduced sesame into America, and that it took hold first in South Carolina, where an estimated 40 percent of all slaves were imported. By 1730, South Carolina was producing sesame oil.[15]

Today America imports forty thousand tons of sesame seed each year. With over one hundred thousand seeds to a pound, that's a lot of seed to bring all the way from Africa, Southeast Asia, and Latin America. We grow thirty-eight thousand acres of sesame ourselves, half of it in Texas. Most of this is for sesame seed buns. Sesame, however, is labor intensive, and efforts to make it a viable crop in America have concentrated on breeding cultivars that retain their seed upon maturity rather than shedding them, such retention suiting mechanical harvesting.

America was not always in love with sesame seed buns. Until World War II, it was sesame seed oil that interested us, but the war and alternative oils— cottonseed and soybean—undermined sesame oil's appeal. In 1954, however, Washington, D.C., resident Dorothy Koteen changed America's eating habits when her "Open Sesame Pie" won the sixth annual Pillsbury Bake-Off Contest. Within the week, American grocery stores sold out of sesame seed, reordered in bulk, and began a national love affair.[16] Imports soon doubled, and McDonald's, and then everyone, decided they had to have sesame seeds on their hamburger buns.

Another African crop, the cowpea (*Vigna unguiculata*), also known as southern pea, black-eyed pea, brown-eyed pea, callivance, cherry bean, frijol, China pea, Indian pea, cornfield pea, crowder pea, field pea, and purple hull, is one of the world's more important legumes. Thanks to its high-protein content, drought resistance, and nitrogen-fixing abilities, the cowpea is popular among the poor wherever it is grown. George Washington Carver, better known for promoting the peanut, also touted the cowpea as "both a bank and a mortgage—lifted to the poor man." Another called it "the sheet anchor of the southern farmer."[17]

Like other crops, the cowpea's ancestral home eluded historians for years. It is so ubiquitous that Africa, Asia, and South America have each been argued as its continent of origin, as its popular names China and Indian pea suggest. But plant geneticists favor Africa, for it is there that the cultivated cowpea's wild ancestor thrives and where the plant exhibits its greatest genetic variety—both criteria of a point of origin. Somewhere in sub-Saharan Africa, the cowpea was domesticated. Its use then spread east to India, where cowpeas are so common that India was long thought the place of origin.

It spread further east, to China and Japan, but not, interestingly enough, to Europe, perhaps because of the relatively inhospitable climate. The Arabs, who obtained cowpeas via African connections, appear to have introduced it to Europeans. Northern Europeans came to know of cowpeas through the African slave trade, which resulted in its early importation to the New World. Native Americans were so quick to use the nutritious vegetable that early North American explorers thought it indigenous. In 1700 John Lawson traveled from Charleston, South Carolina, up the Santee River and into North Carolina. Of Indian agriculture he observed, "the kidney-beanes were here before the English came being very plentiful in the Indian corn fields." Lawson may call cowpeas "kidney beans," but he is not referring to the familiar kidney beans of today. Those are *Phaseolus vulgaris*, which are indigenous to South America. Sloane's size reference ("not so big as the smallest field pea") suggests that he is describing cowpeas, not kidney beans, since cowpeas look pretty much like a miniature kidney bean. Lawson's remark that they "were here before the English came," if fact, suggests the Indians obtained them from early explorers. That the bean was "very plentiful in the Indian corn fields" made people suppose that it was native and rendered it useless for barter. In 1666, Virginia forbade colonists from paying taxes in "Indian peas," and Thomas Jefferson, who is credited with the first known use of the word *cowpea*, thought them native to America. It was a French explorer of the Mississippi River valley, Le Page du Pratz, who correctly theorized that the Indians' "Appalachian bean" came over the mountains from the Carolinas with the English, who had acquired them from the slaves from Guinea.[18]

The cowpea found America sufficiently amiable that it became naturalized. Indian tribes and rural southerners cultivate varieties long fallen out of favor with the industrial farmer. The United States, although a Johnny-come-lately to the cowpea, nonetheless contributes to its worldwide genetic variation. And wild escapees have established themselves east of the Mississippi as well as in Texas. The Southern Weed Science Society classifies the plant as invasive.[19]

Because some cowpea varieties tend to ripen over a long period, they are especially useful in subsistence farming. Farmers can plant them at one time, and then harvest at their leisure. That the leaves and flowers are as edible as the seeds increases the plant's value. But it is the cowpea's nitrogen-fixing ability that make it the poor farmer's true friend; "What clover is to the North and West as a means of improving the fertility of the soil, the cowpea is to regions south of the clover belt," proclaimed one agriculturalist in 1909.[20] While all plants require nitrogen to grow and while it is plentiful in the atmosphere, few organisms can use it in its atmospheric form. Enter "nitrogen-fixing bacteria," which can convert nitrogen gas to usable forms. Soil bacteria make nitrogen available to plants by inhabiting root nodules, or swellings, exchanging nitrogen for protection—swellings that can be easily seen by examining the roots of the clover that no doubt grow on your lawn.

The South is the center of America's cowpea culture, with over eighty thousand hectares under cultivation. Athens, Texas, laid stake as "The Blackeyed Pea Capital of Texas," after local businessman J. B. Henry started growing cowpeas in commercial quantities around 1910. Several canning companies opened up in the 1930s and 1940s, and Neiman-Marcus touted Athens's pickled blackeyes as "Texas Caviar."[21] But for truly Texas-sized production figures, you have to go to Africa. There, Nigeria, the undisputed world champion, grows 2.1 million of the estimated 3.3 million tons of cowpeas accounted for worldwide each year.[22]

Africans use all parts of the plant—eating seeds, leaves, and roots and feeding cattle the stems. The leaves, boiled like spinach, can be dried and stored for later use, and judicious harvesting does not greatly affect seed production. The leaves are often more nutritious than the beans. Americans tend to eat only the seeds, reserving the rest for cattle and hogs. We eat cowpeas both green and dried. The green are usually frozen or canned, although some people roast them like peanuts. The dried are sold as is. *Vigna unguiculata* is known by a number of names. Those derived from shape are called either kidney or crowder, the fuller kidney being more spaced out in the shell and the crowder being more crowded and pinched. They may be sold as either beans or peas. If marketed by color, they may be black-eyed, brown-eyed, cream, purple, or pink. Whatever their market name, and there are seven thousand different cultivars housed at the International Institute for Tropical Agriculture, they're all *V. unguiculata*, as are the yard-long, asparagus, and catjang beans.[23] These last two are subspecies that hail from Asia. The yard-long bean, or asparagus bean, is an extremely long climbing bean, and the catjang is a bush bean, whose name comes from Malay *kachang*, pea or bean.[24]

Whatever you call a cowpea, if you're truly southern, you know it as a key ingredient of Hoppin' John, a de rigueur New Year's Day rice and bean dish. Purported to bring at the least good luck, Hoppin' John's combination of legume and grain provides a nutritious alternative for those unable to afford meat. When combined with collard greens, the meal is said to insure its diner as much money in pennies and greenbacks as he eats in cowpeas and collards. The combination of beans, rice, and leafy greens just might hearken back to Africa, where rice and bean dishes are common and where cowpea leaves are used in cooking.

Nobody knows the origin of the Hoppin' John name or the recipe. Some people find it interesting that Limpin' Susan, another oddly named dish, which is made with rice and okra, also contains an African vegetable. Although certain white southerners surmise that they eat both dishes in memory of genteel poverty that followed the Civil War, antebellum recipe books prove that both dishes were popular with whites long before Reconstruction. Historians think these and other southern foods reveal the pervasive influence of African culinary traditions on southern cooking. Similar dishes exist in West Africa and in New World cultures that are heavily indebted to African culture, such as in Brazil and the Caribbean. Few serious etymologists accept the folk claim that Hoppin' John memorializes the spontaneous, or enforced, hopping of children around the dinner table when served beans and rice. Some argue that Hoppin' John is a corruption of the French term *pois a pigeon*, or pigeon pea (*Cajanus caja*), which is the West Indian culinary equivalent of cowpeas. Experts disagree on whether pigeon peas originated in India or Africa, but all agree the pea came to the New World with African slaves. Also known as Congo pea, no-eye pea, dhal, gandule, and gandure, pigeon peas are popular with Puerto Ricans, whose *arroz con gandures*, or rice with pigeon peas, is so in demand among transplants to the mainland that America imports canned pigeon peas from Kenya.[25] An alternative explanation is that Hoppin' John is a corruption of *bahatta kachang*, a supposed polyglot term for rice and beans.[26]

Made with cow or pigeon peas, Hoppin' John's guarantee of good luck just might echo African attitudes towards the peas. Ethnobotanist James A. Duke, well known for his studies of Central American botanical uses, states that "cowpeas are sacred to Hausa and Yoruba tribes of Nigeria, and are prescribed for sacrifices to abate evil and to pacify the spirits of sickly children."[27] Someone with a sense of humor may have named the Limpin' Susan dish, a seemingly deliberate reversal of Hoppin' John. Susan may be limping for reasons more intimate than dinner; okra's shape has given rise to an American folk tradition that the vegetable is an aphrodisiac, something Zimbabweans also believed: "Ndebele men are not permitted to eat it because delele [wild okra] is said to weaken them physically and sexually. Men from the Shona clans have no such qualms."[28]

A Green Nightmare

The Un-American Lawn

North America has thirty-two million acres of grass. There are more acres of lawn than corn. Ostensibly a symbol of suburban leisure, the lawn is actually a labor intensive monoculture annually consuming three million tons of fertilizer and sixty-seven million pounds of pesticides, and it is responsible for the use of five hundred and eighty million gallons of gasoline. Every year mowing collectively produces 50 percent of the waste entering landfills and as much pollution as 3.5 million cars.[1] All-American though it may be, little about the lawn is native to America.

Lawns have been a status symbol since they first became popular among eighteenth-century English aristocrats anxious to create gardens with a more natural look than the hitherto popular French formal gardens. Armies of workers kept these lawns trimmed. Blenheim Palace in England employed fifty men to scythe its lawn, and aristocrats on both sides of the Atlantic relied on sheep and cattle to keep their lawns fashionably short. Then, in 1830, in Gloucestershire, England, engineer Edwin Beard Budding built the first successful hand-powered reel mower. In 1842 a Scotsman patented a forty-two-inch-wide horse-drawn mower. Americans were copying the English lawn mower by the 1850s, and affordable gas-powered mowers appeared at the end of the century.[2]

Garden hoses, which are merely miniaturized fire hoses, came into popularity in the second half of the nineteenth century. Jan van der Heiden of Amsterdam invented sewn leather fire hoses in the 1670s, and early Dutch fire trucks carried sewing kits to make on-the-spot repairs. Philadelphian's James Sellars and Abraham Pennock replaced stitches with rivets in 1807, permitting higher water pressure and greater hose lengths. Charles Goodyear's 1839 invention of vulcanized rubber soon made fire hoses even longer, stronger, and less prone to leaks. Inventive minds soon shrank these hoses to domestic proportions, and the garden hose was born, as was its adjustable spray nozzle, also borrowed from firefighters.[3] With the addition of simple, water-powered sprinklers in the 1870s,

A nineteenth-century lawn. Frank J. Scott, *The Art of Beautifying Suburban Home Grounds of Small Extent* (New York, 1870).

the lawn care industry was ready to boom. And it did, along with the first great rush to the suburbs.

The newly popular trolley and commuter train systems of the late 1800s permitted the creation of America's first suburbs. The new suburbanites avidly followed the gardening advice of people such as Andrew Jackson Downing, Calvert Vaux, Frederick Law Olmsted, and Frank J. Scott. Born to a professional gardening family in Newburgh, New York, Downing wrote his classic *Treatise on the Theory and Practice of Landscape Gardening, Adapted to North America* in 1841 at the age of twenty-six, began editing the *Horticulturist* in 1846, and published *Architecture for Country Houses* in 1850. His distinguished career, which included designs for Hudson River estates and the grounds of the United States Capitol, the White House, and the Smithsonian Institution, ended in 1852 when the steamboat he was on blew up while he was racing a rival on the Hudson River. But before his death, Downing impressed on Americans and on landscape designers in particular the attraction of a lawn. Englishman Calvert Vaux, who practiced landscaping with Downing until Downing's death, later became partners with Frederick Law Olmsted and assisted in the design of New York's Central Park. The park's landscapes are heavily indebted to Downing's advice: "Plant spacious parks in your cities, and unclose their gates as wide as the gates of morning to the whole people."[4]

But it was Olmsted and Vaux's 1868 collaboration on a planned Chicago suburb, Riverside, that would shape American suburbia for a century. Riverside, a "suburban village," exemplified the designers' desire for a "naturalistic" suburb, utilizing curving roads, large public areas, and careful landscaping. Individual houses that had one-hundred-foot lot lines and thirty-foot setbacks could not have walls. Front lawns ran together in an evocation of republican community and openness. Olmsted explained in 1870 that "probably the advantages of civilization can be found illustrated and demonstrated under no other circumstances so completely as in some suburban neighborhoods where each family abode stands fifty or a hundred feet or more apart from all others, and at some distance from the public road." A description of the ideal front lawn also appears in Downing disciple Frank J. Scott's *The Art of Beautifying Suburban Home Grounds*: "A strip twenty feet wide and a hundred feet long may be rendered, proportionally, as artistic as the landscape vistas of a park." Scott further explained, "The beauty obtained by throwing front grounds open together, is of that excellent quality which enriches all who take part in the exchange, and makes no man poorer. . . . It is unchristian to hedge from the sight of others the beauties of nature which it has been our good fortune to create or secure."[5]

Scott warns suburbanites, "A smooth, closely shaven surface of grass is by far the most essential element of beauty on the grounds of a suburban home" and *"no lawn can be brought to perfection if cut less often than once a week,"*[6] advice one might still get at a neighborhood lawn-care store. Scott assumes homeowners will "swing a lawn scythe or roll a lawn machine." The scythe dictating the minimum size of a lawn, "for a piece of lawn in a place where a scythe cannot be swung, is not worth maintaining. Rolling mowers by horse or hand power have been principally employed on large grounds; but the hand machines are now so simplified and cheapened that they are coming into general use on small pleasure grounds, and proprietors may have the pleasure of doing their own mowing without the wearisome bending of the back, incident to the use of the scythe."[7]

But what kind of grass was one to cut? A mix of Rhode Island bent grass, creeping bent grass, red-top, sweet vernal grass, Kentucky bluegrass, and white clover, according to Scott.[8] All alien. All part of what was known to early colonists as "English grass," to distinguish it from native American grasses. Not that everyone agreed—or yet agrees—that all these grasses are foreign.

Kentucky bluegrass (*Poa pratensis*) came to the New World as a forage crop, but it spread so rapidly that many colonists thought it native. Peter Kalm noted that bluegrass and white clover were growing as hay crops outside Montreal in 1751, and historians surmise that French Canadians took both with them into Indiana and Illinois. From there it spread into Kentucky, whose rolling limestone regions proved especially welcoming. Settlers from the colonies to the east passed through the state and spread both the seeds and the name, Kentucky bluegrass, which gradually edged out the traditional English names of smooth meadow and June grass.[9] A visit to any lawn store will confirm that *P. pratensis* is possibly America's favorite lawn grass, at least in cooler regions. Nativists bent on restoring pristine prairies detest bluegrass, which often outcompetes native grasses and establishes minimonocultural empires. But most of us love it, as did John James Ingalls of Kansas, who proclaimed in 1872 in *Kansas Magazine:* "One grass differs from another grass in glory. One is vulgar and another patrician. There are grades in its vegetable nobility. Some varieties are useful. Some are beautiful. Others combine utility and ornament. The sour, reedy herbage of swamps is baseborn. Timothy is a valuable servant. Redtop and clover are a degree higher in the social scale. But the king of them all, with genuine blood royal, is blue grass."[10]

Often planted with bluegrass, both in colonial days and now, white clover (*Trifolium repens*), a legume, is a nitrogen source for soil and a nutritious fodder for grazing animals. Like its companion bluegrass, colonists mistook white clover for a native, though Native Americans did not: "I am told that it is never met with far back in the woods, but immediately on their being cleared away, either by fire or otherwise, it takes possession of the ground; which should prove that it was natural to it; that the seed lies there but cannot vegetate till the ground is cleared; but again I have been told, that by some tribes of Indians it is called 'white man's foot grass,' from an idea that wherever he has trodden, it grows; which should prove at least that it had not been known in the country longer than the white man."[11]

White clover was not the only import that Native Americans associated with white people. Longfellow's Hiawatha chants about pale-face tagalongs, "Wheresoe'er they move, before them / Swarms the stinging fly, the Ahmo, / Swarms the bee, the honey-maker." Thomas Jefferson notes that Indians called the honeybee the English fly, and J. Hector St. John de Crevecoeur, whose 1782 *Letters from an American Farmer* provides an early account of American customs, explains, "The Indians look upon them with an evil eye, and consider their progress into the interior of the continent as an omen of the white man's approach: thus, as they discover the bees, the news of the event, passing from mouth to mouth, spreads sadness and consternation on all sides." Hiawatha also speaks of the plantain: "Wheresoe'er they tread, beneath them / Springs a flower unknown among us, / Springs the White-man's Foot in blossom." Both narrow and broad-leafed (*Plantago lanceolata* and *P. major,* respectively), followed Europeans worldwide, and Native Americans and the Maori of New Zealand called it the "white-man's foot."[12] Native Americans' laments have given way to nativist excoriations. Those interested in preserving a pre-Columbian landscape have labeled white clover an invasive weed. Nevertheless, like its fellow traveler bluegrass, white clover can be purchased nationwide, and is probably growing, if not on your front lawn, then on the shoulder of the nearest highway.

Scott's recommended bent grasses—creeping bent grass (*Agrostis palustris*), Rhode Island or colonial bent grass (*A. tenuis*), and redtop (*A. alba*)—are still popular. Both suburbanites strolling their yards and golfers setting up on the putting green stand on creeping bent, a fine-bladed grass best adapted to cool climates. Rhode Island, or colonial bent grass, was apparently first remarked upon in Roger Williams's letter to John Winthrop in 1647. It is a popular lawn grass today and has been claimed over the years as both a native and an alien, with alienists having the current edge.[13]

But redtop, so called because of its reddish panicles, is the bent family's true controversial member. Widely planted—often with white clover—as a hay and pasture grass, redtop varies greatly depending upon the environment. This was its curse in the nineteenth century, since it grew well for some and not for others. William Richardson of Ireland first popularized it as a hay grass in 1807. Redtop, or fiorin grass as Richardson termed it after its Gaelic name *fiorthann,* quickly became controversial. Writing in 1863 to beleaguered Confederates desperate for homegrown solutions to shortages of nearly everything, Frances Porcher noted, "The *Agrostis stolonifera latifolia* (*Fiorin*) is considered by many in England as the best and most productive grass to sow on wet meadows; it is said to yield enormous crops, and it vegetates during the cold portions of the year. It has been a subject of much discordant opinion." Agriculture expert James Buckman explained in 1865, "This plant has been much extolled for the meadow; but our experience shows it to vary in value according to the nature of the position in which it is placed; as thus, in an irrigated meadow it sends up a large quantity of quite rich pasturage, whilst in poor or dry districts its herbage is hard and harsh, and not at all relished by cattle or sheep."[14]

Scott's final species, sweet vernal grass (*Anthoxanthum oderatum*), is responsible for the distinctive smell of newly mown hay. The grass contains a crystalline compound, coumarin, that has such a distinctive fragrance that the French make a perfume from it called flouve oil after its French name, *flouve odorante.* Formerly a food additive in everything from margarine to ice cream, the Food and Drug Administration banned coumarin in the United States fifty years ago after it was found to damage the liver and possibly cause cancer. But those who buy cheap vanilla in Mexico are probably still ingesting it unwittingly, since coumarin—not vanilla—is the primary flavoring agent of this too-good-to-be-true bargain. While commercial coumarin is either synthetic or derived from tonka tree beans, which are native to tropical America, the compound exists in many plants, including lavender, cinnamon, strawberries, cherries, and sweet clover. Although banned as a domestic food additive, coumarin continues to be added to tobacco for flavoring and to perfumes for the odor.[15]

Scott's lawn grasses can still be found in your local lawn and garden center. Purists, however, have come to dislike the appearance of mixed species lawns. The U.S. Department of Agriculture (USDA), in cahoots with professional golf and tennis associations, spent years and millions of dollars developing specialized grass species. Golf courses and lawn tennis clubs subsidized government research that improved strains of grass, to which the Garden Club of America gave its seal of approval. Americans learned that one's lawn should be "a plot with a single type of grass with no intruding weeds, kept mown at a height of an inch and a half, uniformly green, and neatly edged."[16] Suburbanite disciples soon realized that such miracle lawns were, if not completely impossible, then nearly so. There simply is no single species of grass that does uniformly well in shade and sun, dry and wet, compacted and loose, low traffic and high traffic areas. But there are those of us who try. More than twenty-six million households in 2000 paid a professional to help them with their lawn.[17] Confronted with the impossible, more and more lawn professionals tout mixed-species lawns that are tailored to an individual's needs. Which is to say, we're back to what our great-great-grandparents, following Scott's advice, planted a hundred years ago when they adapted pasture grasses to lawns.

While Scott's other recommendations remain available if you live in the north, you're probably more likely to find shade-tolerant fescue and rye supplementing the basic bluegrass. The USDA lists dozens of fescue species growing within the United States. Many are both native and of limited range, as their names indicate: Alaska, alpine, Arizona, California, Hawaiian, southwest, tundra, and Washington. Others, often the more widespread varieties, are imports, including several lawn and pasture varieties. Two of the more common alien fescues, tall (*Festuca arundinacea*) and meadow (*Festuca pratensis*), are European and, hence, popular with northern farmers and homeowners, since these species survive freezing. But both are invasive. Caretakers of prairie lands warn that both tall and meadow fescue can crowd out native grasses. Given their ubiquity in the continental United States and continued popularity with seed suppliers, eradication is impossible except in tightly controlled, relatively small areas.[18]

The most popular American cultivar of tall fescue, Kentucky 31, grows on millions of acres of southern lawns and pasture and owes its discovery to a sorghum syrup contest. Invited in 1931 to judge a Menifee County, Kentucky, syrup contest, University of Kentucky agronomist E. N. Fergus took a look at a "miracle" grass growing on W. M. Suiter's farm. Despite a severe drought, Suiter's hillside field was lush green. Fergus took some seed back to the university, and in 1943 Kentucky 31 was released. Touted as a panacea for southern farmers, Kentucky 31 today grows on an estimated thirty-five million acres. But it is an alien. Its original home is unknown, although Menifee County legend has it that the grass arrived as packing for a load of English bone china sometime in the nineteenth century. Unfortunately for farmers, stowed away within the grass was a symbiotic fungus, *Epichloe typhina*. The fungus appears to be the key to Kentucky 31's amazing vigor, rendering infected plants unpalatable to a variety of insects and nematodes. But it also sickens animals grazing on infected fescue. Several years after planting Kentucky 31, farmers noticed that their cattle came up lame and appeared sickly, while mares feeding on the fescue aborted more frequently and gave less milk. The so-called Fescue War commenced, with agricultural experts defending and attacking Kentucky 31 in increasingly acrimonious terms. The cause of fescue foot and fescue toxicity, however, remained a mystery, until a Georgia cattleman noticed in the 1970s that cattle grazing fescue in one field grew sick but those in another did not. Researchers discovered that the fescue in one field was rampantly infected with the fungus. Comparative tests in Alabama demonstrated that cattle grazing on noninfected fescue gained nearly twice as much weight as those grazing on infected fescue. Kentucky 31 was well on the way to pariahdom. Researchers today are trying to breed a fungus that imparts protection from insects but doesn't harm cattle.[19]

Ryegrass is the third most popular lawn grass in northern mixtures. Both tall and meadow fescue have recently been reclassified as ryegrasses, transforming *Festuca arundinaceum* into *Lolium arundinaceum* and *Festuca pratensis* into *Lolium pratensis*. If you're confused, pity the poor scientist who must remember that these have changed and that both were also once known as *Festuca elatior*; and ryegrass has a propensity for hybridizing within its own ranks and with fescues. The *real* ryegrass, the one you're most likely to encounter in a bag of seed, is either perennial ryegrass (*Lolium perenne*) or annual ryegrass (*Lolium multiflorum*), although there are those who will tell you that these are two varieties, not two species. For those with a lawn, the main difference is the distinction of perennial versus annual, although even that can vanish.

What you don't want mixed in with your ryegrass seeds are the seeds of darnel, *Lolium temulentum*, which are supposedly the tares of Jesus' parable: "Allow both to grow together until the harvest; and in the time of the harvest I will say to the reapers, 'First gather up the tares and bind them in bundles to burn them up; but gather the wheat into my barn.'"[20] An alien weed, darnel now grows throughout all fifty states, having been brought over as a contaminant with wheat seeds. Darnel so resembles wheat that the two are virtually indistinguishable. The only real cure for a contaminated crop was to use it as hay, rather than risk planting even more darnel the next year. Modern technology has had more success in separating the wheat from the tares. Not that darnel by itself is harmful; it is a grass and its seeds are edible. A symbiotic fungus that infects the seeds acts as a human hallucinogen, causing a person to act drunk, hence the French common name, *ivraie*, from *ivre*, meaning drunk. But earlier generations didn't know about the fungus and thought the seeds corrupt. Ryegrass is a corruption of raygrass, which may also come from ivraie, and darnel may derive from archaic words meaning drunk or foolish.

Porcher quotes a description of darnel's effect: "It 'creeps occasionally into our fermented liquors and our bread.' It grows abundantly in cornfields, and is cut with the grain. 'They have been long known to possess narcotic and singularly intoxicating properties. When malted along with barley, which when the grain is ill cleaned sometimes unintentionally happens, they impart their intoxicating quality to the beer, and render it unusually and even dangerously heady. When ground up with wheat and made into bread they produce a similar effect, especially if the bread be eaten hot. . . . The narcotic principle in these seeds has not yet been discovered.'"[21] So common was the accidental, or deliberate, adulteration of wheat and barley that darnel was known locally in England as cheat.[22]

Frank Scott's audience was primarily northern, and so too were his grasses. Southern and western lawn lovers had to await help from the U.S. government to find grasses suitable for their regions. Grass experts divide the continental United States into three broad horizontal bands, based on temperature and rainfall. Scott's colder and damper northern region and the drier and warmer southern region are separated by a transition zone that meanders through the Middle Atlantic states, dips south around mountainous West Virginia, rises northward into southern Ohio, and trends slowly south and west towards northern Arizona. Five grasses dominate southern lawns: bahia, Bermuda, centipede,

St. Augustine, and zoysia. Four, everyone agrees, are alien, while the fifth, St. Augustine grass, has its defenders as a native. Bermuda grass, which came over from Africa, is treated in the chapter on slavery; the other four are discussed here.

A South American native imported into America from Brazil in 1913 for forage, bahia grass (*Paspalum notatum*), its common name deriving from the Brazilian town Bahia, remains popular with southern farmers as pasture. In 1939 in Florida, County Agricultural Agent E. H. Finlayson discovered a bahia grass variety growing among the docks of Pensacola, Florida. It seemed to lend itself as a lawn grass. Highway departments use it to cover roadside verges, with Pensacola and other varieties forming drought-resistant sods with roots as deep as seven feet. Because it chokes out native grasses, several authorities have classified *P. notatum* as an invasive weed. You would think, therefore, that the destruction today of hundreds of thousands of acres of bahia grass would be applauded. But no. Since these acres belong largely to the influential cattle industry, the government of Florida is busy instead trying to eradicate the crickets that are eliminating the bahia grass. Ironically, everything involved in this war of all-against-all is alien: the people, the cattle, the grass, and the insects. Three species of mole cricket—the shortwinged mole cricket (*Scapteriscus abbreviatus*), the southern mole cricket (*Scapteriscus borellii*), and the tawny mole cricket (*Scapteriscus vicinus*)—infest Florida's bahia pastures. These species and the grass they eat are South American, all accidentally imported into the southern United States around 1900 (although bahia grass was also deliberately imported). To save the grass, you must control the cricket; to control the cricket, officials have imported *Steinernema scapterisci*, the mole cricket nematode, a nearly microscopic worm from South America that carries bacteria that is beneficial to the nematode but lethal to mole crickets. The University of Florida obtained a patent for the idea of seeding infected pastures with up to eight hundred million nematodes per acre. Within a week to ten days following the nematode infection, the unlucky mole cricket should die, releasing up to fifty thousand bacteria-laden nematodes, each of which seeks out a healthy cricket to start the cycle again. As far as anyone knows, the nematode infects only the targeted mole crickets.[23]

St. Augustine, or Charleston, grass (*Stenotaphrum secundatum*), may or may not be native, depending on which expert you read. Although it grows wild along the southern Atlantic and Gulf coasts of the United States, its six closest relatives grow in and around the Indian Ocean and the South Pacific. Its closest relative, pembagrass (*S. dimidiatum*), is native to East Africa. One expert cautions that St. Augustine grass's original home is "part of a larger migrational mystery involving . . . other cosmopolitan seashore grasses that lack proven capability of long-range sea dispersal." There are three explanations for its presence in the New World: it is indigenous; Europeans brought it over; or it arrived here—no one knows how—long before 1492. Post-1492 arrival is the obvious explanation, especially since indigenousness seems unlikely given *Stenotaphrum*'s apparent home base in the Indian Ocean. But the varied nature of New World *S. secundatum* requires either a long residence in the New World or multiple introductions after 1492.[24]

Extremely popular in Florida, where it is known as St. Augustine grass, *S. secundatum* was actually first noted as growing in South Carolina in 1788 by botanist Thomas Walter, whose *Flora Caroliniana* is one of the first North American botanical surveys. Now found on all continents except Antarctica, the grass spread rapidly. It was discovered in the Bahamas by 1730, Jamaica by 1750, Brazil by 1767, Hawaii by 1798, and Australia by 1822. Since St. Augustine grass spreads almost exclusively by vegetative means, grass clones carpet vast areas of the Southeast, making the breeding of new varieties difficult. To those accustomed to mowing acres of *S. secundatum*, planting it in a pot may seem absurd. Yet this is precisely what horticulturalists urge you to do with *S. secundatum* var. *variegatum*, variegated St. Augustine grass, which sells for five dollars a plant. This variety is similar to regular St. Augustine grass except that it has white stripes. From time to time, it spontaneously appears in grass exposed to laundry detergent or swimming pool water.[25]

The other two grasses, centipede and zoysia, owe their presence in the United States in part to the efforts of Frank N. Meyer, perhaps the most famous of the USDA's early plant explorers. A twenty-five-year-old Dutchman, Meyer arrived in America in 1901. By 1905 he was in China, hunting down new species and walking over a thousand miles on foot. Meyer made four expeditions to China, from which he brought back over twenty-five hundred species, including forty-five varieties of soybean, laying the foundation for that crop's phenomenal Western success. He also touted the benefits of tofu long before anyone else. Just prior to leaving Peking in 1908, he collected an interesting lemon from a potted plant—the Meyer lemon. Many considered it the best tasting of all lemons. It is a popular garden tree in warm climates and often a component of concentrated frozen lemonade. After examining Chinese and Japanese chestnuts for their resistance to the chestnut blight that was then destroying America's trees, Meyer noted in 1915, "This Japanese chestnut, *Castanea japonica*, might be used as a factor in hybridization experiments together with American, European, and Chinese species to create immune or nearly immune strains of chestnuts," thus starting a breeding experiment that continues today. To the mutual delight and chagrin of many, it was he who introduced America to *Pyrus calleryana*, the Callery or Bradford pear.[26] In 1906 Meyer brought back samples of *Zoysia japonica*, zoysia grass, from Korea. Although *Z. japonica* had been introduced into the States ten years before from Manchuria, Meyer introduced the first plants from Korea. Today a cultivar, *Z. japonica* Meyer, honors him. You've probably read about this variety in advertisements promoting a "super" grass.

American lawns sprout three genera of zoysia, *Japonica, Matrella,* and *Tenuifolia. Japonica,* the hardiest and only zoysia available as seed, is indigenous to temperate eastern Asia, where it has been cultivated for over a thousand years. In Japan, well-cared-for zoysia lawns are traditional settings for outdoor tea ceremonies, especially in the spring. Indeed, one of the common names for *Z. japonica* is "Japanese lawn grass." From farther south in the Philippines, USDA botanist C. V. Piper collected specimens of *Zoysia matrella* in 1911, with the idea of providing a new grass for the southeast coasts of America. Less cold resistant than its Japanese cousin, this Philippine grass, known in America as Manila grass, has finer leaves than *Z. japonica* and, when mowed, makes for a prettier lawn. The third species, *Z. tenuifolia,* hails from the Indian Ocean's Mascarene Islands (Mauritius, Réunion, and Little Rodriguez) and is the least hardy but finest leaved of the three.[27]

While traveling by steamer on the Yangtze River in 1918, Meyer disappeared, probably falling overboard, although there are those who suspect foul play. In his baggage were found *Eremochloa ophiuroides* seeds he had collected in Hunan Province. So it was that centipede grass became Meyer's posthumous gift to southern lawns, where it is known as "the lazy man's grass," thanks to its almost carefree nature. It remains one of the most planted grasses of the southern coastal plain—millions of acres of lawn; all descendants of Meyer's packet of seeds.[28] Unfortunately, the same mole crickets that infest bahia grass are equally partial to centipede. Lawn fanatics have spent millions of dollars each year to eradicate these insects but have succeeded only in creating insecticide-resistant insects whose control requires increasingly potent poisons, which are typically broad-spectrum insecticides, killing all insects, whether harmful or beneficial.

Dirt cheap when sold as centipede, *E. ophiuroides* rises in price when hawked as the ornamental "Chinese love grass," which "forms an 18 inch high, wide-leafed dense clump and loves sun from mid-summer through autumn. Cloud-like drifts of reddish-pink seed heads hover just above the leaves! They become a rich gold as they mature. This plant is great in containers or in a midborder position in the landscape."[29] As with many exotics, centipede outcompetes native plants, especially in disturbed habitats, which has lead several authorities to consider it a weed.

A Sow's Ear from a Silk Purse

The Legacy of Sericulture

Despite four hundred years of effort, the American silk industry has never achieved the success its boosters dreamed it might. But efforts to establish it have introduced alien flora and fauna. Ironically, the species that silk boosters worked hardest to establish have thrived least, while less popular species and escapees have become the objects of massive government-sponsored eradication programs; programs that have, in turn, had untoward effects upon the native American landscape.

The Chinese are generally credited with inventing silk culture. Chinese legend tells of an emperor's wife who first taught people how to rear the silkworm (*Bombyx mori*) on the leaves of the white mulberry (*Morus alba*). As silk was enormously profitable, the Chinese jealously guarded the secrets of its manufacture, and Westerners, confusing silk with cotton, supposed it grew on trees. Two intrepid sixth-century Nestorian monks used a hollow cane to smuggle the first silkworm eggs out of China to Constantinople. From these few egg clusters descended the millions of silkworms that would be raised in Europe over the next twelve hundred years. Europeans did not know of the white mulberry, however, until the fourteenth century, contenting themselves with raising worms on the black mulberry, *M. nigra*, an acceptable but inferior food source for *Bombyx*.[1]

Cold and humid British winters prevented the English from establishing profitable silkworm farms. That eastern North America's winters are far colder did not deter Virginia's colonists when they discovered mulberries in the woods around Jamestown. "There was an assay made to make silke, and surely the wormes prospered excellently well until the master workman fell sick, during which tyme they were eaten with ratts."[2] Despite this inauspicious beginning, silk would remain an American get-rich-quick dream for the next three hundred years. King James I encouraged silk farming not only to promote luxury goods, but also to undermine Virginia's love affair with tobacco. So intent was he to stop cultivation of the noxious sotweed that he required new plantations to plant mulberries. Georgia's promoters so favored silk that Savannah's coat of arms to this day carries a silkworm on its crest. Benjamin Franklin urged the establishment of a silk factory in Philadelphia. And both George Washington and Thomas Jefferson planted mulberries on their plantations.

At first boosters hoped that the American or red mulberry, *Morus rubra*, would prove useful. Native to much of eastern North America from New England south to Florida and west to Iowa and Texas, the red mulberry promised free food for the taking. Native Americans had long cultivated the tree in groves near their villages, harvesting the fruit to eat and using the fibrous inner bark to make garments. Indeed, the remnants of De Soto's ill-fated sixteenth-century expedition, taking their cue from Choctaw squaws, included ropes made from this bark and used to rig the vessels they built to travel back to Mexico. But *Bombyx* silkworms, although they will eat red mulberry leaves, do not like it, preferring those of their natural food tree, the white mulberry.[3]

In 1522 Cortez imported both *Bombyx* worms and *M. alba* to Mexico, making him perhaps the first person to introduce sericulture to the New World. English colonies in North America established groves of white mulberry following Jamestown's founding nearly a hundred years after Cortez. Hopeful farmers also planted the black mulberry, *M. nigra*, but it proved too tender to survive New England winters. Farther south, though, escapees of both white and black mulberries naturalized. The white became rather common in the eastern United States, while the more tender black mulberry remained restricted to the warmer south. Today the white mulberry grows throughout the continental United States and Hawaii, outcompeting and hybridizing with the native red mulberry, which is actually in decline in some areas. Although watchdog groups classify the tree as moderately invasive, many consider it a weed. Nevertheless, it is still commercially available.

The year 1776 replaced English speculators with American, and the boondoggle continued. Like all things American, it also grew in scope, setting the stage for the 1830s "mulberry mania." William Robert Prince was the fourth generation to run the family's nursery in Flushing, Long Island. A restless entrepreneur, Prince introduced osiers, sorghum, the Chinese yam, and merino sheep into the United States. He also helped found Sacramento, California, on a gold-prospecting trip out West, promoted American viticulture, wrote books on grapes, apples, and roses, and fueled both the mulberry and ailanthus manias of the nineteenth century. His great-grandfather started the Linnaean Botanic Garden in 1737, which the modest Prince renamed as William R. Prince and Company. The 113-acre nursery is where the miracle mulberry,

Morus multicaulis, was first grown in America. A quicker-growing, larger-leaved variety of the white mulberry, *M. multicaulis* was brought from the Philippines to France in 1824, and Prince imported it into America in 1826. William Kendrick, author of *American Silk Growers Guide*, took it from there to his nursery in Newton, Massachusetts, "and gradually marvelous stories of its value spread from town to town and from state to state. Nurserymen gave up all other business to propagate the South Sea novelty; farmers covered their land with the trees, and all eastern America, converted into one great mulberry plantation, was to become the rival of the Orient and of Europe in the production of silk. Plants brought fabulous prices, and the north, the south, and the west struggled with each other to secure them in the auctions rooms of eastern cities," single trees selling for five dollars apiece.[4]

Among those who hitched their fortunes to silk were religious utopians. The Shakers, credited with introducing silk farming to Kentucky, never managed to make much money from their efforts, but the Harmonists did. Founded by German-born George Rapp, the Harmonists were a communal, celibate community awaiting Christ's imminent return. Settling first in Harmony, Pennsylvania, in 1804, they moved to New Harmony, Indiana, in 1815, and then back to Pennsylvania in 1824 to a town they christened Economy. Rapp's granddaughter Gertrude (he already had children when he decided to become celibate) became nationally known for the sericulture she started in 1827, which flourished until the 1850s, when cheaper foreign silk led the Harmonists to quit silk. Another utopian drawn to silk was George Benson, whose Northampton Association of Education and Industry in Massachusetts practiced communal ownership of the equipment and buildings necessary to silk farming. Although short-lived, the Northampton Association lasted long enough to provide Sojourner Truth a temporary home and a permanent calling, mixing as it did Garrisonian abolition with business.[5]

Both the Massachusetts legislature and the U.S. House of Representatives published manuals on the silk industry, and the U.S. Treasury commissioned a 220-page report on silk manufacture. Silk promoter Jonathan Cobb's 1831 *A Manual Containing Information Respecting the Growth of the Mulberry Tree with Suitable Directions for the Culture of Silk* proved so popular that it went through four editions by 1839, and Congress ordered two thousand copies. Cobb himself built a silk mill in 1837 that produced some thirty-five thousand dollars of sewing silk a year.

Ward Cheney, a New Jersey nursery and cocoonery operator, promoted *M. multicaulis* through his monthly *American Silk-Grower and Farmer's Manual*. He moved to South Manchester, Connecticut, where in 1838 he started what would become the largest silk mill in the United States. Although Cheney's cocoonery failed, the Cheney Silk Manufacturing Company became famous as a model mill town and hosted tours of its workers' quarters. Cheney built boarding houses for the single workers and individual cottages for married workers complete with gas, running water, and garden plots. He also built schools, a sixty-thousand-dollar public hall, and a free library.

Prince, too, built a cocoonery to profit from his trees. But neither he nor his fellow speculators took into account the vagaries of nature and the economy. Quieted by the economic crisis of the panic of 1837, mulberry mania plunged when the severe New England winter killed off hundreds of thousands of trees. It disappeared completely when disease eliminated most of the survivors. John Brown, of later abolitionist fame, went bankrupt when his dreams of a silken fortune from land speculation in Franklin Mills, Ohio, bottomed out.[6] By 1839 speculators were stuck with a million unwanted trees. Seedlings that had sold for five dollars apiece two years before couldn't fetch a dollar. Even Prince's cocoonery went bust. Some ancient trees alive today are said to be the living legacy of Prince's project. In addition to these and wild descendants of long-forgotten nurseries, mulberry madness also littered our maps with Mulberry Groves, Hills, Farms, Rows, and Streets, reminders that our ancestors were as gullible as we when it comes to wasting money on harebrained schemes.

Another unintended legacy of silken dreams is the paper mulberry, *Broussonetia papyrifera*. Native to east Asia, the small tree has a fibrous inner bark, which the Chinese used to make paper around 100 C.E. This skill and the tree spread east to the Pacific islands, transported by Polynesians who made bark cloth, and west to Samarkand, from where in 751 conquering Arabs carried them across North Africa to Moorish Spain. From there both tree and paper made their way into northern Europe. In Asian countries where both silk and paper are made, *Bombyx* silkworms are fed mulberry leaves that remain after the paper is made; the leaves are useless for paper production. Silkworms will eat *B. papyrifera*, although they much prefer *M. alba*. Westerners confused the various species of mulberry, and colonists are thought to have brought *B. papyrifera* to the New World thinking it was *M. alba*. Ancient paper mulberries growing in North Carolina and Virginia are said to be examples of this botanical mistake. Williamsburg, Virginia, has several gnarled specimens that predate the city's founding.

Thomas Jefferson was partial to mulberries. At Monticello he named his slave quarters Mulberry Row, after the native red mulberry trees he planted there to screen the cabins from view. Double rows of paper mulberries lined the circular drive at nearby Poplar Forest. It is curious then that Jefferson, widely touted as a savant, did not know that the *Bombyx* silkworm was a foreign species. In *Notes on the State of Virginia,* he writes, "The silk-worm is a native, and the mulberry, proper for its food, grows kindly."[7] *Bombyx* proved controversial in Monticello's future. Eventually sold to pay off family debts, Monticello wound up the property of James Barclay, of whom Jefferson's granddaughter Cornelia Randolph wrote in 1831, "He is full of schemes; they tell us he intends to cultivate the grape and to rear silk worms and has some plan in his head for making a fortune which I do not know; they say he is a schemer and perhaps may get tired after a time." He did, advertising the place two years later: "It is abundantly supplied with every species of Mulberry, and is perhaps one of the most eligible situations in the world for the lucrative pursuit of the culture of Silk." Jefferson admirers allege that Barclay razed the president's carefully planned gardens and groves to make room for his ill-fated silkworm farm. Barclay descendants reply that their ancestor admired Jefferson and took excellent care of the property. Whatever the case, mulberries returned to Monticello in the 1990s, when they once again graced Mulberry Row. Meanwhile *B. papyrifera* has naturalized itself everywhere east of the Mississippi as well as in the lower Great Plains states, with several states watching it carefully as a potential invasive alien.[8]

While mulberry madness remains a footnote in American botanic history, another of Prince's projects had more serious consequences for the American forest. Prince had growing in his nursery specimens of the *Ailanthus altimissa,* which ultimately helped bail him out of his mulberry morass. Nearly everyone sees something oriental or palmlike in the ailanthus's tall, slender trunk and gracefully arching branches and leaves. Frederick Law Olmsted supposedly urged planting it in Central Park to simulate tropical palms.[9] The tree, native to much of southeast Asia and northern Australia, takes its name, ailanthus, from a Latinized Indonesian *ai lanto,* which means "tree of the gods," an allusion to its rapid growth and height, which can reach eighty feet. Its popular name, tree of heaven, is a mistranslation. The species most common to the United States is A. *altimissa,* or the *really* tall tree of the gods.

William Hamilton, who provided Thomas Jefferson with paper mulberry, is the first person known to have imported the ailanthus into America, bringing it back from England in 1784 to plant as a curiosity. By the early nineteenth century several nurseries, including Prince's, carried the ailanthus as an ornamental. By the 1860s Prince's was shipping trees as far away as Oregon. West Coast gardeners, however, could have found the tree growing in the California Sierras, thanks to Chinese Forty-Niners who brought it with them from China.[10]

Ailanthus glandulosus. Charles F. Millspaugh, *American Medicinal Plants: An Illustrated and Descriptive Guide* (New York, 1887).

Ailanthus mania, like mulberry madness, began in New York City. In the 1830s residents so complained about insects invading their houses through unscreened windows that the city uprooted its linden and horse chestnut trees by the hundreds. "Just at that period, the Ailanthus was growing into notice. It was represented as being from China, of exceedingly rapid growth, with smooth, erect trunk, and long, feathered foliage; indeed, every way so noble as to be styled 'The Tree of Heaven.' Its great recommendation, however, just at that time, was its complete exemption from insects of any and every kind. . . . Every one who inquired about street trees was told of 'the magnificent Ailanthus! It outgrows everything, making eight or ten feet in a year; its leaves are four or five feet long, and it has noble spreading branches; but, above all, no insect will come near it. Good! That is just the tree for streets,' and so one street after another, old streets and new ones, were planted with Ailanthus, until 'up-town' had become completely orientalized with this famous tree of the Gods ('*Gotterbaum*') as the German call it," the *New York Times* recalled in 1852.[11] Henry James also remembered this era, writing in *Washington Square* of that New York address as it appeared in 1835: "It was here that you took your first walks abroad, following the nursery-maid with unequal step, and sniffing up the strange odor of the ailanthus-trees which at that time formed the principal umbrage of the Square, and diffused an aroma that you were not yet critical enough to dislike as it deserved."[12] Baltimore, Boston, and most of America followed New York City's lead, much to Prince's and other nurserymen's happiness and fiscal health, especially since the tree produces an abundance of viable seeds and is easily transplanted as suckers. Then people realized, as had James, that the tree stinks.

Originally partial to the ailanthus because of its rapid growth, leading landscape gardener Andrew Jackson Downing led the attack. His 1841 *A Treatise on the Theory and Practice of Landscape Gardening, Adapted to North America* was perhaps the most influential landscaping book ever published in this country, remaining in print well into the twentieth century. As mentioned previously, Downing was picked to design the grounds of the Capitol, the White House, and the Smithsonian Institution. From his editorial pulpit in the popular magazine *Horticulturist,* he excoriated the ailanthus as "an usurper in rather bad *odor* at home, which has come over to this land of liberty, under the garb of utility, to make foul the air, with its pestilent breath, and devour the soil, with its intermeddling roots—a tree that has the fair outside and the treacherous heart of the Asiatics. . . . Down with the ailanthus! therefore, we cry with the populace."[13]

The ailanthus was a failure as an ornamental, but it resurrected America's silk industry. Hardier and more prolific than the mulberry, the ailanthus tree is fodder for the ailanthus silkworm, *Samia cynthia,* whose large but sloppy cocoons produce a stronger but less luxurious silk than that of *Bombyx.* While the domesticated *Bombyx* silkworm, unable to fly, cannot survive without human support, the wilder and hardier ailanthus silkworm can live outdoors without aid. It is now established in and around many towns in the eastern United States, having survived in the wild when the silk farms responsible for its introduction succumbed.

American interest in the ailanthus silkworm followed Europe's lead. French sericulture suffered a near fatal blow in the 1840s, when an unknown disease decimated the *Bombyx* caterpillars. Desperate researchers seeking a cause and a cure included Pasteur, whose interest in microbes is said to have been piqued by his investigations into the disease. The disease was ultimately called pebrine (from *pebre*, or pepper, for the black spots on sick worms), and was microbial in origin. In 1857 another Frenchman, entomologist Felix Guerine-Meneville, hoping to save a national industry, imported the ailanthus silkworm as a pebrine-resistant source for silk. His success led others to copy him, including Americans. The newly formed U.S. Department of Agriculture commented in its 1862 *Report of the Commissioner of Agriculture,* "Special interest is felt by the department in the propagation and culture of the ailanthus silk worm of China. This insect has been successfully bred in this country during the last season. It will live and grow and spin its silk in the open air in most of the States of the Union, feeding upon the leaves of the ailanthus, hitherto regarded among us as a worthless, if not a noxious, tree. The worm has recently been introduced into France, and has excited an extraordinary interest. The silk of this worm lasts twice as long as that of the mulberry worm, and can be washed like linen. Indeed, in China the garments made from it are often worn by the second generation."[14] But the Civil War intervened, as did the prohibitive cost of labor in the United States, with Asian countries easily undercutting American prices. The silk also was deemed inferior to that produced by true silkworm. The dream of silken fortunes once again unraveled.

Rejected by landscapers and silk farmers alike, the ailanthus became a weed or trash tree, pejorative terms for a plant whose roots predate those of most Americans. Betty Smith tried redeeming it in her 1943 novel, *A Tree Grows in Brooklyn*: "There is a tree that grows in Brooklyn. Some people call it the Tree of Heaven. No matter where its seed falls, it makes a tree which struggles to reach the sky. It grows in boarded-up lots and out of neglected rubbish heaps. It grows up out of cellar gratings. It is the only tree that grows out of cement. It grows lushly . . . survives without sun, water, and seemingly without earth. It would be considered beautiful except that there are too many of it."[15] But few people rallied to Smith's populist defense of the ailanthus, most agreeing with what the *New York Times* had said about the tree a hundred years earlier: "It had become decidedly *common*."[16]

A female gypsy moth. John Comstock, *A Manual of the Study of Insects* (Ithaca, 1901).

Decidedly common and universally loathed is another relic of the silk industry—the gypsy moth. It was loosed upon an unsuspecting nation in 1869 by a well-intentioned dreamer of silken fortunes. Thirty-year-old Frenchman Etienne Leopold Trouvelot immigrated to Boston in 1857 and promptly got bitten by silk fever, which was common at the time. New Englanders who had succumbed to mulberry mania in the 1830s lost everything when northern winters killed off their mulberries trees. Thirty years later people were still looking for a way to provide the American silk-manufacturing industry, then centered in Connecticut, with homegrown silk. The obvious solution was to find a worm and tree that was hardy enough to survive in New England.

Trouvelot began by experimenting with several native American moths whose cocoons resembled that of the ailanthus silkworm. He finally chose the American silkworm, the Polyphemus moth. Five years passed before he got conditions right, but in an 1867 article in the *American Naturalist*, he boasted that two years before, "not less than a million could be seen feeding in the open air upon bushes covered with a net; five acres of woodland were crawling with caterpillar life." Had he but stopped here, his name would not be an anathema today.[17]

But he did not stop. By 1868 he was raising European gypsy moths—which he probably picked up during a visit home in 1866—in a shed in his yard in Medford, near Boston. Trouvelot wanted to breed a superior silkworm moth. After all, fellow Frenchman Guerin-Meneville had managed to do so with the ailanthus silkworm, crossing it with an Indian cousin to produce a hybrid hardier than its parents. Why, though, would a member of the Boston Natural History Society think he could cross the gypsy moth, *Lymantria dispar*, with the silkworm, *Bombyx mori*? Because, in 1868, rather than *Lymantria dispar*, the gypsy moth was classified as *Bombyx dispar*, and hence assumed to be a close cousin to the true silkworm, *Bombyx mori*. Were Trouvelot successful in combining the silkworm's silk with the gypsy moth's hardiness and catholic tastes in food, his fortune would have been made.

Today, however, the gypsy moth is *Lymantria dispar*, a member of the tussock moth family—no kin at all to the silkworm *Bombyx*. Such confusion arose in part because, although Linnaeus promoted his binomial system of nomenclature in the eighteenth century, it was not until the twentieth century that the scientific community reached a consensus on just what characteristics— sexual, structural, function, or familial—were to be used to classify organisms, what names were to be used, and what was to be done with two or more competing names. Despite what you learned or think you learned in high-school biology, the Linnaean system, according to the 1911 *Encyclopedia Britannica*, "is an index to a department of the book of nature, and as such is useful to the student. It does not aspire to any higher character, and . . . cannot be looked upon as a scientific and natural arrangement." Tinkering with the system continues today, both new technologies such as DNA analysis and fads in scientific opinion persuade people to make changes.

Nineteenth-century scientists, therefore, had to take purported relationships between species with a very large grain of salt, which Trouvelot apparently did not. He began with great hopes, little suspecting how later generations would regard his enthusiastic appreciation of *Bombyx dispar*'s—excuse me, *Lymantria dispar*'s—larvae: "What a destruction of leaves this single species of insect could make if only a one-hundredth part of the eggs laid ever came to maturity! A few years would be sufficient for the propagation of a number large enough to devour all the leaves of our forests."[18]

Since the true silkworm and the ailanthus silkworm are not closely related, Trouvelot failed to breed a superior worm. But before he gave up, he lost several gypsy moth egg clusters. Some say they simply fell through an open window, others say that a storm broke the window and they fell out. Either way, one could indirectly blame medical science for the gypsy moth's presence. Screens were uncommon on windows until the end of the nineteenth century, when the British bacteriologist Sir Ronald Ross proved mosquitoes carried malaria—a discovery that would garner him the 1902 Nobel Prize for Medicine and create a run on window screens. The *Oxford English Dictionary* credits an 1895 Montgomery Ward and Company catalog with the first use of "window screen." Had

Ross made his discovery earlier, we might have been spared both Trouvelot's gypsy moths and the ubiquitous ailanthus, which, you will recall, replaced the bug-laden linden and chestnut trees.

With a new world before them, Trouvelot's worms were fruitful and multi-plied and multiplied and multiplied. Trouvelot, however, quit as a breeder of worms, turned his eyes heavenward, and became a Harvard astronomer, return-ing in 1882 to France, where he died an acclaimed stargazer in 1895—the same year "window screens" entered the language. Meanwhile his missing gypsy moths were busy becoming as numerous as the stars. By 1888 worried Massa-chusetts agricultural experts were aware that gypsy moths were on the loose, and in 1889 the moths swarmed through Trouvelot's old neighborhood, where alarmed residents collected them by the bucketful, but to no avail.

Despite both state and federal efforts, nothing could stop the moth. Natu-rally occurring predators and parasites usually restrain it in its native environ-ment, although even there it can devastate forests, as it did several times in the nineteenth century. But so seemingly benign in Europe is the moth that lepi-dopterists in nineteenth-century Britain even bred it for release in an attempt to bolster its numbers. Experts calculate that it has been expanding the radius of its range in America by some ten miles annually since 1869. By 1880 it had infested 400 square miles of Massachusetts, by 1905, 2,500 square miles in four states, and by 1974, 200,000 square miles in the U.S. and Canada. A three-year study in Pennsylvania showed a geometric explosion; 10,000 infested acres in 1969 became 100,000 in 1971 and 900,000 in 1973. Despite a succession of quarantine and inspection laws designed to corral it, the gypsy moth has ridden north and northeast on the prevailing winds, and leapfrogged south and west, hitching rides on recreational vehicles and campers, which prompted inspectors routinely to set up shop in popular camping spots to catch the vagrants.[19]

Nor was Trouvelot the only person accidentally to loose Mothra on America. In 1920 a New Jersey agriculture inspector discovered gypsy moths that he determined had come from the Netherlands ten years earlier with a load of blue spruce. In 1993 a German container ship in Wilmington, North Carolina, was infested with European and Asian gypsy moths as well as a hybrid of the two.[20]

When not carried interstate by vacationing campers, the gypsy moth nor-mally travels far only as a newborn caterpillar. These miniature monsters spin a thread of silk and launch themselves into the wind, "ballooning" up to thirty-five miles across country and as high as two thousand feet. Only as caterpillars are they destructive. Adult moths never eat, a characteristic shared by all mem-bers of the tussock moth family. But each egg mass harbors from 150 to 1,500 caterpillars-to-be, and each caterpillar eats a good square foot of leaves a day for eight to ten weeks. That's 560 square feet of leaves per caterpillar. Sites on Long Island have recorded twenty thousand egg cases per acre. What a mass of frass such munching worms must pass.[21]

Little stops them. Most of Canada remains unscarred because the North American variety's eggs don't survive well below zero degree centigrade, though even the Eskimo must pause when learning of Siberian egg cases that have survived at negative forty-one degrees centigrade. From the 1890s until World War II, government exterminators' weapon of choice was lead arsenate—a poison as deadly to mammals and bees as it was to the increasingly resistant gypsy moth caterpillar. DDT replaced lead and arsenic following World War II, with a standard application of one pound for every acre. This continued for nearly twenty years, until Rachel Carson's *Silent Spring* forced its stateside ban in 1963. Since then, use of biological controls has assumed a major role.

Various birds—crows, grackles, robins—regularly dine on moths. Several species of mice and the gray squirrel make serious inroads into areas overpopulated with the gypsy moths. But the gypsy moth enjoys relative immunity in the States, having no real enemies other than humans. Desperate public officials have combed the gypsy moth's native haunts for predators and parasites. They've discovered over a hundred, mainly ground beetles and wasps. One wasp species practices an exquisite torture, laying its eggs inside a living caterpillar, with the wasp's progeny then borrowing out through the caterpillar's skin. But success is hit or miss. In the thirty-five years since being released, no Asian wasp introduced to control the moth's numbers has survived in America. A Japanese fungus that may be the last best hope against the moth disappeared for some seventy years. This fungus, a virus, and a bacterium are stars in today's arsenal.

Discovered in 1915, the bacterium *Bacillus thurungiensis*, when occurring in sufficient quantities, kills gypsy moth caterpillars by infecting their digestive systems. While most other life forms, including humans, have neutral to acidic digestive systems, lepidopterans have alkaline systems, which are home sweet home to *Bt*, as the bacterium is known. Unfortunately *Bt* doesn't care whose guts it congests, killing beneficial caterpillars as well as gypsy moth caterpillars.[22]

Partner in the war against gypsies is a virus that, if eaten, attacks a cell's ability to make proteins. *Borrelinavirus reprimens* causes "wilt" in caterpillars. Infected individuals become sluggish and swollen and wilt and droop, hanging head downwards from their perch while their cuticle skin begins leaking body fluids teeming with the infectious virus. Unlike *Bt*, *B. reprimens* attacks few other species of caterpillar.[23]

But the biological champ is the fungus *Entomophaga maimaiga*, a relative of bread mold. Native to Japan, it was first released in the United States in 1910, when *E. maimaiga*–infected gypsy moths were deliberately freed near Boston. Nothing happened, although the fungus may have caused moth die-offs in the 1930s. Rereleased in 1989, it has since proven effective in several major moth die-offs. As its genus name *Entomophaga* suggests, this fungus kills by feeding on the caterpillars' insides. Its species name, *maimaiga*, is the Japanese common name for the gypsy moth. At first spreading southward along the East Coast from worm to worm and by spores, *E. maimaiga* now has gypsy moth eradicators happily spreading it throughout their woods. One drawback is that it takes up to a week to kill its host, which all the while munches away on leaves. Another is that, unlike the bacteria *Bt* and the virus *B. reprimens*, the fungus remains a relatively permanent feature of the environment, and its effect on other lepidopterans is unknown.[24]

The effect of another biological control agent was equally unfortunate. *Compsilura concinnata*, a small European fly, like all members of the Tachinid family, parasitizes other insects. To control the gypsy moth, the federal government released it in thirty states between 1906 and 1986. While its maggots do parasitize gypsy moth caterpillars, consuming them from the inside out, they also attack one hundred and eighty other insect species, including harmless and beautiful American silkmoth caterpillars like the giant promethea and cecropia. These two species were so numerous a hundred years ago that their cocoons were collected by the hundreds, but they have since precipitously declined in the Northeast. No one knew why until researchers in Massachusetts discovered that *C. concinnata* infected American silk moth caterpillars at least as effectively as it did gypsy moth caterpillars. But nothing can be done; *C. concinnata*, like the gypsy moth, is here to stay.[25]

Other control programs include releasing sterilized males, which reduces gypsy moth numbers but is costly and slow. Also, fecund females mate with naturally occurring virile males so that any success is temporary. Pheromone-baited traps are phenomenally successful, but impractical for eradication programs, although commonly used to measure the spread of gypsy moths. Homeowners try to save individual trees by wrapping tree trunks with burlap, which the caterpillars use for shelter at night. Vigilant tree lovers then collect and kill the larvae.

Gypsy moths are not particular about what they eat. While this seemed a desirable trait to Trouvelot as he tried to breed a cheaper silkworm, it is the despair of those trying to kill or contain an insect that can gnaw the leaves of over five hundred different tree species, is partial to some fifty or more, and positively adores oaks. Ironically the mulberry is not among its favorites. Though devastated, northeastern forests actually harbor numerous tree species unpalatable to the gypsy moth. Disaster, though, looms for the oak and pine forests in much of the South. What the moth doesn't kill outright, it weakens. Two or three years of devastation so depletes a hardwood's reserves that it is easy prey to bark beetles and root rot. Studies show that 58 percent of oaks are killed within three years of an infestation, while denuded evergreens usually die the first year. Already, the long, southwest-reaching ridges of the Appalachian Mountains are being devoured. Tourists on Virginia's Skyline Drive and Blue Ridge Parkway pass through leafless forests even in midsummer.[26]

The gypsy moth will not destroy America's forests. But it will permanently alter their composition, sending reverberations throughout an ecosystem already reeling from chestnut blight, Dutch elm disease, the woolly adelgid, and acid rain. Virginia, where I live, has been fighting the gypsy moth for years. Each year the front lines are farther south and nearer home. In the last decade of the twentieth century, Virginia newspaper accounts took on the pessimistic tones of the doomed. Despairing homeowners tried using burlap in vain. The falling frass sounded like rustling leaves, and the worms crawled in and the worms crawled out, before, behind, above, between, below. The skittish closed their windows at night, lest they awaken wrapped in a silk cocoon. Then, in 1995, overnight, like Zenacharib's army, the pests died off at the hand of God, disguised as the fungus *E. maimaiga*. The year of the great die-off, gypsy moth caterpillars defoliated 850,000 acres of Virginia forest. For the next four years, officially they ate nothing. But *E. maimaiga* is not magic, though it seemed like it at the time, and gypsy moth numbers have once again swollen to dangerous heights, ravaging 71,000 acres in 2000.[27]

Everywhere I have lived in the South bears traces of America's love affair with silk. Palmlike ailanthus fringe the forest's edge outside my window, and though no ailanthus moths inhabit my ailantery, I can see them when I visit Washington, D.C., in the summer, their caterpillars chewing their way along ailanthus leaflets. Eradicators regularly spray for gypsy moths along the nearby Blue Ridge Parkway, and the Virginia Forest Service sells trees it advertises as resistant to gypsy moth depredations. Although the mulberries growing in my fields are, I believe, *M. rubra*, I can always drive over the mountain and into Tidewater and Williamsburg, where there are white mulberries so stooped with age they must be propped up. I grew up near Silk Hope and now live ten miles from a Mulberry Hill. Nearby Monticello has its Mulberry Row and my childhood had Dr. Seuss's *And to Think That I Saw It on Mulberry Street.*

Psychedelic Gardens

What Grandmother Grew in Her Backyard

Chances are that your garden harbors plants with potent mind-altering abilities, some of which you know about, others of which you are unaware. Some may be illegal just to possess. Many plants either accumulate or produce chemical compounds to help them in their perpetual battle against predators, which would eat them to death. All our kitchen herbs, for example, derive their culinary attractiveness from compounds that the plants produce to deter herbivores. It just happens that the primate *Homo sapiens* likes the taste of, say, mint and so has carried it throughout the world, selecting the mintier individuals to propagate, and breeding new species along the way. Some of these chemicals do more than taste good; they can cure us, alleviate our pains and aches, and even bend our minds. To this day the world relies on plants to fill its medicine cabinet. Before nineteenth-century industrialized drug production, many gardens included a medicinal section, where plants known for their beneficial effects were grown. As large-scale medicine manufacture took over, we forgot these plants' medical uses but kept many for their beauty, just as explorers brought back to our gardens plants whose beauty disguised their medicinal properties.

So it was that nobody in the west had any reason to suspect the psychic properties of morning glory (*Ipomoea violacea*). Close relatives like field bindweed (*Convolvulus arvensis*), which grows throughout Europe (and now America, thanks to inadvertent colonization), are entirely without hallucinogenic properties, as are the American native sweet potatoes (*I. batatas*) and *I. jalapa*, a famous nineteenth-century remedy for constipation. Unsuspecting gardeners fell in love with *I. vioilacea*'s ephemeral beauty, transplanting it throughout the temperate world, where it has become, some say, the world's most commonly planted flower and, in the eyes of farmers and governments, a noxious and invasive weed. It was so pervasive in our grandmothers' gardens that one common name is granny vine.

Drug companies bent on developing new pharmaceuticals accidentally discovered *Ipomoea*'s hallucinogenic properties while studying herbal remedies for a variety of ills. One such remedy was ergot, used to control bleeding in childbirth. Ergot is a fungus that infects grasses, deforming seeds to several times their normal size and creating misshapen purplish bodies that farmers thought resembled cockspurs—hence the name ergot, from the French *argot* for spur. Since its size depends directly on the size of the grain it infects, ergot is most often noticed in larger grained cereals such as rye, although it infects dozens of different grasses. The fungus produces several mind-altering alkaloids. It caused the mysterious Holy Fire of the Middle Ages, when hundreds of people were seized with uncontrollable tics and convulsions. Some victims lost their arms, legs, and sanity. Today historians think these mass manias came from eating bread baked with infected rye. The victims suffered from either convulsive or gangrenous ergot poisoning, the first causing muscle spasms and delirium, the other causing gangrene that resulted from constricted blood vessels in the extremities. But prior generations thought ergot a curse from God or the devil. A consensus that ergot was fungal in origin was not reached until the nineteenth century.[1]

Holy Fire, so named because sufferers felt as if their limbs were on fire, was also known as St. Anthony's fire because monks of the Order of St. Anthony ran a chain of hospitals to tend the victims. Gaston de la Valloire, a pious Frenchman, founded the order in the eleventh century following the miraculous cure of his son after Valloire prayed to St. Anthony. The order is perhaps best remembered today from sixteenth-century German painter Matthias Grünewald's horrific depiction in *The Temptation of St. Anthony*, a panel in the Isenheim altarpiece that was commissioned for an Antonite hospital in Alsace. Thrown back on the ground, St. Anthony is surrounded by hallucinogenic demons and a lesion-covered human, probably a representation of convulsive and gangrenous ergotism.[2]

Lethal in large doses but medicinal in small quantities, ergot was used for centuries to induce labor. It became an international commodity, and Maud Grieve discusses the merits of Austrian, German, Norwegian, Russian, Spanish, Swedish, and Swiss ergots, proclaiming Russian the best but Spanish the largest. New York state physician John Stearns popularized ergot, which he called *Pulvis parturiens (Secale cornutum)*, among American physicians, but as early as 1824 another doctor, David Hosack, counseled against using ergot to hasten childbirth, although he suggested its use to prevent postpartum bleeding —for which it is still used today.[3]

In the late 1930s, while attempting to synthesize a drug based on the effects of ergot but that was more manageable, Swiss chemist Albert Hofmann manufactured lysergic acid diethylamide, whose first name, lysergic, is Greek for "from ergot" (*lys* and *ergic*). After accidentally ingesting the drug, which now is commonly know by its acronym, an intrigued Hofmann decided to experiment and, on April 19, 1943, took the first deliberate LSD trip. Drug aficionados quote his bucolic description: "Now, little by little I could begin to enjoy the unprecedented colors and plays of shapes that persisted behind my closed eyes. Kaleidoscopic, fantastic images surged in on me, alternating, variegated, opening and then closing themselves in circles and spirals, exploding in colored fountains, rearranging and hybridizing themselves in constant flux." What are ignored are the sentences preceding this happy vision: "A demon had invaded me, had taken possession of my body, mind, and soul. I jumped up and screamed, trying to free myself from him, but then sank down again and lay helpless on the sofa. The substance, with which I had wanted to experiment, had vanquished me. It was the demon that scornfully triumphed over my will. I was seized by the dreadful fear of going insane."[4] LSD's father thus experienced both the first good and bad trip. Hofmann's discovery soon fell into the hands of Timothy Leary and the CIA, although they would use the drug for quite different purposes, Leary seeking to expand Western consciousness, the CIA seeking a royal road to mind control. By the mid-1960s LSD was illegal in the United States.

LSD led Hofmann to investigate other hallucinogens. It was he who identified the active ingredients in morning glories. The first westerner known to have theorized morning glories' hallucinogenic properties was Harvard Botanical Museum director Richard Schultes. He argued in 1941 that this Mexican native was the plant that Spanish chronicler Francisco Hernandez described in his 1651 *Rerum Medicarum Novae Hispaniae Thesaurus, seu Plantarium, Animalium, Mineralium Mexicanorum Historia*: "Oliuhqui, which others call coaxihuitl or snake plant, is a climber with thin, green, heart-shaped leaves. . . . The flowers are white, fairly large. . . . The seeds are roundish. . . . When the priests of the Indians wanted to visit with the gods and obtain information from them, they ate of this plant in order to become inebriated. Thousands of fantastic images and demons then appeared to them."[5]

Schultes argued that oliuhqui is today's *Rivea corymbosa* (or *Turbina corymbosa*), which Mexicans still use as a psychic medicine. They associate and use it with what they call tlitliltzin, with *R. corymbosa* being paler in color and "female" and tlitliltzin being black and "male." In 1959 Hofmann was sent samples of both *Rivea corymbosa* and *Ipomoea violacea*; he determined both to contain potent hallucinogens. While scientists received with great skepticism Hofmann's analyses of the seeds as natural sources of LSD-related alkaloids, Dutch drug users did not. Hofmann recounts, "We were apprised by two Dutch wholesale seed companies that their sale of seeds of *Ipomoea violacea*, the ornamental blue morning glory, had reached unusual proportions in recent times. They had heard that the great demand was connected with investigations of these seeds in our laboratory, about which they were eager to learn the details. It turned out that the new demand derived from hippie circles and other groups interested in hallucinogenic drugs. They believed they had found in the oliuhqui seeds a substitute for LSD, which was becoming less and less accessible." That morning glory seeds remain a relatively minor drug, Hofmann explains, is due to their bad taste, their tendency to cause nausea, and their lesser hallucinogenic properties, as well as their tendency to produce "mental emptiness, . . . anxiety and depression."[6]

Rivea corymbosa and *Ipomoea violacea* grow in Mexico and the extreme southern United States. The USDA labels both as native, while asserting that *I. tricolor*, the morning glory vine, which grows freely as far north as Massachusetts, is "probably introduced." Linnaeus is credited with first naming *I. violacea*, and Spanish botanist Antonio Jose de Cavanilles first named *I. tricolor* in 1794. Ethnographers maintain that the two species are the same, with one expert noting twelve scientific names for the species.[7] Just to confuse us, the USDA distinguishes between *I. violacea* and *I. tricolor* in its Plants Database but considers the two as synonymous in its Germplasm Information Resources Network (GRIN).[8] *Ipomoea tricolor*, whether a variant of *I. violacea* or not, has definitely spread far beyond its original boundaries, being present in nearly everyone's garden. Seed companies have been offering packets of *I. tricolor* since the nineteenth century, regularly concocting new varieties to ensure continued sales—a necessary duty since morning glories reseed themselves. By 1900 we were growing a late-blooming version of what became the favorite variety when introduced in the 1930s as "Clarke's Early Flowering Heavenly Blue." In the 1940s Ferry-Morse Seed Company began selling a white variant of "Heavenly Blue" called "Pearly Gates," and in 1960 California plant breeder Darold Decker began promoting a variegated blue and white version of this variant that he called "Flying Saucers."[9] Despite both the suggestive names and drug-circle rumors, Heavenly Blue, Pearly Gates, and Flying Saucers were intended to promote flower sales, not seed consumption, and there is no evidence that the seeds of these varieties were more hallucinogenic than other varieties of *I. tricolor*. Anyway, the odds are that those red and purple morning glories growing uninvited along your fence aren't *I. tricolor*; they're probably tall morning glory (*Ipomoea purpurea*), an alien imported from tropical America that is now growing throughout the United States. It is a prohibited noxious weed in Arizona and is as potent a hallucinogen as *I. tricolor*, according to drug sources.[10] It may be yet another variety of *I. tricolor*, so confused and confusing is the morning glory family.

Papaver somniferum, the oriental or opium poppy, has long been the world's primary pain reliever as well as a beautiful flowering plant and a favorite of your Victorian great-great-grandmother. A self-seeding annual found throughout most of the United States, *P. somniferum* was both common and innocuous enough to be featured in Frank L. Baum's *The Wonderful Wizard of Oz*, where Dorothy and Toto fall asleep "in the midst of a great meadow of poppies. Now it is well known that when there are many of these flowers together their odor is so powerful that anyone who breathes it falls asleep, and if the sleeper is not carried away from the scent of the flowers, he sleeps on and on forever. But Dorothy did not know this, nor could she get away from the bright red flowers that were everywhere about; so presently her eyes grew heavy and she felt she must sit down to rest and to sleep."[11] Baum exaggerates *P. somniferum*'s soporific possibilities, but these traits prompted Linnaeus's species name *somniferum*. Before our war on drugs, the poppy and its opium enjoyed a more distinguished reputation. The ancient Sumerians praised it, as did the Egyptians, Greeks, Romans, Indians, Chinese, and Europeans. Although excoriated and anathematized today, opium nevertheless remains indispensable to modern pharmacists, both morphine and codeine being its derivatives.

Widespread opium addiction and its association with China is a product of international trade. Opium is remarkably adapted to trade. It is lightweight, durable, and immensely profitable, and its analgesic and addictive qualities ensure a loyal and ever-expanding clientele. Arab traders first introduced opium to the Far East fourteen hundred years ago. The Spanish brought tobacco and pipe smoking to the region during the colonial period; Dutch traders in Taiwan combined the three, and the Chinese learned from them.[12] But it took the British to make what had hitherto been a minor problem a major catastrophe. India had long been China's primary opium supplier. But when the British seized control of the subcontinent, they regulated, then expropriated, the production of opium, both dramatically increasing supplies and making it the lynchpin of their eastern empire's profitability. Exports to China averaged 340 tons in 1811 and 1,841 tons in 1829.[13] Chinese attempts to stem the flood culminated in the Opium Wars of 1839–42 and 1856–60, with British greed wrapping itself in the mantle of free trade and civilization to demand a China open to opium. By 1906 India was exporting thirty million dollars a year in opium, with 80 percent of this being shipped directly to China. Americans grabbed what they could of the action, including Yankee trader Warren Delano, who helped oversee the importation of Turkish opium into Canton, China, for the Boston-based shipper Russell and Company. Returning to the states, Delano, the grandfather of Franklin Delano Roosevelt, settled in New York. Other Americans getting rich off Chinese misery included America's first four millionaires: John Jacob Astor, Elias Hasket Derby, Stephen Girard, and Joseph Peabody.[14]

Not that Western opium manufacturers ignored addicts nearer home. That the nineteenth century was the great age of opium addiction is the direct result of laissez faire principles in trade and medicine. Prior to Bayer's discovery of aspirin, opium was the world's primary pain reliever. All countries, east and west, imported tons of it. Western countries were disinclined to make the wholesale addiction of their population a government goal—although this was Britain's aim in China—but opiates were everywhere. Much research fastens on the white, middle-class female addict, as much for the salacious fantasies first encouraged by the antiaddict crusades of the period as for the prescription records that give historians a paper trail to follow. An 1854 New Jersey prescription book, for example, reveals opium to have been the most commonly prescribed drug, present in over 50 percent of all prescriptions.[15] Women were especially likely to be addicts because doctors routinely prescribed morphine during childbirth, with women hiding their subsequent addiction by drinking over-the-counter, opiate-laced nostrums. The poor also had access to enough real opiates to obviate Marx's observation regarding religion's analgesic properties. Opiates formed the basis of almost all pain relievers, from cough drops to cancer nostrums. Mothers quieted colicky infants with patent medicines laced with opium—Godfrey's Cordial, Street's Infants' Quietness, Atkinson's Infants' Preservative, and Mrs. Winslow's Soothing Syrup—hooking addicts early on. The literati sang the praises of opium eating, and doctors thought the drug a panacea.

Rime of the Ancient Mariner author Samuel Taylor Coleridge is perhaps England's most notorious opium addict, partly because he told us about it in a note to his poem "Kubla Khan":

> In consequence of a slight indisposition, an anodyne had been prescribed, from the effects of which he fell asleep in his chair. . . . The Author continued for about three hours in a profound sleep, at least of the external senses, during which time he has the most vivid confidence, that he could not have composed less than from two to three hundred lines; if that indeed can be called composition in which all the images rose up before him as *things*, with a

parallel production of the correspondent expressions, without any sensation or consciousness of effort. On awakening he appeared to himself to have a distinct recollection of the whole, and taking his pen, ink, and paper, instantly and eagerly wrote down the lines that are here preserved. At this moment he was unfortunately called out by a person on business from Porlock, and detained by him above an hour, and on his return to his room, found, to his no small surprise and mortification, that though he still retained some vague and dim recollection of the general purport of the vision, yet, with the exception of some eight or ten scattered lines and images, all the rest had passed away like the images on the surface of a stream into which a stone has been cast, but, alas! without the after restoration of the latter![16]

Though Coleridge's anodyne is no doubt a famous bright spot to generations of students suffering through British literature, teachers find equally powerful the image of "a person on business from Porlock." Many an overwrought professor has cursed the man from Porlock's various incarnations. Coleridge's anodyne was laudanum, a mixture of alcohol and opium, which was said to have been introduced to the West by the early-sixteenth-century German alchemist and/or quack Philippus Aureolus Bombastus Theophrastus Paracelsus von Hohenheim, who also lent details of his larger-than-life escapades to the Faust legend, gave us the word *bombast*, and, not incidentally, was said to have died of an overdose of his own painkiller, laudanum.

Addiction plagued Coleridge most of his adult life, as the epitaph he wrote for himself suggests: "O lift one thought in prayer for S.T.C. / That he, who many a year with toil of breath, / Found Death in Life, may here find Life in Death." His friend Thomas De Quincey wrote English literature's most famous description of opium-eating in his *Confessions of an English Opium-Eater*, in which he sings opium's praises: "Here was a panacea, . . . for all human woes; here was the secret of happiness, about which philosophers had disputed for so many ages, at once discovered; happiness might now be bought for a penny, and carried in the waistcoat-pocket; portable ecstasies might be had corked up in a pint-bottle; and peace of mind could be sent down by the mail," only to later discover "an Iliad of woes" in addiction.[17]

Americans too succumbed in droves. A Massachusetts doctor noted in 1872 that Vermont, New Hampshire, Connecticut, Florida, California, and Arizona all produced opium, with "ten acres of poppies being said to yield, in Arizona, twelve hundred pounds of opium," in addition to official imports estimated at 225 tons a year in the 1870s.[18] Philadelphia was a national center of morphine manufacture, morphia being hawked as a cure for opium addiction.[19] In addition to middle- and lower-class female addicts, America is rumored to have suffered from an army of addicts resulting from the Civil War. Just how many addicted veterans burdened postwar America remains contentious. One historian alleges, "In 1865 there were an estimated 400,000 young War veterans addicted to Morphine. . . . The returning veteran could be . . . identified because he had a leather thong around his neck and a leather bag [with] Morphine Sulfate tablets, along with a syringe and a needle issued to the soldier on his discharge. . . . This was called the 'Soldier's Disease.'" Skeptics note that this graphic description, written 110 years after the war, for a book published by the National District Attorney's Association, has little historical basis. These critics claim that "soldier's disease" became a bugaboo of middle-class America during World War I, not the Civil War, and that newfangled hypodermics were not a recognized Army issue, either for addicted veterans or Union Army physicians, of whom only an estimated 19 percent even knew how to use them.[20]

Not even the invention of the hypodermic escapes controversy. Most histories credit Scottish doctor Alexander Wood with the first use of a needle to inject morphine subcutaneously in 1853. In the same year, however, French veterinarian Charles-Gabriel Pravaz of Lyon used a similar needle to treat arterial aneurysms, leaving priority up for grabs. In any case, Englishman Christopher Wren used a quill feather and pig's bladder to inject dogs with opium, wine, and beer in 1665. Several physicians—Irish, French, and German—had used various instruments—knives, razors, and glass straws—to inject opiates subcutaneously before either Wood or Pravaz. Despite the confusion, it was the Frenchman who won the ultimate recognition. "Pravaz syringe" became the name for the new medical instrument.[21] Whatever the facts, the hypodermic would have been a new medical instrument for doctors on both sides during the Civil War and, being new, almost unknown to blockaded southern physicians. Nevertheless, as Woods's experiments suggest, the hypodermic's invention was intimately tied to opiates, Woods having sought a more direct means of delivering pain relief to victims.

Such relief was more powerful than ever, thanks to German pharmacist Friedrich Wilhelm Adam Sertürner's 1805 isolation of morphine, the active ingredient of opium, which he named morphium after Morpheus, the god of dreams in Ovid's *Metamorphoses*. Later scientists introduced the term *morphine*, which was current in English by 1828, a year after Heinrich Emanuel Merck began selling morphine over the counter, which was the genesis of today's international pharmaceutical giant Merck.[22] Incredibly morphine—essentially concentrated opium—was promoted as a cure for opium addiction in the mid–nineteenth century. So disastrous was this treatment that Bayer pharmaceuticals, looking for a magic bullet, lighted upon diacetylmorphine. Diacetylmorphine was first isolated in 1874, and Bayer began marketing it in 1898 as a nonaddictive morphine alternative under the brand name Heroin, which, as we now know, was also a disaster. Fortunately for Bayer, a year later it marketed acetylsalicylic acid under the trademark Aspirin and made a bundle.

American doctors slowly became aware that their morphine prescriptions were the cause of addictions at the same time that the number of Chinese immigrants to America rose dramatically. Medical chagrin coupled with racist attitudes toward Chinese opium dens led to the gradual stigmatization of opium and its derivatives. Couple this with Protestant temperance agitation against all things pleasurable, and you wind up with the 1914 Harrison Narcotics Act, which, seeking to regulate narcotics, became the first salvo in what is now a multibillion dollar war on drugs. Thanks to increasing more comprehensive regulations, *Papaver somniferum* is now illegal within our borders—which someone needs to tell the plant, since the *Flora of North America* records its growing wild in Greenland, Canada, the Southwest, the Northwest, the Northeast, and the Middle Atlantic states. The USDA lists it as established in thirty-four states and labels it as both noxious and invasive.[23] Although the plant is illegal, its seeds are not, a result of a biological quirk that renders the seeds useless as a narcotic and the fact that we like poppy seed bread. The poppy seed that we have in our kitchens is *Papaver somniferum* and is entirely legal as long as we don't plant it. This makes one wonder just what a mainstream seed company expects us to do with packet descriptions such as "Giant Seedpods Make Unforgettable Everlastings! Lavender blooms in spring are followed by giant purplish seedpods! . . . Easy to grow in full sun."

Many know sweet calamus, or sweet flag, as either a garden plant for boggy areas or as the "scented herbage of [Walt Whitman's] breast." But to those interested in things more psychoactive than gardening and poetry, *Acorus calamus* is North America's answer to LSD, cocaine, and heroin. Formerly a member of the American pharmacopeia, where it served to mitigate upset stomachs and excessive flatulence and to flavor drinks, *A. calamus* fell from official favor when researchers discovered it caused cancerous tumors in rats but rose in favor with those seeking legal highs.

Sweet calamus may be either of two closely related plants, *A. calamus* or *A. americanus*. The latter is native to North America; the former is a European import. Widely used in the Old World, *A. calamus* may have been an ingredient in the holy oil recipe that Yahweh gave Moses, as written in Exodus and assuming the translation of ancient Hebrew is accurate: "Take thou also unto thee . . . pure myrrh . . . sweet cinnamon . . . sweet calamus . . . of cassia . . .

and of oil olive: And thou shalt make it an oil of holy ointment." Used to perfume a variety of oils and unguents in the classical world, calamus appears to have been grown in gardens as well as harvested wild: "A garden inclosed is my sister, my spouse; a spring shut up, a fountain sealed. Thy plants are an orchard of pomegranates, with pleasant fruits; camphire, with spikenard, Spikenard and saffron; calamus and cinnamon, with all trees of frankincense; myrrh and aloes, with all the chief spices." Jeremiah mentions "sweet cane from a far country," and Ezekiel refers to Tyre's trade in calamus, which was perhaps due in part to the potency of the local variety, since Pliny, speaking of calamus, claims, "that of Syria passeth all the rest, . . . there grow both sweet Calamus, and also Squinanth or Iuncus Odoratus (*i.e.* the Sweet-rush)."[24]

Europeans imported calamus until Carolus Clusius, the botanist best remembered for having introduced tulips to Holland, brought it with him from Vienna in 1593, and he grew and shared it with European herbalists. England's John Gerard wrote, "the root of Calamus drunk . . . helpeth the pain in the side, liver, spleen, and breast. . . . The juice strained with a little honey, taketh away the dimness of the eyes, and helpeth much against poison."[25]

Acorus calamus came west with Europeans colonizing the Americas. Today it grows throughout the northeast and central United States, its range so overlapping with the closely related A. *americanus* that many thought the two the same plant, until Constantine Samuel Rafinesque called the native species A. *calamus* variety *americanus*. Colorful and irascible, Rafinesque was born in Constantinople of European parents. He lived in America as a young man, but then moved back to Europe, where he established a family, only to abandon them in a return to America, where he taught college in Kentucky, lectured in Philadelphia, became obsessed with American Indian history and linguistics, wrote some 220 books and pamphlets, and identified more than six thousand new species of plants and animals. The last accomplishment Asa Gray termed a "monomania." Most of Rafinesque's many species' names have fallen from favor, although *Cynomys ludovicianus* (prairie dog), *Odocoileus hemionus* (mule deer), and A. *americanus* remain in use.[26]

A. *americanus*'s range is restricted to the northernmost tier of states and Canada, whereas A. *calamus* grows in nearly every state except the Rocky Mountain states and Florida. American calamus today often marks the site of a former Indian village or camp, the Native Americans having widely traded and planted calamus for a variety of uses. Adored by muskrats, A. *americanus* was planted to attract them and is colloquially known as muskrat or rat root. A commonly used human digestive, calamus root also works as a stimulant. Northeastern Indians, who chewed two-inch-long root sections to invigorate themselves on long treks, passed the habit on to Canadian fur trappers and possibly American poet Walt Whitman. Some speculate that Whitman nibbled away at calamus while hiking Long Island before discovering more poetic uses for the root. After the Union blockaded access to traditional medical supplies, the surgeon general of the Confederacy issued in 1863 the *Standard Supply Table of the Indigenous Remedies for Field Service and Sick in General Hospital*, which included calamus as an "aromatic, stimulant and stomachic."[27]

Sweet flag recently became a relatively well-known hallucinogen in the West. Adherents claim its use extends into remote antiquity, although proving these allegations is difficult. In drug circles a widely reported allegation is that North American Indians ate ten-inch-long calamus roots to induce hallucinogenic trips, but this apparently rests largely on a dubious anecdote originating in the 1960s. Analysis has shown that the roots contain compounds whose affects on humans are similar to those of amphetamines. One online merchant advertised, "The key ingredient in Bliss Extra is the Aserone contained in its Calamus extract. Aserone is converted into TMA-2, which is the basic building block from which most modern amphetamines were originally derived. The Ecstasy like hallucinogenic properties of the Aserone, together with the stimulating properties of the Sida extract, makes [*sic*] Bliss Extra the first true Ecstasy alternative."[28] Touted as a "legal" high, aserone products are sold in alternative shops and by some herbalists. But many vendors offer caveats to potential customers, since it must be eaten to work and because in 1968 the U.S. Food and Drug Administration banned aserone and its primary source, calamus, as a food additive after tests showed they caused cancer in laboratory animals. Subsequent testing indicated that European and Asian calamus contained the carcinogenic culprit, beta-aserone, while American calamus's alpha-aserone did not cause cancer.[29] However, since both species grow in America, American-grown products may not, in fact, be safe.

Our grandparents also grew in their gardens another psychedelic plant, *Datura stramonium*, for both its beauty and medicinal value. Thomas Jefferson was invited to grow it, and datura found its place in "ghost gardens," which contains only white-flowered plants. The most famous ghost garden is probably Vita Sackville-West's still-extant White Garden at Sissinghurst Castle in England.[30] Decidedly dangerous, datura fell from favor, although lately it and its South American relatives, the angel trumpets, or *Brugmansia*, have enjoyed a resurgence in popularity. Angel trumpets are showier but frailer cousins of datura, a quick growing annual that easily reseeds itself and became a poor man's version of the hothouse angel trumpet. Its popular name, jimsonweed, memorializes the antics of soldiers who made the mistake of eating it while stationed

Datura stramonium, Charles F. Millspaugh, *American Medicinal Plants: An Illustrated and Descriptive Guide* (New York, 1887).

at Jamestown, Virginia. Robert Beverley's *The History and Present State of Virginia* reports, "The Jamestown weed (which resembles the thorny apple of Peru, and I take to be the plant so called) is supposed to be one of the greatest coolers in the world. This being an early plant, was gathered very young for a boiled salad, by some of the soldiers sent thither to quell the rebellion of Bacon; and some of them eat plentifully of it, the effect of which was a very pleasant comedy; for they turned natural fools upon it for several days: one would blow up a feather in the air; another would dart straws at it with much fury; and another stark naked was sitting up in a corner, like a monkey, grinning and making mows at them; a fourth would fondly kiss and paw his companions, and snear in their faces, with a countenance more antic than any in a Dutch droll. In this frantic condition they were confined, lest they should in their folly destroy themselves; though it was observed that all their actions were full of innocence and good nature. Indeed, they were not very cleanly, for they would have wallowed in their own excrements if they had not been prevented. A thousand such simple tricks they played, and after eleven days returned to themselves again, not remembering anything that had passed."[31]

Whether soldiers ate the leaves despite or because of knowing the effects is unknown. Civil War doctor Porcher claims, "The plant while young and tender is readily collected and eaten as a salad by soldiers in camp." But what came to be called "Jamestown weed" was a powerful mind-altering plant known to both Indians and colonists. Beverley includes a description of the local Pamunkey and Appomattox Indians' initiation ritual for young men called *huskanawing*: "The principal part of the business is, to carry them into the woods, and there keep them under confinement, and destitute of all society for several months, giving them no other sustenance but the infusion, or decoction, of some poisonous, intoxicating roots; by virtue of which physic, and by the severity of the discipline which they undergo, they became stark, staring mad; in which raving condition, they are kept eighteen or twenty days." Anthropologists suspect these "poisonous, intoxicating roots" were *Datura*, which was—and still is—used extensively throughout the Americas as a ritual intoxicant. Peruvians used related species of *Datura* as an anesthetic during their trepanning surgeries, when they would successfully operate on the skull, as well as for numbing those who were buried alive as escorts for the dead. The Aztecs employed yet other *Datura* in their religious rituals, using the seeds, which were kept on the altars, for visions and oracles. Indians of the American Southwest also used *Datura* in religious initiations, giving rise to the common name, sacred thorn apple.[32]

Colonists, too, were aware of *Datura*'s powers for good and evil. Charles Thompson, secretary of the Continental Congress, wrote in his additions to

Thomas Jefferson's 1785 *Notes on the State of Virginia:* "There is a plant, or weed, called the Jamestown weed, of a very singular quality. The late Dr. Bond informed me, that he had under his care a patient, a young girl, who had put the seeds of this plant into her eye, which dilated the pupil to such a degree, that she could see in the dark, but in the light was almost blind. The effect that the leaves had when eaten by a ship's crew that arrived at Jamestown, are well known."[33] Although Jefferson might have left out *Datura* from his *Notes,* he knew the plant well enough to be leery of its effects. When a correspondent sent him a poisonous plant for Jefferson's gardens, Jefferson politely declined it, writing, "I have so many grandchildren and others who might be endangered by the poison plant, that I think the risk overbalances the curiosity of trying it." But he went on to describe a suicide potion made from *Datura:* "The most elegant thing of that kind known is a preparation of the Jamestown weed, Datura-Stramonium, invented by the French in the time of Robespierre. Every man of firmness carried it constantly in his pocket to anticipate the guillotine. It brings on the sleep of death as quietly as fatigue does the ordinary sleep, without the least struggle or motion. Condorcet, who had recourse to it, was found lifeless on his bed a few minutes after his landlady had left him there, and even the slipper which she had observed half suspended on his foot, was not shaken off." Condorcet's recipe is lost, but he remains well known. Mathematician, historian, and human rights advocate Condorcet abandoned his privileged position to support the French Revolution in its infancy. However, opposing the execution of the king, he fell from favor and fled, only to be arrested and thrown into prison, where, according to Jefferson, he committed suicide.

Lauding Condorcet's suicide potion as admirable, Jefferson opines, "It seems far preferable to the Venesection of the Romans, the Hemlock of the Greeks, and the Opium of the Turks. I have never been able to learn what the preparation is, other than a strong concentration of its lethiferous principle. Could such a medicament be restrained to self-administration, it ought not to be kept secret. There are ills in life as desperate as intolerable, to which it would be the rational relief, e.g., the inveterate cancer." Revolutionary that he was, Jefferson cannot help adding, however, that "as a relief from tyranny indeed, for which the Romans recurred to it in the times of the emperors, it has been a wonder to me that they did not consider a poignard in the breast of the tyrant as a better remedy."[34]

The Old World was equally aware of *Datura*'s powers. The scientific name *Datura* is Linnaeus's Latinized version of the common Hindi word for the plant, *dhatura.* While some Indians used the plant as an aphrodisiac, others had more sinister applications. A hereditary band of religious devotees called Thuggees (from which we get the word *thug*) reportedly used *Datura stramonium* to knock out victims, whom they then robbed. While some popular accounts today allege that these thugs murdered their unconscious victims, nineteenth-century accounts differ, distinguishing among murdering thugs, robbing thugs, and poisoning thugs. Joseph Dalton Hooker, the director of Kew Gardens, a botanical collector and world traveler and long-time friend of Charles Darwin, wrote in his 1854 *Himalayan Journals,*

> I had the pleasure of meeting Lieutenant Ward, one of the suppressors of Thuggee (*Thuggee,* in Hindostan, signifies a deceiver; fraud, not open force, being employed). This gentleman kindly showed me the approvers or king's evidence of his establishment, belonging to those three classes of human scourges, the Thug, Dakoit, and Poisoner. Of these the first was the Thug, a mild-looking man, who had been born and bred to the profession: he had committed many murders, saw no harm in them, and felt neither shame nor remorse. His organs of observation and destructiveness were large, and the cerebellum small. He explained to me how the gang waylay the unwary traveller, enter into conversation with him, and have him suddenly seized, when the superior throws his own linen girdle round the victim's neck and strangles him, pressing the knuckles against the spine. . . . The Dakoit (*dakhee,* a robber) belongs to a class who rob in gangs, but never commit murder — arson and housebreaking also forming part of their profession. . . . The Poisoners all belong to one caste, of Pasie, or dealers in toddy: they go singly or in gangs, haunting the travellers' resting-places, where they drop half a rupee weight of pounded or whole *Datura* seeds into his food, producing a twenty-hours' intoxication, during which he is robbed, and left to recover or sink under the stupifying effects of the narcotic. He told me that the *Datura* seed is gathered without ceremony, and at any time, place, or age of the plant. He was a dirty, ill-conditioned looking fellow, with no bumps behind his ears, or prominence of eyebrow region, but a remarkable cerebellum.[35]

The toddy that the poisoners sold was palm sap, often fermented and hence alcoholic, and it is the source for the word *toddy,* as in rum toddy. Between the alcohol and the half a rupee's weight of *Datura* seeds (about a third of an ounce), it's no wonder the victim nodded off for twenty-four hours. And given *Datura*'s reputation for poisoning people who eat it, it's no further wonder that some victims never woke up.

The thugs were a hereditary group of ritual murderers whose crimes were religious acts of devotion offered up to Bowanee (or Kali), goddess of destruction and disorder, best known to Westerners as a naked female with wild hair, adorned with a necklace of severed heads and earrings of dead children, her mouth bloody and filled with fangs. Thugs or Phansigars (from *phansna*, to strangle) transcended caste and religion. Even strictly monotheistic Muslims worshiped Bowanee; fathers initiated their sons into a cult so secret no woman ever knew what her husband and sons were doing when they would vanish for weeks at a time. Wandering India in large groups, they passed themselves off as travelers, pilgrims, and merchants. The thugs insinuated their way into the confidences of fellow travelers, whom they then strangled and buried. If the British accounts are to be believed, which they certainly were in the nineteenth century, the thugs averaged forty thousand victims a year, throughout three centuries— twelve million dead in all. Cornish-born William Sleeman first exposed the cult in 1830, taking years to convince his fellow Brits of its existence, and then it took years more to eradicate it, using informers to arrest hundreds of cult members and then sentencing these to exile or prison.[36]

The most infamous thug was the elusive Ameer Lee, whose eventual arrest and confession appeared in Sleeman's report and formed the basis for the character who provided Western readers deliciously terrifying entertainment: Feringhea, "le chef des Thugs, le roi des Etrangleurs," as Jules Verne describes him in *Around the World in 80 Days*. To reach his land, as Phinneas Fogg did while traveling through India, was no easy feat: "They came upon vast tracts extending to the horizon, with jungles inhabited by snakes and tigers, which fled at the noise of the train; succeeded by forests penetrated by the railway, and still haunted by elephants which, with pensive eyes, gazed at the train as it passed. The travellers crossed, beyond Milligaum, the fatal country so often stained with blood by the sectaries of the goddess Kali. Not far off rose Ellora, with its graceful pagodas, and the famous Aurungabad, capital of the ferocious Aureng-Zeb, now the chief town of one of the detached provinces of the kingdom of the Nizam. It was thereabouts that Feringhea, the Thuggee chief, king of the stranglers, held his sway. These ruffians, united by a secret bond, strangled victims of every age in honour of the goddess Death, without ever shedding blood; there was a period when this part of the country could scarcely be travelled over without corpses being found in every direction. The English Government has succeeded in greatly diminishing these murders, though the Thuggees still exist, and pursue the exercise of their horrible rites."[37]

Feringhea is the child of Philip Meadows Taylor, whose 1839 novel, *Confessions of a Thug*, was based largely upon Ameer Lee's confession. In it he turned the character into the nineteenth century's incarnation of Europe's horrified fascination with Asian villains. Feringhea in turn inspired Sax Rohmer's insidious Doctor Fu Manchu and others. So utterly fascinating was Taylor's book that a young Queen Victoria asked for and received the page proofs so she might be titillated before her subjects were. Eugène Sue's 1845 *The Wandering Jew* transforms the Hindu Indian into a mesmerizing half-breed whose vision of thuggery recalls in the twenty first century Osama Bin Laden: "Bowanee will always watch over us, intrepid hunters of men! Courage, brothers, courage! The world is large; our prey is everywhere. The English may force us to quit India, . . . but what matter? We leave there our brethren, secret, numerous, and terrible, as black scorpions, whose presence is only known by their mortal sting. Exiles will widen our domains. 'Brother, you shall have America!' said he to the Hindoo, with an inspired air. 'Brother, you shall have Africa!' said he to the negro. 'Brothers, I will take Europe! Wherever men are to be found, there must be oppressors and victims—wherever there are victims, there must be hearts swollen with hate—it is for us to inflame that hate with all the ardor of vengeance! . . . That all who are not with us may be our prey, let us stand alone in the midst of all, against all, and in spite of all. For us, there must be neither country nor family. Our family is composed of our brethren; our country is the world."[38]

If true, this is all deliciously horrifying. That there were Thuggees, no one disputes. But critics, such as Kevin Rushby, argue that the ranks of Thuggee devotees and victims were swollen with bandits and common murderers in an unconscious British effort to remake a "hideous" India in the image of a staid and proper Britain. Sleeman's efforts to break what he saw as a vast conspiracy of terror resulted in a stronger British presence and the 1871 Criminal Tribes Act, which codified the notion of hereditary criminal castes and classes. This is why Hooker was so interested in the skulls of the thugs he saw in India: "His organs of observation and destructiveness were large, and the cerebellum small" and "no bumps behind his ears, or prominence of eyebrow region, but a remarkable cerebellum." The consensus of many in the West at the time was that there was a biologically determined criminal class of humans that were identifiable through phrenology, the science of reading the skull. In 1833 Edinburgh, Scotland, scientists determined that seven severed thug heads that they had studied showed clear signs of criminality. It was supposed that, properly applied, phrenology could identify born criminals, who could then be removed to someplace far away, like Australia, while lawful society could go about its business. That Thuggees share much with today's international terrorists has not escaped social scientists, who wonder if there are quite as many Osama Bin Ladens as the authorities, intent only on our safety, insist.[39]

Our grandparents also grew another drug plant associated with terrorism, though this one was found not in grandmother's garden, but in grandfather's fields. For more than three hundred years, *Cannabis sativa*—marijuana or hemp—was a major part of American agriculture, so major that its wild descendants are now an eradicable part of our landscape. The 1913 USDA *Yearbook* reports, "Hemp is abundant as a wild plant in many localities in western Missouri, Iowa, and in southern Minnesota, and it is often found as a roadside weed throughout the Middle West."[40] It's true. I've driven by miles of Nebraska railroad embankments and cornfield ditches green with it.

Uncle Sam spends millions each year in a pointless battle against this exotic species. Each year thousands of agents spread out across the nation looking for pot plants. In Virginia's Shenandoah Valley, where the stuff is cultivated, agents take to the skies in helicopters. Authorities bamboozled the public with tales of super-secret ray guns that could separate a dope plant from the rest of nature with its ultraviolet signature, but, in fact, keen-eyed agents look for the dark green plants against the dull background of browning corn. It's big news around the valley when they pull up a few dozen plants. What would they do with miles of weed?

Alleged contributor to the Republic's decline, *C. sativa* was once the pride of Uncle Sam. As recently as World War II, the government encouraged farmers to grow weed, giving them the seed. Back before nuclear subs, plastic, and high tensile steel, ropes kept the world's navies sailing. And *C. sativa* was source for most rope. Called hemp, its cultivation was a national-security issue. Both Walter Raleigh and King James envisioned growing hemp in the New World; William Byrd wanted to drain Virginia's Great Dismal Swamp and plant it with *Cannabis*, and both Thomas Jefferson and George Washington grew it. But let Uncle Sam tell the story. In *Hemp for Victory*, a World War II propaganda movie, we learn that

> a 44-gun frigate like our cherished Old Ironsides took over 60 tons of
> hemp for rigging, including an anchor cable 25 inches in circumference.
> The Conestoga wagons and prairie schooners of pioneer days were covered
> with hemp canvas. Indeed the very word *canvas* comes from the Arabic word
> for hemp. . . . But now with Philippine and East Indian sources of hemp in
> the hands of the Japanese, and shipment of jute from India curtailed, Ameri-
> can hemp must meet the needs of our Army and Navy as well as of our Indus-
> try. In 1942 patriotic farmers at the government's request planted 36,000 acres
> of seed hemp, an increase of several thousand percent. The goal for 1943 is
> 50,000 acres of seed hemp. . . . As for the United States Navy, every battleship
> requires 34,000 feet of rope. . . . American hemp will go on duty again: hemp
> for mooring ships; hemp for tow lines; hemp for tackle and gear; hemp for

countless naval uses both on ship and shore. Just as in the days when Old Ironsides sailed the seas victorious with her hempen shrouds and hempen sails. Hemp for victory.[41]

Makes me want to go out and grow my bit for America.

Hemp prices rose and fell according to the fortunes of war. The War of 1812 helped American dealers after Britain cut our defense contractors off from European sources, and the Kentucky variety of seed was touted as world-class quality. In 1824 *Old Ironsides* herself pitted her ropes and sails spun from American hemp against a Russian ship with Russian hemp cordage and canvas. Unhappily for us, "after being thus worn for nearly a year, it was found, on examination, that the Russian rope, in every instance, after being much worn, looked better and wore more equally and evenly than the American." A century later, the USDA, concerned over the declining quality of American-grown hemp, began a breeding program under the direction of Lyster H. Dewey, who mixed and matched Kentucky hemp with reputedly superior Chinese, Japanese, and Smyrna hemps.[42]

World War I saw a rise in hemp production and reputation, but both fell precipitously with peace. Hemp became the "killer weed." Uncle Sam turned from promoting its growth for industrial use to prohibiting its growth for recreational use. With the change in attitudes, came a change in names. Hemp was called marijuana. Ironically, hemp had once before been known as a killer. The ropes that held up sails had also suspended necks. Shakespeare has Pistol beg for Bardolph's life, "let man go free / And let not hemp his wind-pipe suffocate." But Henry V, the kind of man who never smoked a joint, lets his erstwhile comrade swing from the fatal tree.

Because hemp was now dope, and dope illegal, the farmers that heeded Uncle Sam's clarion call had to pay a symbolic dollar in federal taxes and keep records for the Bureau of Narcotics. *Hemp for Victory* warned, "This is hemp seed. Be careful how you use it. For to grow hemp legally you must have a federal registration and tax stamp. This is provided for in your contract. Ask your county agent about it. Don't forget."

Although there's dope and there's dope. Today's dealers want *C. sativa* high in *cannibis* and low in fiber. A hundred years ago Americans wanted a high-fiber, low-dope variety. These two contrary uses of hemp have endured thousands of years, ever since people started smoking dope and hanging dope smokers. Today there are two recognized kinds of *Cannabis*—*C. sativa* and *C. indica*. The former is a high-fiber, low-dope hemp, the latter a low-fiber, high-dope hemp. The difference between the two was known, but not entirely clear,

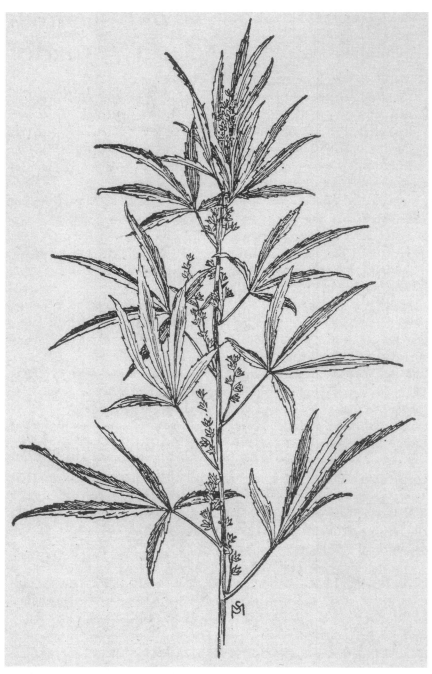

Cannabis sativa. Ada E. Georgia, *A Manual of Weeds* (New York, 1920).

Cannabis indica. Charles F. Millspaugh, *American Medicinal Plants: An Illustrated and Descriptive Guide* (New York, 1887).

to many in the nineteenth century. Porcher wrote, "*Cannabis sativa.* . . . The value of this plant for manufacturing purposes, for making ropes and cordage, is well known. . . . I have not been able to ascertain whether the juice of the plant, as cultivated here, possesses the intoxicating properties of the East India species (*C. Indica*), though it has been asserted that 'water in which it is soaked becomes violently poisonous.'"[43] What may have been a minor point of curiosity in 1863 became a major legal issue to Americans a century later, when possession of *C. sativa* was made illegal. If *C. indica* is merely a variety of *C. sativa*, then you're in trouble. If, however, *C. indica* is a different species, you're free to light up. Botanical opinions vary on the issue, though most botanists today lean to the one species, two varieties, school of thought—to the frustration of dealers and the delight of cops.

Whatever the species, cannabis was and remains a drug. Tetrahydrocannabinol, or THC, is the active ingredient of marijuana. Science tells us that THC, absorbed by the blood, triggers certain cannabanoid neuron receptors, whose function appears to be to create a variety of sensual effects. This means that the stuff will give you a "buzz" if you smoke it, eat it, or drink it.

A 1918 pharmacist's recipe book, *The Dispensatory of the United States of America*, stated that

> Cannabis is one of the most important of our remedies, but, like our best agents, it must not be used indiscriminately, but its cases should be specifically selected. The great indication for cannabis (the keynote) is *marked nervous depression*. . . . Owing to a special action upon the reproductive apparatus, it is accredited with averting *threatened abortion*. . . . Cannabis is said in many cases to increase the strength of the uterine contractions during parturition, . . . without the unpleasant consequences of ergot, . . . By its control over the mental functions, it controls lascivious thoughts, dreams and desires, and is, therefore, of some value in *nocturnal seminal emissions*. Probably its control over urethral irritation contributes to its value here. In this manner *impotence* is said to have been cured by it. Cannabis has some reputation as a remedy for *chronic alcoholism*, and for the cure of the *opium habit*.[44]

The Dispensatory reads like a user's guide, carefully distinguishing between *gunjah, hashish,* and *bhang*—all versions of marijuana. Marijuana itself is Mexican Spanish, possibly from the Native American Nahuatl word for prisoner, *mallihuan,* but probably not from the Spanish name, Maria-Juana. Typically, terms for the drug are foreign, suggesting an alien, illicit origin, while licit use elicits English terminology. Thus hemp is solid Old English, with cousins in Dutch and German. Linguists trace hemp back to a hypothetical Germanic *xanipiz,* related to the Greek word for hemp, *kannabis,* the languages trading "k" with "h" and "p" with "b"—with or without the aid of marijuana.

The Hindu sacred text *Rig-Veda* talks of a sacred drink called "soma," whose affects are similar to those of cannabis. (Aldous Huxley would use soma for the euphoric drug in *Brave New World.*) Other's have seen cannabis masquerading as the biblical Song of Song's calamus and as Homer's nepenthe. Such associations are not universally accepted. But cannabis does make an undisputed appearance in Marco Polo's account of the Old Man of the Mountain's elite corps of assassins, whose very name is a corruption of *hashish,* their drug of choice:

> The old man . . . had caused a certain valley between two mountains to be enclosed, and had turned it into a garden, . . . [and] fashioned it after the description that Mahommet gave of his paradise, to wit, that it should be a beautiful garden running with conduits of wine and milk and honey and

water, and full of lovely women for the delectation of all its inmates. . . .
Now no man was allowed to enter the garden save those whom he intended
to be his ashishin. . . . he would introduce them into his garden, some four, or
six, or ten at a time, having first made them drink a certain potion which cast
them into a deep sleep, and then causing them to be lifted and carried in. So
when they awoke, they found themselves in the garden. . . . So when the old
man would have any prince slain, he would say to such a youth: "Go thou and
slay so and so; and when thou returnest my Angels shall bear thee into paradise. And shouldst thou die, natheless even so will I send my angels to carry
thee back into paradise." . . . And in this manner the old one got his people to
murder any one whom he desired to get rid of. Thus, too, the great dread that
he inspired all princes withal, made them become his tributaries in order that
he might abide at peace and amity with them.[45]

Baudelaire and others so sang the praises of cannabis that its consumption
became de rigueur among Continental bohemians. Lewis Carroll's hookah-
smoking caterpillar in *Alice in Wonderland* records the drug's popularity in
English circles. American expatriates—Paul Bowles, William S. Burroughs, and
Allen Ginsberg—touted *kif,* North Africa's term for cannabis.

Hemp may yet rehabilitate itself. Marijuana enthusiasts on the Internet tout
it as an ecological godsend. Hemp, they say, needs no chemical insecticides
and little fertilizing, unlike cotton. It also uses much less water than does cotton, which we seem to like to grow in deserts. Hempen cloth is softer, warmer,
more absorbent, three times stronger, and more durable than cotton. When
we've finished extracting the fibers, we can use what's left over for paper, thus
saving forests, which don't grow as fast as does hemp. The government needn't
worry about dope freaks; science has managed to breed dopeless varieties of
dope! So no one's going to pocket stray leaves for illicit purposes.[46]

With any luck, hemp may once again enjoy the fame it did when François
Rabelais touted its powers:

Without it kitchens would be a disgrace, tables repellent, even though they
were covered with every exquisite food, and beds pleasureless, . . . Without it
millers would not carry wheat to the mill, or carry flour away. Without it, how
could advocates' pleadings be brought to the sessions halls? . . . plaster be carried to the workshop . . . water be drawn from the well? . . . Would not official
documents and rent-rolls disappear? Would not the noble art of printing disappear? . . . How would church bells be rung? . . . All the woolly trees of Northern India, all the cotton plants of Tylos on the Persian Gulf, of Arabia, and of
Malta have not dressed so many people as this plant alone. By it bows are

strung, arbalests bent, and slings made. . . . By its powers of catching the waves of the air, vast merchant ships, huge cabined barges, mighty galleons, ships with a crew of a thousand or ten thousand men are launched."

Who but a dope would disagree?

Bad Air and Worse Science

Malaria's Gifts to America

Malaria may well be the deadliest disease humanity has ever encountered. Experts guesstimate that the disease has killed more people throughout history than have wars. Today 250 to 300 million people worldwide are infected, and 2.5 million of these die each year. Prior to World War II, the United States was also cursed with malaria. During the Civil War 50 percent of white and 80 percent of black Union troops are estimated to have contracted malaria. The Centers for Disease Control estimated that six hundred thousand Americans contracted the disease in 1914. Only the government's concerted efforts and the miracle pesticide DDT eradicated malaria in the States. Before drugs and drainage conquered it, people desperate to prevent or cure malaria imported plants purportedly capable of combating the disease. Their descendants are still with us.[1]

Malaria is a gift from Old World to the New, there being no record of its having been present in the Americas prior to the arrival of Europeans. Not that malaria leaves any telltale skeletal signs. Nevertheless, none of the pre-Columbian Central American written records describes an illness similar to malaria. Within a few generations of 1492, however, malaria spread throughout the Americas, helping to kill off native peoples who were not immune and spurring white Europeans to import allegedly immune black Africans into malarial districts.

Microscopic parasitic protozoans called plasmodia cause malaria. The plasmodia infect not only people, but also a variety of mammals, birds, reptiles, and mosquitoes. Four kinds of plasmodia infect humans: *Plasmodium vivax, P. malariae, P. ovale,* and *P. falciparum*—and each causes a different response in its human host. *Plasmodium vivax* and the relatively rare *P. ovale* cause similar symptoms known as benign tertian malaria, since it doesn't kill and its fevers reappear every other, or third, day. *Plasmodium malaria* causes quartan malaria, with fevers repeating every fourth day. *Plasmodium falciparum* is the deadliest plasmodium, causing malign tertian malaria, whose fevers' timing resembles that of benign tertian malaria, but whose intensity often results in death. Mosquitoes carry the plasmodia from one infected person to another, injecting them into the blood stream along with anticoagulants in their saliva when they bite us. Only female mosquitoes, which need blood to produce eggs, bite; the males are inoffensive nectar feeders. Only members of the *Anopheles* mosquito species infect humans. Other animals have their own plasmodia and mosquito species. Pre-Columbian America had *Anopheles* mosquitoes. They may have been annoying, but, without malaria, they were not dangerous. However, when these mosquitoes bit Europeans and Africans infected with malaria, they acquired the plasmodia and passed them on to other humans, and an American epidemic ensued.[2]

Not that anyone understood then the connection between mosquitoes and malaria. That was a nineteenth century medical triumph. Indeed, at least one person thought mosquitoes helped prevent malaria. *Harper's Weekly* told its readers in 1875, "According to the recent revelations of a physician, the mosquito has been shamefully abused, and instead of being a plague, should be regarded as a public benefactor. The mosquito was created for the purpose of driving man from malarial districts. Its presence is a warning; but if man will not heed the warning, what does this public benefactor do? Why, it injects hypodermically a little liquid, which serves a double purpose—it renders the blood thin enough to be drawn up by the hungry insect, thus affording him a good meal; and as this liquid contains the principles of quinine, a useful homeopathic dose is thus administered."[3]

Both popular and scientific opinion held that malaria was caused by "miasmas" that arose from decaying organic material in stagnant or polluted water. These miasmatic vapors—bad air, or, in Italian, *mala aria*—were said to cause fevers in humans. The Pontine Marshes outside Rome were so notoriously malarial that the Italian-derived word *malaria* won out over earlier terms, such as *ague* and *fever*, in the English language. Eighteenth-century writer Horace Walpole's 1740 observation about "a horrid thing called the mal'aria, that comes to Rome every summer and kills one," is the first known use of the word in English.[4] Malarial control consisted of eliminating standing or noxious water, avoiding or countering miasmas, and counteracting malarial fevers with a variety of drugs. *Anopheles* mosquitoes prefer to feed at dusk and after dark, so "night air" was considered especially dangerous.

None of these remedies was particularly effective. It was a New World plant that would provide the first genuine malarial cure. Legend has it that in 1638 Spanish doctors, desperate to cure the dying countess of Chinchon, the vice queen of Peru, used a native American bark recipe and affected a miraculous cure. The Spanish imported quantities of the bark into Europe, where it became known as "Jesuits' bark." Another legend claims that the arch-Protestant Oliver Cromwell died after refusing to use this Catholic remedy. In 1742 Linnaeus named the genus *Cinchona* after the viceroy's wife, and it became the sovereign cure for malaria.[5]

But the quality of bark varied considerably, there being several species of *Cinchona*, and purveyors were not above adulterating their wares. In 1836 Englishman Charles Ledger, fascinated with the Peruvian forest, discovered an especially potent species, now known as *C. ledgeriana*, and tried to interest the British government in propagating it. Ignored, Ledger turned to the Dutch, who eagerly planted the trees in their colonies in Java, cornering the world market in cinchona bark. Indeed, so important were these Javanese plantations that their seizure by the Japanese in World War II spurred the Allies into manufacturing a replacement, chloroquine.[6]

A tropical plant, *Cinchona* cannot grow in the continental United States or Europe. But that did not stop enterprising entrepreneurs from seeking to discover alternatives. As anyone who has drunk quinine water knows, quinine—the active ingredient of cinchona bark—is bitter. Its bitterness is one trait that many of the purported malarial cures shared.

One of the first to discover an alternative to cinchona bark was English clergyman and amateur physician Edmund Stone. Casting about for a replacement for the scarce and costly cinchona, Stone lighted upon the bark of the white willow, *Salix alba*. In a April 23, 1763, letter to the Royal Society, he wrote, "An account of the success of the bark of the willow in the cure of agues." While willow bark did not actually cure malaria, it did reduce both the pain and fever associated with the disease, containing what we now call salicylic acid—the active ingredient in aspirin. Willow's painkiller qualities had been known to the ancient Greeks, but Stone's rediscovery appears to have sparked new interest in the tree.[7]

European scientists isolated salicylic acid from willow bark in 1829, but the required dosage caused vomiting. Friedrich Bayer and Company of Germany managed to isolate a more potable form, acetylsalicylic acid, in the 1890s. Bayer aspirin is still one of the best-selling pain relievers on the market. The only reason we don't have to capitalize *aspirin*, which Bayer and Company coined, is because the Versailles Treaty ending World War I specifically forced Bayer to give up the trademark. Ironically, modern studies indicate that the white willow actually has lower concentrations of salicylic acid than many of its cousins, but, since modern aspirin is generally synthetic, it doesn't really matter from a pain relief point of view.[8]

The white willow, native to Eurasia, grows fifty to eighty feet tall and two to four feet in diameter in wet habitats and was used in basket making and charcoaling. Colonists brought it with them to America, but Stone's discovery stimulated plantings of willow wherever it would grow. Today S. *alba*, widely distributed throughout the United States, is considered a potentially invasive plant in several states. Nevertheless, it is widely available and used both as an ornamental and for windbreaks.

Nor was the white willow the only willow used. All willows contain varying amounts of salicylic acid, so all were fair game for importation, or, if native, cultivation. The white willow was a decidedly plebeian tree, associated as it was with basket making and the lower classes. A much more respectable willow was the weeping willow, *Salix babylonica*, whose trailing tresses not only looked prettier than the white's stubby branches, but whose family roots reached back to the Bible and ancient China. Linnaeus named the weeping willow after the tree described in Psalm 137, "By the waters of Babylon we sat down and wept when we remembered thee, O Sion! As for our harps, we hanged them up upon the willow-trees that are therein." Plant historians now think this tree was likely the Euphrates poplar, *Populus euphratica*, indigenous to the Middle East and common along the banks of both the Euphrates and Jordan rivers, unlike the weeping willow, which comes from China and probably had not yet been brought west. But colonists didn't know this, and the legacy of their enthusiasm for the willow remains with us in the guise of the trees and blue willow china, first produced by Thomas Minton in 1780 in England, but soon so popular that even the Chinese wound up imitating it.

Legends—none of which seems reliable—have grown up regarding the willow's arrival in both England and the United States. Eating figs with the Lady Suffolk (or opening a crate of Turkish fig; it depends on who's telling which version), the Restoration poet Alexander Pope supposedly noticed that the basket in which the figs lay had a still-green shoot. He planted the shoot in his garden at Twickenham on the Thames, and the first weeping willow was grown in England. So popular was Pope's garden and tree that in 1807 the proprietor had the gardens razed to discourage visitors. Today all that remains is Pope's grotto, an elaborately decorated underground room, and a number of riverside willows. This makes a great story before which the probable truth pales. Pope's neighbor in Twickenham was a Mr. Vernon, whose mercantile job took him to Turkey, whence he probably imported the first tree and generously gave a cutting to Pope.

Undissuaded by prosaic reality, Americans have traced Pope's tree to America. A Revolutionary-era British officer is said to have brought with him a sprig from Pope's tree, intending to plant it on lands he would seize from the soon-to-be-defeated Americans. Himself defeated and forced to return to England, he gave his sprig to a victorious John Custis, George Washington's son-in-law, who planted it at his Potomac River plantation, Abingdon, whence cuttings made their way throughout the colonies. Abingdon lies under today's Washington National Airport, where no willows grow.[9]

The nineteenth century's most famous weeping willows may have been the two that grow on St. Helena above where Napoleon was buried in 1821. So famous was the association that the weeping willow was known to many as the Napoleon willow. Visitors to St. Helena's would take sprigs home to plant. Boston, Provincetown, and Newport all had willows that were said to have grown from such sprigs. Washington, D.C.'s riverside weeping willows are also said to descend from Napoleon's willows. But graveyards were the weeping willow's true home. Victorians filled cemeteries with the trees and depicted them on headstones, many of which still survive.

While willows invaded the eastern shores of America, another tree would make its beachhead on the West Coast. The 1849 prospectors who flooded California in search of gold did not use the individualistic pans shown in the cinema. They constructed industrial-sized hydraulic mining machines that sluiced millions of gallons of river water, rock, and gravel downhill, eroding land that was already denuded of trees to meet the miners' insatiable lumber demands, including the construction of spillways for hydraulic mining operations. California promoters sought ways to reclothe these barren hills and canyons, and eucalyptus proved an attractive choice.

Three hundred eucalyptus species are native to Australia, and all but about ten are endemic to the Australian continent. Among these is the Tasmanian blue gum, or *Eucalyptus globulus*, introduced to the west by the French. In 1791 the French sent an expedition under the command of Antoine Raymond Joseph de Bruni D'Entrecasteaux to search for an earlier, missing expedition. Entrecasteaux, governor of French Mauritius, home of the dodo bird, died of scurvy, and his expedition was wracked by the political turmoil in France, the common sailors siding with the revolutionaries and the officers with the monarchy. So grievous were the divisions that the officers gave the ships over to the Dutch in 1794 to prevent their being used by the Revolution. Entrecasteaux died the year before. Prior to his death, however, he sailed the coast of Tasmania in a vain search for his missing compatriot. There his naturalist, Jacques Julien Houton de Labillardiere, gathered samples from a eucalyptus tree new to western science. It was a tree he would christen *Eucalyptus globulus*, using the existing genus name and creating the species name because the seeds of the

A eucalyptus tree. Julia E. Rogers, *The Tree Book* (New York, 1905).

tree reminded him of clothing buttons then popular in France. Accompanying him on the expedition was Felix Delahaye, who would become head gardener for the Empress Josephine at her country retreat, Malmaison. The empress was an avid gardener, and she and Delahaye grew over a hundred Australian plants in her gardens, including *Eucalyptus globulus*. In addition to plants, they raised black swans, kangaroos, and emus.[10]

The French introduced *Eucalyptus globulus* to Europe as an ornamental tree, but a German promoted its antimalarial properties. Twenty-two-year-old German-born Ferdinand Jakob Heinrich Mueller immigrated to Australia in 1847, after receiving a first-rate botanical education in Germany. Mueller explored the hinterlands of Victoria and became its first government botanist. Among his thousand publications was the 1876 masterwork, *Forest Culture and Eucalyptus Trees*, which claimed the eucalyptus grew faster and taller than even California's redwoods, was equally impervious to insect damage, provided ideal lumber, and prevented malaria. Thanks to Mueller, the blue gum was planted in Europe, North and South Africa, Spain, Portugal, South America, Hawaii, and California. For his efforts he was made a German baron and a British knight, was decorated by France, Spain, Denmark, and Portugal, and was known as "the prophet of the eucalyptus."[11]

The eucalyptus became the darling of botanical promoters. *Harper's Weekly* told readers in 1871 that the tree was valuable "especially on account of its alleged virtues as a remedy for fever. It furnishes a peculiar extractive matter, or alkaloid, called eucalyptine, said by some to be as excellent a remedy against fever as quinine. In Spain its efficacy in cases of intermittent and marsh fevers has gained for it the name of 'fever-tree.'"[12] Mueller had been the first to suggest that the eucalyptus's perfume might disinfect fever regions. An obliging science provided the explanation. Australian entrepreneur Joseph Bosisto began distilling oil of eucalyptus in 1854 and soon was using forty-seven tons of eucalyptus leaves a week. Bosisto theorized and the American chemist C. Kingzett confirmed "that the eucalyptus as a fever-destroying tree, owes its power to the oil which finds its way into the atmosphere. This oil has antiseptic properties . . . enormously intensified . . . as soon as the oil is oxidized by atmospheric oxygen in contact with moisture." The "peroxide of hydrogen" formed by the action of air and moisture upon the volatile oils of the eucalyptus was said to be "capable of oxidizing a correspondingly large amount of organic matter, rendering it harmless—for instance, vegetable matter which may be undergoing decomposition and producing malarial fever."[13]

In addition to its ability to counteract malarial decomposition, the eucalyptus was also popular because its prodigious uptake of water dried out land and thus prevented malaria mosquitos from breeding in the first place. In 1857 Mueller sent seeds to France, which were then planted in Algeria, where the trees there helped dry out marshy areas. In the Roman Campagna, monks who planted eucalyptus trees claimed the trees because of their desiccating property soon made the place habitable year round. Some noted that the drying out led to the disappearance of the mosquito. *Harper's* reported, "The tree prefers a marshy soil, in which it grows to a great height very rapidly. It dries the earth under it by the evaporation from its leaves, and shelters it from the sun, thus preventing the generation of marsh miasma." And it opined, "it may be well to consider it in California and Arizona."[14]

Mueller's promotional campaign took the eucalyptus to every viable climate worldwide. The man sometimes credited with introducing *E. globulus* to California is legendary clipper ship captain Robert H. Waterman. Born in New York City in 1808, a twelve-year-old Waterman departed on a ship bound for China and never quit sailing. Skipper of the world's first clipper ship, the *Sea Witch*, Waterman set a seventy-seven day record for the Canton, China, to New York run, sailing an impressive 358 miles in one day. In a four-way clipper ship race from New York to San Francisco via Cape Horn, he came in first in ninety-seven days. He is supposed to have imported and sold eucalyptus trees as ornamentals in the early 1850s while serving as port warden and inspector of hulls for the port of San Francisco.[15]

Whether or not Waterman was the first to import eucalyptus we will never know. There were plenty of Australians in Gold Rush California. Since all East Coast sea traffic had to round the tip of South America to reach California, it was easier to import items from Australia than to order them from New York City. The plant soon became popular in California. By 1857 eucalyptus trees were on sale in an Oakland nursery and became so popular and cheap that in 1871 one nursery advertised blue gums for ten cents a seedling. Speculators took to planting large tracts of eucalyptus with an eye toward cashing in on its value as lumber. Individual nurseries boasted of selling five thousand seedlings in a day and two hundred thousand in a year. The California Agriculture Board promoted "artificial forests," and one newspaper gave away bags of seed to new subscribers. The president of Santa Barbara College, Ellwood Cooper, promoted the tree in speech and print, publishing *Forest Culture and Eucalyptus Trees* in 1876, "the only complete and reliable work on eucalypti published in the United States," and heavily indebted to Mueller's work.[16]

California immigrant Abbot Kinney promoted the eucalyptus in the 1890s. Having made a fortune in cigarettes while on the East Coast, Kinney traveled the world, visiting Australia, where he no doubt first came to know the eucalyptus.

He moved to California and made a second fortune in real estate. His most enduring monument is Venice, California—a West Coast attempt to recreate the Italian town, canals and all. While alive, Kinney enjoyed fame as a eucalyptus promoter, and his 1895 book *Eucalyptus* became a bible for eucalyptus speculators.[17]

California enjoyed a eucalyptus boom in the first decade of the twentieth century. Fueled by reports of the imminent exhaustion of American timber and buoyed by eucalyptus's rapid growth, speculators planted hundreds of thousands of acres in seedlings. The Santa Fe Railroad created an entire forest to supply its future railroad tie needs, and Jack London put in a hundred thousand seedlings. State forester George Lull enthused, "the long-despised eucalypts will be greater wealth-producers than the orange." California planted seven and a half million seedlings in 1911. Unfortunately for the enthusiasts, eucalyptus did not live up to its reputation. While old growth eucalypti in Australia were indeed valuable timber trees, the young trees of California proved susceptible to rot and were liable to split. The Santa Fe Railroad and others abandoned their "artificial forests," which would later become subdivisions in a booming California land market.[18]

Once ensconced in California, *E. globulus* spread, establishing itself in pure stands and excluding native flora by overcrowding and as a result of the chemicals it concentrates in the soil. These nearly pure stands of *E. globulus* pose severe fire threats because of the tremendous amount of flammable litter that accumulates under the trees, as the Berkeley fires of 1991 demonstrated. Before white settlement, the Oakland / Berkeley Hills area supported an open oak-tree savannah and even a redwood grove. But these trees were felled and replaced with eucalyptus trees, which were touted as excellent timber trees and windbreaks. The eucalyptus found the habitat congenial and soon became naturalized. When people began to build houses in the eucalyptus groves, a disaster was inevitable. In 1991 the groves exploded into fire, killing twenty-three people and destroying thirty-four hundred houses. Environmentalists today include those who would remove all alien species, and the Berkeley fires added fuel to their "only American" arguments. But California's eucalyptus trees are here to stay; they are too widespread to eradicate, too liked by too many, and actually beneficial to native species such as the Monarch butterfly, which prefers to overwinter in eucalyptus groves.

Equally controversial are Hawaii's eucalyptuses, which arrived during the 1870s "eucalyptus craze." They were planted on Maui as part of a reforestation effort. So popular were they that, between 1908 and 1933, over two hundred thousand were planted yearly. Large ranches, such as the 330,000-acre Parker

Ranch, led the effort to reclothe Hawaii in eucalyptus forests. But the tree's voracious appetite for water lowered water tables in ranching country. Aggressively growing, the eucalyptus also shaded out native Hawaiian plants. Today commercial eucalyptus forests, planted to provide pulp for the voracious Asian market, are targets of protests by those seeking to protect Hawaii's native flora and fauna. But more widespread than protests are advertisements extolling the beauty and fragrance of eucalyptus groves and allees.[19]

If aromatic trees such as the eucalyptus could prevent malaria, it followed that noxious-smelling trees might promote malaria. By such scientific logic hangs the rise and fall of the ailanthus tree. Silkworm fanciers introduced *Ailanthus altissima* to the United States in an unsuccessful effort to establish a silk industry based upon its associated silkworm. As an alien species, the ailanthus had few natural enemies in the Americas and hence its branches remained relatively bug free, which drew the attention of city planners in the days before window screens. In addition to being bug free, the ailanthus was also a rapid grower—an attractive quality for someone interested in lining city streets with trees. It also was rumored that the tree absorbed the odors responsible for malaria. Charles F. Millspaugh, author of *Medicinal Plants,* recounts that the ailanthus "has caused more newspaper comment than any other now planted in this country. . . . About the year 1800 it was brought into this country, and soon grew in public favor as an ornamental tree for lawns, walks and streets; later on it became in greater demand on account of its supposed property of absorbing from the atmosphere malarial poisons; under this new idea the tree became a great favorite in cities and large towns, especially as its growth was rapid and its beautiful foliage pleasing. The occurrence, however, of several severe epidemics, especially in the larger cities, set people thinking—might not this tree, which so fully absorbs poison, also throw off toxic effluvia? may it not store up the noxious gases and again set them forth in the flowering season? Certainly the staminate flowers smell bad enough to lay any disease to their emanations."[20]

The battle played out in the pages of the *New York Times.* The ailanthus, correspondents wrote, "stole the hearts of the people; especially those who were fond of a shade, but did not fancy waiting through the life-time of a generation to enjoy it. . . . So it became the favorite and most popular of all trees in newly settled villages, about farm-houses that had been neglected, and in streets lately graded." However, people began to suffer "ailanthus fever," whose primary symptoms—congestion and headache—suggest to us hay fever, but to nineteenth-century alarmists a variety of malaria. "The foul effluvia which the leaves of the Ailanthus tree absorb are all emitted again in a condensed essence by the flowers of the same tree. . . . no insect will feed on its foliage, and so poisonous is the odor that it emits that no bird will build its nest in its branches, or even light upon them." Children were especially vulnerable to ailanthus fever; one correspondent had five children "all ill, at the same time, and all by the poisonous effluvia of this loathsome Ailanthus tree—two of them fling their branches across the window of my nursery, filling the room with their poisonous odor. Fainting and vomiting attended in all these five cases. Both my physicians traced this illness of my children to *the poison* of the Ailanthus—And I have not a doubt of it. I had no remedy. The trees are not mine." Millspaugh reports, "A war upon the trees followed, both wordy and actual, which almost banished them from the country."[21]

Ironically, the ailanthus's purported deadly properties had been a matter of record for some hundred years. Scottish horticulturalist Philip Miller, eighteenth-century curator of the Chelsea Physic Garden for sixty years and author of the influential *Gardener's Dictionary*, had named the tree *Toxicodendron altissima* —the very tall poison tree—because it gave him headaches. But Miller preferred a rival classification system to that of Linnaeus, and not everyone accepted his nomenclature. What Miller had warningly called *Toxicodendron*, a Frenchman christened *Ailanthus*, the two names fighting for precedence until this century when they were combined as *Ailanthus altissima*.

Ailanthus sufferers often compared their tree to the upas. The upas—Malay for poison—tree's deadly aromatic effects were made known in a 1783 *London Magazine* article, which purported to be the translation of a Dutch surgeon's travel account to the Spice Islands but was in fact English fiction. The surgeon's narrative embroidered upon the fact that there really is a upas tree, *Antiaris toxicaria*, from which the Malay extracted poison for their poison darts. But the real tree is no match to its fictive cousin, whose effluvia was deadly to all animal and plant life within twelve miles so that tree perforce stood alone in a barren valley, surrounded by the bones of its victims. The surgeon interviewed a

priest, who lives on the nearest habitable spot to the tree, which is about fifteen or sixteen miles distant . . . employed by the Emperor to reside there, in order to prepare for eternity the souls of those who, for different crimes, are sentenced to approach the tree, and to procure the poison. . . . Malefactors, who, for their crimes, are sentenced to die, are the only persons to fetch the poison; and this is the only chance they have of saving their lives. . . . They are then provided with a silver or tortoise-shell box, in which they are to put the poisonous gum, and are properly instructed how to proceed, while they are upon their dangerous expedition. Among other particulars, they are always told to attend to the direction of the winds; as they are to go towards the tree before the wind, so that the effluvia from the tree are always blown from them. . . . They are afterwards sent to the house of the old priest, to which place they are commonly attended by their friends and relations. Here they generally remain some days, in expectation of a favourable breeze. During that time the ecclesiastic prepares them for their future fate by prayers and admonitions. When the hour of their departure arrives the priest puts them on a long leather cap with two glasses before their eyes, which comes down as far as their breast, and also provides them with a pair of leather gloves. . . . The worthy old ecclesiastic has assured me, that during his residence there, for upwards of thirty years, he had dismissed above seven hundred criminals in the manner which I have described; and that scarcely two out of twenty returned.

As absurd as this folderol sounds today, when it was offered in the interest of "Natural History and the advancement of science," many believed it. Charles Darwin's grandfather Erasmus Darwin memorialized the tree in verse, describing where "Fierce in dread silence on the blasted heath / Fell Upas sits, the Hydra-Tree of death." The upas became a metaphor. Byron in *Childe Harold* describing death and disease as "This boundless upas, this all-blasting tree." America's Emerson begged, "Swing me in the upas boughs, Vampyre-fanned, when I carouse," and abolitionists cursed "the upas tree of slavery."[22]

The more scientifically inclined sought to explain the tree's virulent nature. James Richardson wrote in his 1872 *Curiosities of Plant Life*, "In the low valleys of these islands [Indonesia], surrounded by the most brilliant and majestic forests in the world, this splendid tree flourishes, the trunk free of branches to a height of perhaps eighty feet, and bearing aloft a superb crown of foliage. But woe to the traveler that touches the milky juice which the bark is ever ready to spurt forth. It is one of the most acrid of vegetable poisons. The deadly habitat of this tree has greatly helped to increase its evil reputation. In many places where the trees abound, the deep valleys (ancient volcanic craters) are filled with a dense, life-destroying atmosphere of carbonic acid gas, which rises from the soil, and which the natives attribute to exhalations from the trees themselves, telling fearful stories of their far-reaching virulence." Carbonic acid gas is carbon dioxide, which asphyxiates. One did well to give wide birth to trees with kin such as this.[23]

Poor ailanthus, from malarial cure to cause in twenty years. And then to cure again. Science has now conscripted the ailanthus in its war against malaria. Today researchers claim the tree—a member of the largely tropical Quassia family, from which we get quassia, a bitter substance used medically and as an insecticide—produces compounds that kill the malarial plasmodium. Malaria isn't the only thing ailanthus kills; its stewed roots make a herbicide potent enough to kill off pea, corn, grasses, cress, and pigweed seedlings. Like many plants the ailanthus concentrates in its tissues chemicals that occur in the soil, chemicals that it can tolerate but that other plants often cannot. Over the years it literally poisons competing species, establishing large stands of pure ailanthus. Science calls this chemical warfare allelopathy, and the jungle-trained ailanthus excels at it. Early enthusiasts were thus right to suppose the ailanthus an antimalarial agent. They erred, however, in breathing rather than imbibing its properties.[24]

None of these nineteenth-century arborial cures really worked. Not until fifty years ago did the United States succeed in eliminating malaria from within its borders. Today drainage projects undertaken to dry up wetlands that are breeding areas for mosquitoes and the liberal use of DDT are betes noires of the environmentalist movement. In the 1940s and 1950s, however, these tactics were greeted with enthusiasm. Osprey and bald eagle eggs aside, they were a success. The United States did eliminate malaria within its borders. However, an ambitious United Nations program to do the same worldwide failed. Only vigilance has kept America malaria free, and this freedom is now endangered. The United States averages around one thousand known cases of malaria each year. These are generally due to healthy people contracting malaria abroad and bringing it back, previously infected people entering the country, pregnant mothers passing it on to their infants, blood transfusions, and accidental import of malarial mosquitoes. During the Vietnam War returning soldiers were a leading source of malarial infection. Recently immigrants from malarial countries to the south have been tied to malaria. The descendants of those who first brought malaria to these shores are now themselves threatened. Like the first Old World immigrants five hundred years ago, the infected are bitten by *Anopheles* mosquitoes who ingest the plasmodia and spread them to the healthy. Malaria-infected mosquitoes have been found breeding recently in both Georgia and Virginia, and more will follow.

Airplanes and globalization also conspire to spread the disease. "Baggage malaria" results from air travelers inadvertently closing malarial mosquitoes inside their suitcases, only to release them upon returning home. Even environmental-friendly recycling efforts can boomerang. Asian automobile tires imported into America in the 1980s for remanufacturing brought with them the Asian tiger mosquito, *Aedes albopictus*, which has since spread throughout the Southeast. Innocent of spreading malaria, the tiger mosquito has been implicated in spreading dog heartworm, eastern equine encephalitis, dengue fever, encephalitis, yellow fever, and West Nile virus.

If foreigners and foreign imports bode ill for the United States, then it's only fitting that foreign plants come to the rescue. Enter *Artemisia annua*, source of the Chinese miracle drug qinghaosu. Clinical trials suggest that this drug kills chloroquine-resistant strains of *P. flaciparum*, the deadliest of the four human-infecting plasmodia. Chinese scientists discovered the drug in the 1970s while seeking new cures for malaria, which was devastating North Vietnamese troops during the Vietnam War. Their inspiration came from studying neglected texts of Chinese herbal cures. All the rage in natural-remedy circles and the object of serious medical research today, *A. annua* turns out to be the cousin of *Artemisia absinthium*, wormwood (named because of its ability to expel worms and known for its bitterness), and the source of the now-illegal absinthe. According to the 1898 *King's American Dispensatory*, "Previous to the introduction of cinchona it was largely employed in *malarial intermittents*, and was at one time a popular remedy for *jaundice*."[25] *Artemisia absinthium*'s powers derived from the same source as did the upas tree's—gaseous exhalations, although, in wormwood's case, the gas was good, as *Harper's* explained to readers, "According to recent discoveries in chemistry, ozone is generated in immense quantities by aromatic plants and flowers, such as mint, lavender, heliotrope, etc. It is the belief of chemists that whole districts can be freed from the deadly malaria infecting them by simply covering them with aromatic vegetation." Both wormwoods, of course, are widely naturalized in the United States.[26]

Bioterror

Older Than You Think

In the fall of 2001, letters containing anthrax appeared in news media offices in Florida, New Jersey, and New York, in Microsoft offices in Nevada, and in the U.S. Senate in Washington, D.C. Five people died from anthrax, twenty-five survived, and perhaps ten thousand had to take precautionary antibiotics for two months. The rest of us became uncomfortably aware of the possibilities of biological terrorism. As dastardly as they might have been, the 2001 anthrax attacks were neither our first nor our deadliest biological attack. Bioterror in America is older than the United States.

Perhaps the earliest and certainly the most infamous act of deliberate bioterrorism in America was an attack perpetrated by the British on the Delaware Indians. When French North America became British following Britain's victory over France in the seven-year-long French and Indian War, the British soon angered Indians by absolutely refusing to continue the French practice of supplying Native Americans with weapons and ammunition. This, coupled with the British awarding Indian lands to Europeans in violation of treaties, led to the 1763 rebellion named after its Indian leader, Chief Pontiac. Several tribes allied with Pontiac, sacking all the British forts in Ohio Country except Fort Detroit and Fort Pitt. With Detroit under siege, a delegation of Delawares approached Fort Pitt, where Pittsburgh now stands, to demand their retreat. The fort's captain was Simeon Ecuyer, a Swiss mercenary recruited to become a member of the Sixtieth (Royal Americans) Regiment of Foot, a British unit composed primarily of Americans. Knowing reinforcements were on the way, Ecuyer refused the demand and gave the Indians a dubious gift: "Out of our regard to them we gave them two Blankets and an Handkerchief out of the Small Pox Hospital. I hope it will have the desired effect."[1] Within a year smallpox was raging within the Delaware tribe and spread south into Creek and Choctaw country and west into the Plains.

Ecuyer handed out the blankets in either May or June of 1763. A month later the commander of all British forces, Lord Jeffrey Amherst, and Colonel Henry Bouquet, commander of forces in Pennsylvania, exchanged letters on the subject, Amherst querying, "Could it not be contrived to send the small-pox among these disaffected tribes of Indians? We must on this occasion use every stratagem in our power to reduce them." Bouquet replied, "I will try to inoculate them . . . with some blankets that may fall into their hands, and take care not to get the disease myself." Neither Amherst nor Bouquet was at Fort Pitt when Ecuyer distributed the blankets, and Bouquet did not relieve the fort until August. That Ecuyer and Amherst came up with the idea independently of each other strains credulity, and popular history has laid the blame squarely with Amherst. Nor was he alone in so attacking Indians. His successor, General Thomas Gage, approved using "sundries . . . to convey the Smallpox to the Indians."[2] Assuming Amherst were the culprit, where did he get the idea? Fifteen years earlier, the French had blamed the British for deliberately spreading the smallpox that decimated the French-allied Micmac Indians of Nova Scotia. In 1758 Amherst landed there, charged with taking the primary French fort in the area, Fort Louisbourgh—which he did, opening up the St. Lawrence Valley to a British invasion and making such a name for himself that he became commander of British forces in North America. Perhaps he learned in Nova Scotia from British perpetrators or street rumor the possibilities of biological warfare.

While we may look back with distaste at Ecuyer, Amherst, and Bouquet, their white contemporaries did not. Amherst became a hero of the colonists for defeating Pontiac, and both New York and Connecticut named towns after him. As late as 1943, Hervey Allen's bestseller, *The Forest and the Fort*, portrayed both Ecuyer and Bouquet as heroes. Nor did the French and Indian War mark the end of rumors that bioterror was used against Native Americans. Popular accounts of the Trail of Tears accuse the United States of deliberately exposing the exiles to cholera in order to kill them. While a third to a half of the people being forced westward died en route, that they were knowingly exposed to cholera in order to kill them is another matter. The disease entered the Mississippi River valley in 1832 via New Orleans. Choctaw removal began the next year, and the disease spread north along the Mississippi, killing thousands of whites and Indians alike. The Cherokee, having appealed their removal, did not leave until 1838; four thousand of the eighteen thousand who left for Oklahoma died on what the survivors termed the Trail of Tears. Despite the appalling death rates, only rumor alleges a deliberate plot to eradicate the Indians by disease. Nor do later rumors that the government deliberately avoided vaccinating Indians hold water. While numerous accounts indicate that epidemics soon

Lord Jeffrey Amherst, British commander during the French and Indian War. Gilbert Parker, *Old Quebec, the Fortress of New France* (New York, 1904).

followed the introduction of white goods into Indian hands, there is no proof that the infection was deliberate. Not that people don't think the worst. Forty-Niners headed overland to California were killed by Indians who thought the whites had deliberately infected them with cholera.[3]

During the British invasions of Nova Scotia, Colonel Edward Cornwallis had offered a ten- then fifty-pound bounty for every scalp or prisoner brought in during 1749–52. "It would be better to root the Micmac out of the peninsula decisively and forever," he wrote in a letter.[4] Cornwallis had a nephew, Charles, who also joined the British army. It is this Cornwallis who, as commander of the British forces in the South, surrendered at Yorktown in 1781, ending the American Revolution. He was but one among a number of British officers who, the Americans alleged, used smallpox as a weapon against the colonists. Smallpox and camp fever broke out among the British forces during the siege of Yorktown, killing twenty-seven thousand of the thirty thousand blacks who had joined with Cornwallis in order to escape slavery, according to Thomas Jefferson. Colonists believed that the British evicted their black allies throughout the siege in order to spread smallpox among the American troops. The *Pennsylvania Gazette* charged on November 14, 1781, that "Lord Cornwallis's attempt to spread the smallpox among the inhabitants in the vicinity of York, has been reduced to a certainty . . . and must render him contemptible in the eyes of every civilized nation." Benjamin Franklin repeated the charges in 1786. Perhaps America's Cornwallis learned his tactics from Nova Scotia's Cornwallis.[5]

Yorktown was but the last site of such British tactics, if you believe the colonists, but the same charges surfaced during the sieges of Boston and Quebec. Americans were far less likely to have suffered smallpox as children than were the British. So a smallpox epidemic inevitably killed more Americans than British. So devastating was smallpox that Washington eventually had to inoculate his entire army, and in secret too, because he feared the British might find out and attack while everyone was sick in bed and because popular sentiment had it that the inoculation would kill you. Of course, the British denied they ever used such tactics. Just as they denied they had any connection with the other infamous biological attack of the Revolution—the Hessian fly.

That we even call the smaller-than-an-ant Hessian fly Hessian is thanks to politics. Fired with revolutionary patriotism and incensed over his economic losses in farming, George Morgan decided to insult the mercenaries that George III had sent over during the American Revolution, explaining, "The name of Hessian Fly was given to this insect by myself and a friend early after its first appearance on Long Island, as expressive of our sentiments of the two Animals —We agreed to use some industry in spreading the name to add, if possible, to the detestation in which the human insect was generally held by our yeomanry and to hand it down with all possible infamy to the next generation as a useful national prejudice—It has now become the most opprobrious term our language affords and the greatest affront our chimney sweepers and even our slaves can give or receive, is to call or be called Hessian."

Morgan was remembering the summer of 1786, when his farm near Princeton, New Jersey, which had been restored after Hessian mercenaries had sacked it during the Revolution, was overrun with "white worms" in the wheat. These worms so sapped the stalks that the wheat failed to produce seeds properly. The damage was so devastating and widespread that the New York governor asked the legislature to address "the fatal ravages" of the fly. Alarmed editorialists warned that "the whole continent will be over-run—a calamity more to be lamented than the ravages of war" and taking their cue from Morgan and others, spread the "fact" that "the Hessians (or the Jews or the Turks) have brought over thousands of little *insects*, on purpose to destroy this country." The British were terrified that their wheat fields would fall to the fly and thus banned American wheat imports in 1788, coincidentally harming the recently independent Americans and lining the pockets of the farming leaders of the Privy Council. However, poor wheat harvests throughout Europe that year led to bread shortages and revolutionary fervor in France, which the Privy Council feared more than they relished profits, and it lifted the ban in 1789.

Thomas Say provided the first scientific description of the Hessian fly. He chose *destructor* for its specific name in recognition of its ravages in American wheat fields. Nationalism colored scientific descriptions of the bug throughout the nineteenth century, with German and American entomologists especially divided on the insect's origin. The term *Hessian fly* implicitly accused the Germans of bringing it to these shores, though whether done deliberately or accidentally was a matter of debate. European scientists, faced with the prospect in 1788 of the fly's importation from America, were unable to identify it and had to rely on American accounts. This should have settled the issue. But not until the end of the century did a consensus arise that *Phytophaga destructor* probably hailed from western Asia, made its way into Europe, and traveled from there to America. Ironically, it was George Washington's military successes that secured its arrival here. The British, having lost the wheat fields of New Jersey, were forced to import shiploads of wheat and with the wheat came the Hessian fly.[6]

Seventy years later, the American Civil War occasioned charges of bioterrorism against both sides. General Sherman, who many southerners consider an unredeemable evil, was the victim of Confederate attempts to poison water supplies. Not that the Union escaped blame; their schemes still ravage southern agriculture 140 years later. In his 1875 *Memoirs*, Sherman, writing about his pursuit of General Johnston's Confederate troops, recalls, "On the 8th [of July, 1863] all our troops reached the neighborhood of Clinton [Mississippi], the weather fearfully hot, and water scarce. Johnston had marched rapidly, and in retreating had caused cattle, hogs, and sheep, to be driven into the ponds of water, and there shot down; so that we had to haul their dead and stinking carcasses out to use the water."[7] Such has been the practice of retreating forces since Roman days, in hopes of spreading disease and denying the enemy water. But Sherman mentions no casualties from drinking the polluted water. In any event the Union had suspected the South as early as 1861 of poisoning its troops. Soldiers in the Union's occupying armies were warned in the war's first year to accept no food or water from unknown civilians, and sporadic accounts of poisonings surfaced from time to time in newspapers.[8] But it was not until 1863 that U.S. Army General Order No. 100 outlawed such practices, "The use of poison in any manner, be it to poison wells, or food, or arms, is wholly excluded from modern warfare."[9]

Southerners, of course, accused the North of bioterrorism and had at least circumstantial evidence to back up the allegations. A devastating pest of several crops, the orange and black harlequin bug, *Murgantia histrionica*, native to Central America, was found in Texas at the end of the Civil War. Southern farmers, reeling from the loss of slaves, the war, and their Confederate currency, suspected that the Union had deliberately introduced the pest to further undermine southern agriculture.[10] Only anecdotal evidence supports the allegation, but regardless of how they got here, the bugs proved an agricultural disaster, having since spread from coast to coast and as far north as New England, although they threaten crops only in the warmer South.

Polluted water and stink bugs pale before what the *New York Times* characterized as "an outrage against humanity, calling for . . . the universal execration of mankind." This was Confederate doctor Luke P. Blackburn's plot to spread yellow fever throughout the major cities of the North and among the occupying Union troops in the South.[11] Born in Kentucky, where he also practiced medicine, Blackburn became an expert on yellow fever, working during the epidemics of 1846, 1853, 1854, 1855, and 1856 and in the Bermuda epidemic of 1864.[12] In Bermuda, he filled ten trunks with the vomit-covered blankets and sweat-stained clothing of those who had died of the fever. He transferred the trunks first to Canada and then into the United States, where accomplices distributed them to unwitting clothing stores and charities. Blackburn also prepared a valise of yellow fever and smallpox-infected clothes that was to be sent to Abraham Lincoln. Lee's surrender rendered Blackburn's efforts pointless.

But Lincoln's assassination encouraged a paranoid Union to find conspiracies everywhere, and Blackburn's plot came to light through separate investigations in Bermuda, Toronto, and Washington, D.C. In Bermuda a parade of witnesses testified in May 1865 to the Confederate government's knowledge of and possible involvement with Blackburn's collecting, storing, and shipping of the infected items.[13] A Toronto trial the same month acquitted Blackburn of having violated any Canadian law, due to lack of proof. Although no one produced any of the infected clothing, Blackburn's attorney never denied the conspiracy. Blackburn's main accuser in Toronto, Godfrey J. Hyams, later testified in Washington, D.C., before the commission investigating Lincoln's assassination. Hyams's testimony in Toronto and Washington was identical. He stated that Blackburn had hired him to smuggle the trunks into Boston, New York, Philadelphia, Washington, Norfolk, and points south. To protect himself from infection, Hyams was told to "smoke strong cigars and chew camphor."[14] Hyams's testimony was supported by others who identified him as the "J. W. Harris" who had sold trunks of clothing to an auctioneer and clothes dealer. Nothing, however, came of the government's attempt to link the "Great Fever Plot" with the assassination, despite the government's assertion "that the rebel chief, Jefferson Davis, sanctioned these crimes, committed and attempted through the instrumentality of his accredited agents in Canada . . . upon the persons and property of the people of the North, there is positive proof on your record." Nor, although widely believed, was another allegation. "It it's a matter of notoriety that a part of his [Hyams's] statement is verified by the results at Newbern, North Carolina, to which points he says, a portion of the infected goods were shipped, through a sutler, the result of which was that nearly two thousand citizens and soldiers died there, about that time, with the yellow fever."[15] Hyams received a federal pardon, and Blackburn returned to Kentucky, where he became Democratic governor in 1879, thanks in large part to his heroic efforts to help people during the 1878 yellow fever epidemic. His political fame resurrected stories of "the gentle specimen of Southern chivalry, who is charged with trying to import yellow fever into the infant schools and orphan asylums of New-York, Philadelphia and other cities, in order to destroy as many of the Northern people as possible." To which Blackburn replied, "The statements are lies, and I don't care a d— —n for all the Republican comments in Christendom." But Blackburn's refusal to explain just what he had been up to in 1864 was accompanied by his apparently damning assertion that "a physician, by his knowledge of disease and medicine, has the same right to slay an enemy as a General has with an army and ammunition." This statement did little to clear the name of a man whose tomb declares him a "Good Samaritan."[16]

Yellow fever was a natural choice for Blackburn, given both his familiarity with the disease and its virulent nature. Endemic to much of the West Indies and the Deep South, yellow fever swept through America in periodic waves, killing thousands in the 1690s, 1730s, 1790s, 1840s, and 1850s. Bermuda's 1864 epidemic seemed a southern trump card delivered by a friendly heaven. No one knew what caused or cured yellow fever; symptoms included sweating, vomiting, the oozing of blood from every orifice, and jaundice, the color of which gave the disease its name. In the days before germ theory, fevers were believed to result from atmospheric corruption, miasma that arose from rotting vegetable matter in low-lying areas. Bad air was the cause, and good smelling air a preventative, thus nosegays of strong scented herbs—or cigars and camphor—could keep you safe, and foul-smelling clothing sicken you, which explains Blackburn's interest in Bermuda's filthy clothes; he wanted them, not for their germs, but for the miasma trapped within them.

Not until 1900 did U.S. Army doctors under the command of Major Walter Reed prove that yellow fever, far from being miasmatic, was transmitted by mosquitoes. Purifying the air had no effect upon the disease, which we now know was caused by the yellow fever virus carried by infected female *Aedes aegypti* mosquitoes. Since infected mosquitoes are the means for its spread, yellow fever is not contagious. There is no need to isolate the victim, as was commonly done in Blackburn's day. Appomattox or no Appomattox, Blackburn's plan would have failed—because you can't catch yellow fever from dirty clothes, only from infected mosquitoes.

But you can catch anthrax from sick animals—which is what German bioterrorists hoped would happen to the Allies in World War I. Postwar investigations of possible German sabotage prior to America's official entry into the war revealed that, in addition to more customary and spectacular attempts to blow up American munitions, German agents also smuggled bacterial cultures into the United States. They established biological laboratories to culture diseases and inoculated hundreds, if not thousands, of horses and mules destined for Allied counties in the hope of disrupting Allied transport and spreading epidemics among animal and human populations.

The Germans' primary biological warfare agent in the States was an American. Born in 1884 in Front Royal, Virginia, Anton Dilger was the son of a German immigrant who had served in the Union Army during the Civil War. Dilger moved back to Germany as a child and, while maintaining his U.S. passport, studied medicine at Heidelberg University. In 1915 he returned to America, allegedly to recuperate from the shock of treating children wounded in a French bombing of a church, but actually his intention was to jumpstart a biological sabotage program, since he smuggled into the country several vials of anthrax (*Bacillus anthracis*) and glanders (*Burkholderia mallei*) cultures, the Germans having decided to spread epidemics of anthrax and glanders.[17] Americans now are all too familiar with anthrax after it was distributed through the U.S. mail system in 2001.[18] In 1914 America and the rest of the world were equally aware of glanders, since it infected horses worldwide, revealing its presence in infectious runny noses, coughs, fevers, and pulmonary ulcers.

Dilger grew the bacteria in the basement of a house in Chevy Chase, Maryland, then gave them to Frederick Hinsch, a German sea captain who turned his hand to sabotage after a British blockade trapped him in Baltimore at the start of the war. He was later implicated in the 1916 Black Tom railroad yard explosion in Jersey City. The blast destroyed two million pounds of munitions and eighty-five railroad cars, rained debris on downtown Manhattan and the Statue of Liberty, and was heard ninety miles away in Philadelphia, but killed only three people. Hinsch distributed the bacteria among loyal Germans like himself who were stranded stateside by the blockade, German-Americans still true to the old country, and among disaffected Americans, including a number of dockworkers organized by American J. Edward Felton, a foreman of the North German Lloyd Steamship Line, of which Hinsch was part owner. Felton told investigators in 1930 that he and his crew of ten inoculated horses in Baltimore, Newport News, Norfolk, and New York City. The bacteria were stored in two-inch-long glass bottles stoppered with corks to which sharpened steel needles were attached, their ends resting in the liquid bacteria. Felton and his men would stab the horses while walking alongside their corrals.

Just how many animals died no one knows. The Germans seemed convinced of the program's effectiveness. Some popular accounts suggest epidemics resulted from the inoculations: ships arrived in Europe with thousands of dead animals that were then heaved overboard; the British advance on Baghdad faltered due to glanders. More skeptical analysts, wondering why no saboteur fell ill from accidental infection, question whether Dilger's bacteria were as virulent as he thought. Any glanders or anthrax infections among horses and mules could just as easily have been the result of too many animals in too small a space.[19]

The program lasted only a year. Suspicious government agents interviewed Dilger, who then fled to Mexico. Ironically, he died from influenza in 1918 in Spain during the epidemic that swept across the world the year after the war ended—or was murdered by the Germans, if you believe sensationalist accounts. No one involved in the conspiracy actually committed treason, since war had not been declared. German lawyers after the war denied that the program ever posed a threat to human life, maintaining that anthrax was not communicable to humans. A skeptical *New York Times*, reporting this German defense, appended a short article noting, "In connection with the German attorney's declaration at the Hague that anthrax is not harmful to human beings, it is interesting to recall that a youth of 17 employed at the London docks was certified last week of having died of the disease."[20] Most historians assume the Germans intended both anthrax and glanders to spread from horses to people.

The use of anthrax and glanders as biological weapons continued after World War I, although their avowed targets became people, not horses. Both sides in World War II experimented with the bacteria. The British, fearful of German efforts, perfected anthrax bombs and bullets. Field tests infected Gruinard Island in Scotland so thoroughly that it remained off limits to humans until 1990. The United States planned to produce one million anthrax bombs, using anthrax grown at its base in Vigo, Indiana. But nuclear, not anthrax, bombs ended the war, and the Vigo plant was sold to the Pfizer pharmaceutical company, which uses it to make antibiotics. Ironically, although fears of German biowarfare jumpstarted both the British and American programs, the Germans never made much progress in developing biological warfare.[21]

But the Japanese did. Shiro Ishii, head of Japan's infamous Unit 731 in the two-square-mile walled city of Ping Fan, in occupied Manchuria, perfected weapons utilizing anthrax, cholera, dysentery, glanders, plague, tetanus, tuberculosis, and typhoid. Prisoners were used as guinea pigs. They were locked in rooms with plague-infected fleas, tied to stakes to be infected by exploding bombs, and even cut up alive, their dissected bodies on display. How many people died no one knows. Ishii destroyed Ping Fan before the Soviets could capture it. The United States, although well aware that Ishii and company had used perhaps hundreds of American POWs as living guinea pigs, gave him and his cohorts immunity from prosecution—after collecting as much information as they could about Unit 731's research. Whether you believe that we used this information to make bombs during the Korean War depends on which side you're on. Both China and North Korea insist that the United States used such weapons while we deny it.[22]

Not that we stopped experimenting with various nasty bugs. The last known case of glanders in the United States was that of a thirty-three-year-old microbiologist in 2000 who worked at the U.S. Army Medical Research Institute of Infectious Diseases (USAMRIID) at Fort Detrick, Maryland. He fell sick in March, but it was not until May that lab tests on his liver reveal that he was infected with *B. mallei*—and this was after he had been placed on a respirator. Fortunately for him, his variant of *B. mallei* was susceptible to a couple of antibiotics, and he recovered after several weeks of intensive intravenous treatment. No vaccine exists for B. *mallei*, and before antibiotics 95 percent of those who fell ill died.[23]

Prior to this occurrence, no one in the United States is known to have caught glanders since 1945, when the last of six World War II cases was reported from —where else—Fort Detrick. In 1942 the government picked the abandoned Detrick Field air base outside Frederick, Maryland, as headquarters for a secret wartime biological weapons research center. Detrick was relatively isolated but also near enough to Washington, D.C., that it could be carefully watched. For thirty years Detrick Field—also known as Camp Detrick and Fort Detrick— housed America's bioweapons program until President Richard Nixon shut it down in 1969, declaring the United States would continue research into control of and defense and immunization against biological agents but would "renounce the use of any form of deadly biological weapons that either kill or incapacitate."[24] Relatively moribund after Nixon's shutdown, the U.S. biological warfare program—purportedly entirely defensive in nature—has enjoyed a resurgence of funding and interest following 9/11 and the 2001 anthrax-laced letters. But the renewed interest also has revealed that the government deliberately and secretly violated international law by continuing to make weaponized anthrax and the anthrax-dispensing bombs, despite Nixon's avowal and our signing an international treaty.[25] Fort Detrick also appears connected to the 2001 anthrax plot. In the summer of 2003, the FBI drained ponds near the fort while looking for anthrax and jettisoned lab equipment. They found both. And there are those who suspect both the perpetrator and the anthrax came from Detrick's labs.

Cowboys

And Their Alien Habits

The quintessential American icon, the cowboy, and his accessories—horse, cattle, and tumbleweed—are all alien. The cowboy, being human, is, of course, an interloper in the New World. His accoutrements—hat, horse, saddle, and spurs—are Anglicized versions of those used by his antecedent, the Mexican vaquero (or cowboy, *vaca* being Spanish for cow). The Stetson, named after John B. Stetson, who made the first one in 1865, is a modified sombrero; the Western saddle is an adaptation of that used by Mexican and Californian vaqueros, who also popularized spurs.

Although its ancestors evolved in North America, dying out only ten thousand years ago, the cowboy's horse descended from Spanish horses, Columbus bringing the first ones over to the New World in 1493. Every schoolkid knows that the Indians thought that Cortez's mounted conquistadors were gods; after the conquest of Mexico, horses, indispensable to European civilization, became common. As the Spanish empire expanded northward, so did the horse, with feral numbers often preceding the slower moving humans that migrated north of the Rio Grande. The Pueblo were among the first Indians to tame these wild horses, calling them *mesteno*, or stray, in Spanish, mustang in English. Many remained free and ultimately helped form the huge herds that roamed the Great Plains. Interbreeding with escapees from English colonies to the east, the mustangs numbered an estimated two million by 1900.[1]

The mustang revolutionized the Plains Indians' way of life. But other tribes to the east also domesticated wild horses, developing breeds like the Chickasaw pony from horses Spanish expeditions left behind. De Soto's 1539 expedition set out with 237 horses, none of which left the American mainland. Spanish horses carried Arab, Turk, Barbary, and Andalusian blood in their veins. When these breeds mated with horses from northern Europe that the English brought over, the American quarter horse was born, so named because of its speed on the quarter-mile straightaway, where it was racing by 1674, when the first known race was held in Virginia.[2]

Calm-natured and cow-wise, the quarter horse became the cowboy's favored mount. But its wild cousin, the mustang, competed with cattle for pasture. Modern ranchers took to shooting them from airplanes or rounding them up to sell to rendering plants. In 1971 fewer than seventeen thousand remained. In that same year, Congress passed the Wild Free-Roaming Horse and Burro Act to preserve these "living symbols of the historic and pioneer spirit of the West," thanks to the efforts of Velma Johnston, or wild horse Annie.[3] In 1950 Johnston noticed blood dripping from a horse truck on its way to the glue factory. After following it, she discovered a yearling that had been trampled to death by horses packed so tight they couldn't move. Angered into action by events such as this and the slaughter from airplanes, Johnston helped ban airplane hunting in her Nevada county in 1952, statewide in 1955, and nationwide in 1959. But it took her another twelve years to get the federal government to enforce the ban.[4]

Animal advocates maintain that many of the federal agents charged with protecting wild horses and burros are among the animals' worst enemies. The federal Bureau of Land Management (BLM), on whose lands many of the animals are found, has repeatedly been charged with indifference at best, collusion at worst, in the continued destruction of horses and burros. With no predators other than humans, the animals' populations have soared, despite yearly BLM-sponsored auctions of captured mustangs and burros. Although buyers cannot obtain legal title to their purchases for a year, a measure intended to weed out the unscrupulous, nearly everyone concedes that the majority of animals sold wind up in slaughterhouses. The meat is then shipped to European meat markets, where horse meat has become increasingly popular following the discovery of mad cow disease.

Europe accounted for 70 percent of the world's 140,000 tons of horsemeat imports in 2001, 11,940 tons of which was American horsemeat, down from 19,172 tons in 1995. That's some one hundred thousand horses a year, according to horse enthusiasts.[5] Advocates for the horses prefer euthanasia to butchering, which they describe: "the horses stand in line smelling the blood, sensing the terror. They are electrocuted or speared into the 'kill box' where they shake violently, falling, unable to stand from fear. They are repeatedly bludgeoned with the 'captive dead-bolt' gun which drives a four-inch spike into their skull, rendering the horse not dead but unconscious. Alive and many times still conscious, the horse is then shackled, hoisted, throats slit, bled and dismembered."[6]

It's hard to fault people who oppose driving nails into living horses' skulls, but to give the devil his due it's not that different from what is done to cows, sheep, and pigs. Since eating euthanized horses is illegal, they wind up in the landfill, benefiting no one. There are too many on government lands and too few of us who want to adopt wild mustangs. But it's also hard to find sympathy for the BLM, whose environmental roots, to be kind, are shallow. Long seen as the willing pawn of industrial farming and mining interests, the BLM now wants to halve the number of wild horses and burros on its lands, leaving only thirty thousand, while doing nothing to reduce the number of cattle sharing the same range.[7]

This is only one of a number of controversies that has involved the cowboy's cow since its 1493 arrival in the New World's Caribbean. In 1519, *Bos taurus* arrived in Mexico, and in 1540, Coronado set out on his fruitless quest for Cibola, accompanied by five hundred head of cattle. These were Andalusians, red, black, and white Spanish cattle with large, spreading horns. Many escaped, forming feral herds that came to number in the thousands. Spanish missions spreading north brought with them more cattle, and, as the missions failed, they were replaced by ranches that raised even more cattle. Everywhere in the scrub were wild cattle. Deliberate colonization efforts north of the Rio Grande continued to spread the Spanish cow, which began to interbreed with cattle that came into Texas from the east. While the Texas longhorn was creating itself out west, his distant cousin was busy breeding himself into existence in the south-east, especially in South Carolina, where English cattle interbred with Spanish cattle that strayed or were stolen from Spanish colonies in Florida. Carolina "crackers" headed west with their cattle, which, experts guestimate, provided 25 percent of the longhorn's genes.[8]

Anglos trickled, then poured into Texas. The United States fought and won the Mexican War, taking half of Mexico in the process, and Texas ranchers began looking east and west for markets in 1846–48. The California Gold Rush was one such market, lucrative despite the arduous journey. New Orleans proved an equal and easier market, and soon herds of cattle were being driven east. The Civil War merely increased demand for cattle, the Confederacy requiring vast quantities of beef to feed its armies. As the Union gradually reestablished control of the Mississippi River valley, Confederate markets disappeared, re-placed, at least by the unscrupulous, with equally lucrative Union markets.

The war had demonstrated the feasibility of cattle drives, and peace brought the short-lived but famous era of the Texas cattle drive. Cattle were driven north to railheads in Abilene and Dodge City for shipment east to Chicago. In 1867 thirty-five thousand cattle headed north; four years later, in 1871, six hundred thousand followed them. What sold for four dollars a head in Texas brought eight times that up north.[9]

More than money followed the Texas longhorn northward. In addition to the famous horns, the longhorn also had developed defenses against smaller, but deadlier, predators. Initially plagued by the disease-bearing cattle tick, *Boophilus annulatus*, free-ranging longhorns gradually developed resistance. When they were shipped elsewhere, they took the tick with them, spreading the disease to cattle hitherto unexposed, which then sickened and died. Not that anyone at the time recognized that ticks were the culprit. All that cattlemen knew was that moving cattle spread the mysterious disease, known as "Texas fever." Longhorns were neither the only nor the first cattle implicated. In 1814 James Mease noted that cattle from South Carolina left a trail of fever in herds they mingled with when driven north. North Carolina and Virginia soon restricted cattle entering from regions to their south. Missouri was the first state to take exception to longhorns' propensity to infect healthy herds, passing regulatory laws in 1861. But the post–Civil War cattle drives propelled the issue to prominence, with more and more states passing antilonghorn legislation, especially following the 1868 death of over fifteen thousand head of cattle in Illinois and Indiana following the importation of Texas cattle. When European countries threatened to prohibit imports of American beef, the federal government acted. Recognizing, but not able to explain, the southern connection of cattle fever, a federal investigator for the Department of Agriculture's Veterinary Division, Daniel E. Salmon, invoked a quarantine in 1883. At first the boundary was a line, two hundred miles long, drawn through Virginia, but the quarantine crossed the Mississippi a year later, reached the Rio Grande in 1885, and the Pacific in 1895.[10]

Salmon's quarantine line proved effective, though, at first, nobody knew why. Although some perceptive cattlemen had long suspected ticks might play a role, their suspicions had been pooh-poohed by savants. In 1869 the Department of Agriculture concluded a study that suggested grass might be the culprit, adding, "there is not the slightest foundation for the view that ticks disseminate the disease."[11] Twenty years later, science reversed itself when Department of Agriculture microbiologist Theobald Smith discovered that cattle ticks transmitted the parasite that caused Texas cattle fever. Smith's discovery, the first to demonstrate that arthropods could transmit disease, laid the groundwork for the explanation of malaria, yellow fever, and numerous other arthropod-related diseases. Although Smith did the work, his boss, Daniel Salmon, of the quarantine line, added experimental farm director Frederick Kilbourne's name to the first bulletin of the United States Bureau of Animal Industry, issued in 1893 and titled *Investigations into the Nature, Causation, and Prevention of Texas or Southern Cattle Fever*. In 1886 Salmon had already taken credit for Smith's work, but he was not involved in discovering the bacterium, which we know today as *Salmonella*, named not after its discoverer, Smith, but after a bureaucratic thief. Smith's stolen research was also the first to demonstrate the feasibility of using dead viruses to produce immunity. Smith had proven that pigeons inoculated with heat-killed viruses developed resistance to active bacilli—the basis for vaccines such as those against typhus and polio.[12]

Smith's three hundred-page document on cattle fever proved conclusively that cattle ticks carry microscopic protozoan parasites that cause Texas or southern cattle fever. Infected ticks transmit the parasites by biting their vertebrate hosts. The parasites then enter the animal's bloodstream and, after reproducing, cause fever, anemia, injured spleens, and, in up to 50 percent of cases, death. Uninfected ticks pick up the parasite by ingesting blood from an infected animal. The parasites migrate to the female tick's ovaries, where they are passed on to future generations of ticks, which infect future generations of cattle. Young calves possess a certain level of immunity that early infection encourages, providing lifelong resistance. Thus, cattle born in infected regions remain healthy, while easily spreading the parasites to mature cattle that did not develop the infancy-dependent immunity. With no effective vaccine for the parasite, nineteenth-century America had to attack the arachnid vector, which it did with cattle dips. Robert Kleberg, manager of the immense King Ranch in Texas, proved instrumental in developing the program, writing the Department of Agriculture that "if the tick carries this disease, as your investigation seems to show, I will get rid of the tick." Kleberg dipped twenty thousand head of cattle in a vat he had built earlier to control his cattle's mange and itch and proved tick control possible.[13] So impressed were ranchers and government officials that the United States began a program to extirpate the tick entirely—which it had by 1943, although it persists in Mexico, requiring constant vigilance in a buffer zone established along the border. Today, Texas fever is no longer found in Texas.[14]

In addition to inadvertently spreading cattle fever, America's cowboys also infected hundreds of thousands of miles of our heartland with anthrax, which provided doomsters with plenty to worry about following the anthrax letter scare of 2001. Caused by the bacterium *Bacillus anthracis*, anthrax, according to biological warfare experts, is "the poor man's atomic bomb," being nearly 100 percent lethal if inhaled in sufficient quantities. It is easy and cheap to produce, adaptable to a variety of delivery systems, and a very little goes a very long way—0.02 pounds of anthrax is as effective a killer as 1,763 pounds of sarin nerve gas; 220 pounds sprayed over Washington, D.C., would kill three million people.[15]

Anthrax has plagued humanity since we first domesticated the herbivores it usually infects. Some historians suppose that the "very grievous murrain" from which Egyptian animals suffered and the "boil breaking forth with blains upon man, and upon beast" described in Exodus are among the first recorded outbreaks of the disease. The germ arrived in the New World along with the Spanish and their horses. There are three kinds of anthrax infection. The most common, comprising 95 percent of all cases, is cutaneous anthrax, which infects via breaks in the skin, killing 20 percent of those who remain untreated, whereas treatment saves nearly everyone. Gastrointestinal anthrax, caused by eating infected meat, can kill 50 to 100 percent of those untreated. But inhalational anthrax is the deadliest; 95 percent of those infected die if not treated within two days. Since a symptomless incubation period lasts two to five days, surreptitious infection can devastate populations. While cutaneous and gastrointestinal anthrax are as old as agriculture, inhalational anthrax is very much an Industrial Revolution disease, first appearing as "wool sorter" or "ragpickers' disease" because it was caused by aerosol particles in early textile factories.[16] It is inhalational, or pulmonary, anthrax that is the darling of biological warfare nightmares.

Despite the 2001 attack, anthrax is actually a relatively difficult epidemic to initiate. Prior to modern medical practices, plenty of workers were routinely exposed to large quantities of anthrax spores, but few contracted the disease. Unvaccinated American millworkers "chronically exposed to anthrax" had infection rates of less than 2 percent. In one mill in the 1960s, workers remained healthy despite breathing in six hundred to thirteen hundred spores per eight-hour shift, while in two other mills, fourteen out of one hundred healthy workers were found to harbor anthrax in the nose and pharynx. Comforting though these figures may be, they allay few fears when you realize that when anthrax does strike, it strikes lethally. Ten thousand contracted it in Zimbabwe between 1979 and 1985. In 1979 an accidental release of spores from a Soviet laboratory killed at least sixty-six people in Sverdlovsk. In 1957 nine men at a wool mill in Manchester, New Hampshire, contracted anthrax; four died in what is thought to be the only such American epidemic.[17]

Not that we don't have plenty of anthrax. Conquistador horses, reinforced by infected cattle, spread anthrax throughout the Americas. Native animals caught it, and today buffalo, deer, and elk harbor reservoirs of anthrax throughout their North American ranges. Sporadic anthrax outbreaks occur in so-called incubator zones and anthrax districts. These are old cattle routes—the

Chisolm, Sedalia, Santa Fe, and California trails—along which anthrax-laden cattle carcasses seeded the ground with resistant spores whose descendants continue killing a hundred years later. "In most of the western United States, with a little bit of knowledge and some petri dishes, you can isolate *Bacillus anthracis* from the soil," Harvard Medical School researcher R. John Collier claims. "There's no way it will ever be eradicated from the soil."[18] And what of the anthrax that so terrified us in the fall of 2001? It came from a sick cow in Ames, Iowa, which achieved a sort of immortality by donating its hometown's name to the anthrax strain that the U.S. Army and the so-far-unknown terrorist decided to use. The Ames strain undoubtedly made its way north from Texas inside an unremembered cow whose long-gone remains fertilized the green grass later cow generations ate along with copious quantities of anthrax.

Such anthrax districts were known as "cursed fields" in Europe; "In Auvergne in France there were green mountains, horrible mountains where no flock of sheep could go without being picked off, one by one, or in dozens and even hundreds by the black disease, anthrax. And in the country of the Beauce there were fertile fields where sheep grew fat—only to die of anthrax. The peasants shivered at night by their fires: 'Our fields are cursed,' they whispered." German doctor Robert Koch single-handedly discovered why. Koch, whose wife had bought him a microscope in part for entertainment, became obsessed with minuscule rods—*Bacillus anthracis*—he discovered in the blood of sick animals whose butchered remains he examined. Experimenting, he discovered that all sick mice he examined had the mysterious rods. He isolated and grew the rods and then injected them into healthy mice, which would sicken and die. Autopsies revealed that the rods had multiplied within the infected mice. Koch was the first to enumerate these steps, which may seem self-evident to us, and the process goes by his name—Koch's Postulates—and is the basis for epidemiological research.[19] Koch went on to achieve fame as a researcher of tuberculosis, cholera, leprosy, and a number of other diseases. In 1905 he won the Nobel Prize for Physiology or Medicine. Of his work the committee said, "Only solitary instances occur of one person on his own making so many fundamental and pioneering discoveries, as you have done. By your pioneering research you have found out the bacteriology of tuberculosis, and written your name for ever in the annals of medicine."[20]

Between anthrax and cattle fever, some saw the only solution as keeping Texas cattle out. At first they tried legislation, banning cattle from more and more of the middle and northern plains. "Six-mile laws" forbade cattle (and sheep) within six miles of towns; cattle drives were restricted to a narrow band along the Colorado-Kansas border, with armed vigilantes ensuring enforcement. But nothing worked as well as fences.

Hollywood made the Fence Cutter Wars between cowboy and farmer famous, with the former often assuming the role of unfettered supporter of freedom and the latter a cowardly, mob-minded nabob. Despite Hollywood, the nabob won; today the West is fenced, cowboys drive trucks, and cows are penned up. As Frederick Jackson Turner famously noted, "In a recent bulletin of the Super-intendent of the Census for 1890 appear these significant words: 'Up to and including 1880 the country had a frontier of settlement, but at present the un-settled area has been so broken into by isolated bodies of settlement that there can hardly be said to be a frontier line. In the discussion of its extent, its west-ward movement, etc., it can not, therefore, any longer have a place in the cen-sus reports.' This brief official statement marks the closing of a great historic movement. Up to our own day American history has been in a large degree the history of the colonization of the Great West. The existence of an area of free land, its continuous recession, and the advance of American settlement west-ward, explain American development."[21]

According to Turner, the frontier is "the margin of that settlement which has a density of two or more to the square mile," which means that most Amer-icans never lived there. But myths die hard, and most of us assume both the centrality of the frontier to the making of America and that fences are Amer-ica's antithesis. In an alternate reality, fences settled the Great Plains, and cat-tle drives become the irresponsible brainchildren of agribusinessmen colluding with big railroad interests to exploit cows, cowboys, and public land in reckless pursuit of the gawd almighty dollar. In this movie the farmer is hero. His prob-lem, prior to the invention of barbed wire, was how to fence the treeless West.

Enter *Maclura pomifera*, the Osage orange, or bois d'arc. Although now planted nearly everywhere in the contiguous United States, the Osage orange is native to only a small area of Texas, Oklahoma, and Arkansas, where it grew in river wetlands known as "bodark swamps." French explorers named it *bois d'arc* because the Osage Indians used it in their bows. Americans corrupted the name into bodark. Osage orange is the sole surviving member of its genus. "Osage-orange heartwood is the most decay-resistant of all North American timbers and is immune to termites," which made it attractive to both house builders and fencers in the West.[22] For the thirty years, from 1850 to 1880, America underwent a bois d'arc craze, with westerners making and losing money in a rush to fence in the Great Plains with bois d'arc hedges. "All that is needed is to hack a tree to bits and put them into the ground; each fragment takes root and sends up a flourishing shoot," opined an optimistic enthusiast.

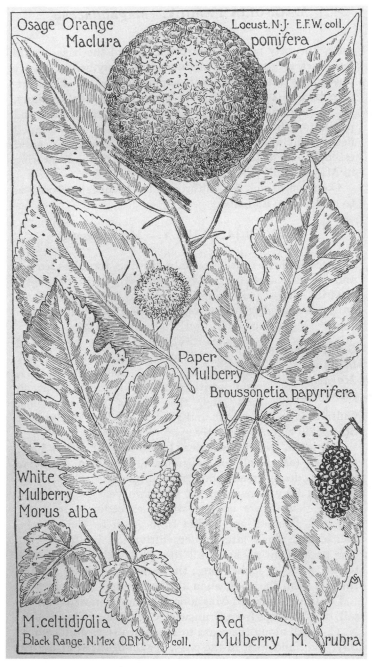

An Osage orange (top). Ferdinand S. Mathews, *Field Book of American Trees and Shrubs* (New York, 1915).

While bois d'arc sprouts easily, a hedge required yearly trimming to become, as advertisers put it, "horse high, bull-strong and pig tight," its dense growth and inch-long thorns supposedly deterring even chickens. Farmers planted over sixty thousand miles of bois d'arc hedge in 1869, and Kansas even paid two dollars for every forty rods of hedge farmers planted. Inhabitants of the tree's native range made twenty-five to fifty dollars a bushel collecting seed in the fall from the trees' grapefruit-looking fruits, with Texans selling one hundred thousand dollars in seeds to farmers in 1868 alone. Midwestern nurserymen began raising plants to sell, and someone invented a bois d'arc hedge trimmer. The future looked rosy.[23] Then Illinoian Joseph Glidden visited the DeKalb County Fair in 1873 and saw Henry Rose's "wooden strip with metallic points." Intrigued, Glidden adapted Rose's design, making the first strand of barbed wire in his farmhouse kitchen. He used a coffee mill to fashion the barbs and a grindstone to twist two strands of wire, one barbed, one plain, around each other and tested the wire by fencing his wife's vegetable garden. Obtaining a patent, Glidden made ten thousand pounds of barbed wire in 1874 and six hundred thousand the next year, and he sold his patent in 1876 for sixty thousand dollars plus royalties. More than fifty million pounds of wire were produced in 1879, and the bois d'arc craze crashed, with many hedges being cut down to provide posts for the new fad.[24]

Today the bois d'arc craze's attenuated roots reach into nearly every state. Escapees from hedges have naturalized themselves in perhaps half of America, greatly expanding the tree's range and ensuring its future survival even as hedges disappear with alacrity. Modern farming techniques favor wide open spaces to fenced-in fields. Some environmental groups, viewing with alarm the rapid demise of what have become increasingly rare wildlife corridors, urge the preservation of remaining hedges—an irony given their recent establishment in the formerly treeless Great Plains.

But the tens of thousands of miles of bois d'arc hedges pale before what remains the most ambitious hedge project in American history—Franklin D. Roosevelt's Shelterbelt Project. It was envisioned as a hundred-mile-wide, climate-altering, Dust Bowl–defeating forest that stretched over a thousand miles, from Canada to Texas. F. A. Silcox, the USDA's chief forester, touted Roosevelt's plan in a 1934 New York Times article as "the largest project ever undertaken in this country to modify climatic and other agricultural conditions in an area that is now constantly harassed by winds and droughts." Running from Canada to Texas and consisting of alternating strips of field and forest designed to create "a more humid belt 100 miles wide in the midst of a region of scant precipitation and recurring droughts," Roosevelt's shelterbelt would realize "a long cherished dream—one inspired by the longings of thousands of dwellers in the Great Plains area—for a strip of woods which might permanently protect their homes and crops from winds that bite in the winter and parch in the summer." With one edge "as far west as trees can be made to grow" and the other where the short grass plains give way to tall grass prairie, the shelterbelt would reduce wind velocity and increase water retention, breaking the back of the Dust Bowl's "black storms," wind-blown soil that darkened skies as far east as New York. Explaining that experiments in both Russia and America had proven that when given protection trees could grow on hitherto treeless plains and steppes, Silcox envisioned a chain of government nurseries that raised "only trees of native origin, or those from the still more arid region to the west." In the north would be green ash, cottonwood, hackberry, elm, burr oak, red cedar, western yellow pine, and blue spruce and in the drier and hotter south, locusts, Osage orange, and native oaks, with willows and poplars in the river bottoms.[25]

Although Roosevelt's ambitious plans were never fully realized, the Civilian Conservation Corps and Works Projects Administration planted two hundred million trees in ten years. Some of those trees remain today, although many have fallen prey to utility companies, widened highways, and agribusiness practices. The trees remaining in Seward County, Nebraska, suggest that the Forest Service's plans were open to change; the primary trees, while including Silcox's pines, white willow, cottonwood, green ash, and honey locust, also include junipers, Siberian elm, Russian olive, sycamore, and wild fruit trees. And, providing shelter from the hot south winds, they run east to west rather than north to south.[26] Attacked as impossible, a boondoggle, and blasphemous, Roosevelt's plains' forests have succeeded so well that, like their predecessor the bois d'arc, some people assume them native and deplore their destruction as environmentally irresponsible.

But no one should deplore the destruction of a cowboy icon both foreign and invasive—the tumbleweed. Roy Rogers's singing cowboy outfit, the Sons of the Pioneers, may have been the primary reason for tumbleweed—*Salsola kali*— becoming a symbol of the American West. Pioneer member Bob Nolan's lyrics —"See them rolling along / Pledging their love with a song / Here on the range I belong / Drifting along with the tumbling tumbleweeds"—not only became the group's most popular song, it also propelled singing cowboy Gene Autry to fame when he sang and starred in the 1935 movie *Tumbleweeds*, the first of some ninety Autry movies. Not that Nolan intended singing about tumbleweeds; he revised his original lyrics about "tumbling leaves" either as a stroke of genius or because nobody could remember the real words.[27]

If how the words came to Nolan remains a matter of dispute, few dispute how tumbleweed itself came to America: the Russians brought it with them. More specifically, Russian religious refugees living in Bon Homme County, South Dakota, imported it in the 1870s in a contaminated shipment of Russian flaxseed. The refugees were Hutterites, followers of Reformation Protestant Anabaptist Jakob Hutter, who chose to live like the first Christians did, communally. Persecuted because they were communists and pacifists, the Hutterites fled Germany and settled in Russia. When new laws forced them to speak Russian and join the military, they came to America, seeking religious freedom in South Dakota. They were ridiculed and persecuted once again. When President Woodrow Wilson permitted Hutterite conscientious objectors, already suspect because they spoke German, to be jailed for their religious beliefs, many of them fled to Canada. Begrudgingly accepted, they were persecuted one more time, under the guise of a 1962 Canadian proposal that "called for the breaking up of existing Hutterite colonies and forcing them to live on individual farms so that they 'can enjoy the freedom of our country.'"[28] Today, rather than being persecuted, the Hutterites are studied by anthropologists interested in the longevity of their communal way of life and by geneticists interested in their relatively isolated gene pool.

The 1880 U.S. Census lists Martin Hofer, one of the original Hutterite refugees, as the local dry goods merchant. But the Hutterites might not have been the first to import Russian thistle. In *Cape Cod*, Henry David Thoreau writes of three trips he made to the peninsula. On the last he observed "saltwort (*Salsola kali*)" growing on the beach. This was 1855, nearly twenty years before the much-maligned Hutterites moved to South Dakota. Although no one doubts their introduction of the weed to the Dakotas, where it became a pest, some anonymous New Englander appears to have already brought the weed to America. Another pre-Hutterite also found *Salsola* in America. In his Civil War *Resources of the Southern Fields and Forests*, Porcher assumes it native and quotes an author who asserts that it "was formerly collected in considerable quantities on our western coasts, and burned to yield soda for the manufacture of glass, and for other purposes. It grows freely from seed, and does not require any great nicety of management, yet never has been carefully cultivated."[29]

Though a weed today, *Salsola* was once an important ingredient in both soap and glass manufacture; one of its common names is glasswort. Boiling *Salsola* ashes with olive oil and brine, soap makers skimmed off and hardened what floated to the top to produce pure, mild soap named after its primary region of production, Castile. Glass makers heated *Salsola* ashes with sand

Russian thistle. Ada E. Georgia, *A Manual of Weeds* (New York, 1920).

until the sand melted, making glass. Forgotten today, *Salsola* was an important industrial raw material, and the Spanish, who dominated the trade, supplied much of Europe with *barilla*, their word for the plant. Unfortunately for barilla brokers, on the eve of the French Revolution, Nicholas Le Blanc perfected a way of manufacturing carbonate of soda—the active ingredient of barilla—from sea salt. Poised to make a fortune, Le Blanc saw his factories confiscated and his process made public. Although he regained his factory, he lost the rights to the process, and, a ruined man, he killed himself in 1806.[30]

But that was two hundred years after the founding of Jamestown, Virginia. And when, in 1608, newly arrived "glasse-men" from Germany succeeded in making glass, sending samples back to London at the end of that year, they made it the old fashioned way, as did their Italian successors. Tourists today can visit the "glass house" at Jamestown. Similar endeavors took place later in New York, Philadelphia, and other sites with access to seaside plants such as *Salsola*. So it is possible that *Salsola* accompanied some would-be industrialist to the New World, its descendants cast out and forgotten when Le Blanc's revolutionary method reached America.[31]

If industry has forgotten *Salsola*, the government has not. Several American governmental agencies consider it both a noxious and invasive weed, whether it is *Salsola kali* (Russian thistle), *S. collina* (slender Russian thistle), *S. paulsenii* (barbwire Russian thistle), *S. soda* (opposite-leaf Russian thistle), *S. tragus* (prickly Russian thistle), or *S. vermiculata* (shrubby Russian thistle); all, as their common names indicate, are from Russia.[32] Government officials first took note of *Salsola* when it began taking over Dakota fields. After the Hutterites accidentally imported it in the 1870s, tumbleweed spread like a tumbling weed. By 1895 sixteen states and Canada reported its occurrence. Today it is found in every state except Alaska. In 1894 Senator Hansbrough of North Dakota proposed Congress allot one million dollars to eradicate the pest within two years. In support the governor of North Dakota claimed three counties had been abandoned because of tumbleweeds, which, he said, covered seventy thousand miles and grew so thickly and prickly that Dakota horses wore leather leggings. A skeptical *New York Times* wondered, "Why not ask Congress to appropriate money for the extirpation of the seventeen year locust?" The philanthropic, albeit ignorant, Philadelphian William D. Riley suggested South Dakota bale the weeds and build a statewide fence out of them to prevent further spread; leftover bales then could be stacked and made into cattle sheds. As the Sioux City *Argus-Leader* remarks of the Philadelphian, "He is kind enough to say that his advice is given to the state without any claim for recompense."[33] Ironically, forty years later, during the Dust Bowl, so many drought-struck farmers fed younger, less prickly tumbleweeds to their cattle that the harvested weed brought five dollars a ton in 1934.[34] More recent tall tumbleweed tales include sixty thousand pounds of weed tumbling into Mobridge, South Dakota, in 1989, and the ominous observation that it was the first plant to reestablish itself at Nevada nuclear test sites.[35]

Salsola's success, like that of many weeds, depended in part upon us. Having brought it to America, we then carried it with us. Railroad cattle cars were its preferred mode of transport and overgrazed lands and roadside verges its preferred residence. Not that the plant isn't capable of getting around quite well on its own, having derived its common name from the mature plant's habit of breaking loose and rolling away with the wind, each plant scattering up to two hundred thousand seeds. A year later, its phantom path grows green with offspring. Unlike many seeds that possess a life-starting food supply for developing seedlings—which is why we and other animals like to nibble them—tumbleweed seeds come empty-handed but precocious into this world, each a coiled-up baby plant ready to grow and get a head start on other plants.[36]

No one seriously thinks of eradicating tumbleweed from America. But some scientists are trying to control it—by importing even more foreign species, this time animals and fungi with a liking for *Salsola*. Known as biological control or integrated pest management, the procedure is fraught with danger, since another pest might be inadvertently unleashed while trying to control the target organism. USDA biologists have identified at least five possible biological controls for *Salsola*: "*Lixus salolae* (a weevil), *Aceria salsoli* (a mite), *Gymnancella* sp. (a moth), *Piesma salsolae* (a plant bug), and *Uromyces salsolae* (a rust fungus)." But that researcher "Rouhollah Sobhian claims more studies are needed on *Gymnancella canella*'s overwintering habitat and host specificity before its value as a biocontrol can be fully ascertained" may send a frisson down the backs of pessimists. "They" are contemplating releasing a new species of caterpillar whose eating habits aren't entirely known.[37]

One can only hope that the researchers communicate better with each other than they do with their public relations staffs. Completely missing from the USDA's list of five biocontrols are two moths studied since the 1970s as tumbleweed controls: the leaf-mining *Coleophora klimeschiella* and the stem-boring *Coleophora parthenica*. The California Department of Food and Agriculture explains, "Both are available for release in California. Beyond its known establishment in central California, there is little information on the effectiveness of *Coleophora klimeschiella*. *Coleophora parthenica* has not been effective in reducing Russian thistle populations. . . . Recent taxonomic reconsideration of *Salsola tragus* and its possible biotypes or subspecies may bring further clarity to the effectiveness of this biocontrol agent."[38] "Taxonomic reconsideration" is a fancy way of saying they're not quite sure what plant group tumbleweeds are related to—and it was taxonomic uncertainty that lay behind the European gypsy moth's disastrous accidental escape into America in the nineteenth century, as explained in "A Sow's Ear."

. . . and Indians

Less Native Than You Think

Adopted hero of many, the Native American is often hailed as the dispossessed guardian of a "natural" America that post-Columbian invaders—plant, animal, and human—despoiled and degraded. While the post-Columbian flora and fauna of the Americas radically changed thanks to the influx of thousands of new species, the idea of Native Americans tending to a pristine America is romantic nonsense. Pre-Columbian human inhabitants of the New World did the best they could to alter the environment to suit their needs and wants, killing off many large mammals in an environmental disaster as yet unmatched in North America, burning millions of acres of woods to create environments better suited to their hunting needs, breeding improved varieties of food crops that they spread far beyond their original homes, and bringing with them from Asia a number of tag-along species.

For a long time archaeologists agreed that people first arrived in the Americas from Asia some ten to fifteen thousand years ago, crossing over a broad coastal plain that was exposed when Ice Age glaciers lowered ocean levels worldwide, an area now covered by the Arctic Ocean. However, recent dating of sites in places as diverse as Virginia and South America suggest humans may have arrived as long as twenty thousand years ago. When they arrived is more than a teapot tempest; the long-popular arrival date coincides with the unexplained die-off of America's Pleistocene megafauna—four-horned antelopes, giant armadillos, giant beavers, bears, bison, camels, horses, mastodons, mammoths, musk oxen, giant sloths, tapirs and their predators, saber-toothed cats, cheetahs, lions, and wolves—all disappearing in a geological wink of the eye. Perhaps America's mammals, unused to human hunters, were exterminated by a "blitzkrieg" of overhunting. If so, then America's "noble savages" killed off more mammals after they arrived than post-Columbians have yet managed. Skeptics prefer the more mundane changing-climate theory, arguing that the end of the Ice Age altered climate, which changed plant communities, which led to herbivore and predator extinctions. Perhaps a combination of the two occurred, the Indian merely offering a fauna already disrupted by climate change its coup de grace. Ecologists believe that there are certain "keystone species" on whose existence numerous other species depend. Remove the keystone, and the entire ecosystem may collapse. The elephant, for example, is critical to maintaining the megafauna-friendly open African savannas; were humans to have exterminated, say, the mammoth, a train of dependent species would have followed it into extinction. Today's killer diseases suggest yet another human-related cause, a cataclysmic epidemic—a hyperdisease—that humans inadvertently introduced, decimating an indigenous megafauna that was as susceptible to extinction as were Native Americans exposed to European human diseases following 1492. But telltale DNA from infected bone tissue has proven as hard to find as have arrow and spear wounds or climate-induced death, and no human-associated disease carrier has yet been identified.[1]

Though the cause of these exterminations is debatable, no one questions the massive environmental transformation that Indians undertook throughout the Americas. The dense Mayan population's agricultural demands undoubtedly transformed the Yucatan's rainforests. Today these forests, winter home to many North American passerine birds, are once again being cleared, which many blame for the plunging numbers of birds visiting our backyards. If so, how many species might have gone extinct when the forests fell a thousand years ago? Revisionist historians' arguments for equally dense human populations in the Amazon Basin seriously undermine the notion of "virgin rainforest" and raise similar questions concerning species' extinctions.

Closer to home, Indians throughout North America used fire to reshape the environment radically. Early explorers recount tales of Indians burning huge swaths of prairie—a seemingly extravagant gesture that, in reality, assured the continuation and expansion of the grasslands. Grasslands, comprising nearly a quarter of the earth's land surface, go by various names: prairie, steppe, pampa, and savanna. Interestingly, the name *savanna* is derived from *zabana*, a Caribbean Indian term the Spanish borrowed. Temperate grasslands such as South America's pampas, Eurasia's steppes, and North America's prairies are typically found in continental interiors subject to extreme temperatures and erratic rainfall. More water generally evaporates than falls, and grasses, which are better adapted than trees to drought and temperature extremes, predominate. North America's prairie is subdivided into three categories: that found east of the Mississippi, the intermediate mixed grass prairie occurring further west on the Great Plains, and the under two-feet tall, High Plains short-grass prairie. Rainfall defines these subdivisions. Intercepting eastward moving, water-laden winds, the

Rockies are thick in snow, while the High Plains short-grass prairie gets only ten inches of rain a year. Farther east, the rain increases again, and the tallgrass prairie averages thirty inches a year. Anyone driving east or west across America can observe these landscape changes, the thickly wooded western flanks of the Alleghenies drying out as the land reaches westward, oak and hickory becoming more common than poplar and basswood, the forests becoming sparser, patchier, the trees shorter, until you realize the grasses have won out and the trees have retreated to river bottoms and towns. And then, farther west, the grasses begin to falter, and sagebrush replaces the grass not already displaced by cornfields.

During the Ice Age glaciers reached south into the Great Plains, their southern terminus roughly marked by today's Interstate 70. North lay a continental ice sheet like that of present-day Greenland. South of this ice sheet a boreal forest grew where today's cornfields replace the "original" prairie. When the glaciers melted, the forest retreated, the prairie advanced, and the West began to look as it does today. Fluctuating climate allowed the prairie to advance eastward into Ohio, creating a "prairie peninsula" that had largely disappeared by colonial days, thanks to more abundant rainfall that favored trees over grasses. But the Native Americans retarded this retreat, lighting yearly fires that burned trees and left grass triumphant long after it should have disappeared. This is known because in the recent past we have chosen to suppress fires and have seen trees replace prairies wherever there is sufficient rainfall. The Indians knew the intimate connection between rain, fire, and grasses long before Western scientists rediscovered it, and they manipulated it to increase game, not grasses.[2]

Perceptive early travelers noted the Indians' use of fire. Sixteenth-century Spanish explorer Alvar Nuñez Cabenza de Vaca said of the natives living in what is now Texas: "The Indians of the interior . . . go with brands in the hand firing the plains and forests within their reach, that the mosquitos may fly away, and at the same time to drive out lizards and other things from the earth for them to eat." The Indians also burned land east of the Appalachian Mountains, although the generally wetter climate there maintained open, parklike forests, not grasslands. In seventeenth-century New England, Roger Williams observed that "this burning of the wood to them they count a benefit, both for destroying of vermin, and keeping downe the weeds and thickets." At the same time, John Smith wrote of Virginia that "a man may gallop a horse amongst these woods any waie, but where the creekes and rivers shall hinder," and Andrew White said of the Potomac's forests, "you might freely drive a four horse chariot in the midst of the trees."[3]

Such environmental reshaping influenced the distribution patterns of plants and animals. Once cleared, regularly repeated fires could maintain forest or prairie. What used to be seen as an untouched wilderness was, in fact, a managed wildlife farm:

> The modification of the American continent by fire at the hands of Asian immigrants was the result of repeated, controlled, surface burns on a cycle of one to three years, broken by occasional holocausts from escape fires and periodic conflagrations during times of drought. . . . So extensive were the cumulative effects of these modifications that it may be said that the general consequence of the Indian occupation of the New World was to replace forested land with grassland or savanna, or, where the forest persisted, to open it up and free it from underbrush. Most of the impenetrable woods encountered by explorers were in bogs or swamps from which fire was excluded; naturally drained landscape was nearly everywhere burned. Conversely, almost wherever the European went, forests followed. The Great American Forest may be more a product of settlement than a victim of it.[4]

That Longfellow's "forest primeval" is a European artifact seems counterintuitive, so ingrained is the "ecologically benign" view of the Indian, a view "influenced by the devastating effect of Old World diseases on native populations. . . . It has been estimated that North America's Indian population collapsed from perhaps 18 million in 1500 to less than 1 million by the late 1700s, when the first waves of American-European settlers poured westward over the Appalachians. Thus, many Indian agricultural lands had two to three centuries to reforest before the first permanent European-American settlers arrived. The landscape looked more "pristine" than it had in more than 1,000 years."[5] Dependent upon a variety of animal and plant species, Native Americans preferred an environmental mosaic to a virgin forest. Mature forests benefited nut-bearing trees, shrubs and brush encouraged deer, and grasslands invited buffalo. Both farming and fuel demands depleted forest resources, and anyone who has looked for firewood around a public campground can appreciate how the twenty thousand inhabitants of Cahokia, across the river from today's St. Louis, packed up and moved on when they ran out of firewood.

The European suppression of fire not only allowed the forest to rebound, it also disrupted animal population sizes. In a controversial 2002 *Atlantic Monthly* article, Charles Mann wrote that although De Soto's 1539 Spanish expedition apparently saw plenty of Indians and few buffalo in the Mississippi River Valley, a hundred years later in the same area, the French explorer La Salle saw few Indians but plenty of buffalo. Because, Mann says, European diseases killed off

Chiefs of the Osage and Assineboin tribes. John S. Kingsley, ed., *The Riverside Natural History* (Boston, 1888).

the Indians, who had been the top predator controlling buffalo populations, buffalo numbers skyrocketed. As did passenger pigeons, which famously flew in flocks "ten miles in width, by one hundred and twenty in length." As archaeologist Thomas Neumann states, according to Mann, the pigeons "'were incredibly dumb and always roosted in vast hordes, so they were very easy to harvest.' Because they were readily caught and good to eat, Neumann says, archaeological digs should find many pigeon bones in the pre-Columbian strata of Indian middens. But they aren't there. The mobs of birds in the history books, he says, were 'outbreak populations—always a symptom of an extraordinarily disrupted ecological system.'" Neumann thinks that there were so many Indians in pre-Columbian North America that they outcompeted the passenger pigeon for its food—fruits and berries. Only after European diseases wiped out native populations did pigeons number in the billions.[6]

But these are merely displaced species, not introduced ones. What evidence is there that the American Indian imported alien plants and animals into North America? Well, there is the Indian peoples, who are no more indigenous to the continent than those who arrived later. And they brought with them another alien mammal, the dog, *Canis domesticus*, which various Native Americans bred into different lines, many still popular today. The Arctic sled dog and pack animal, the husky, has a number of official and unofficial breeds, including the Alaskan malamute and northern Inuit, both named after the native people who originally bred them. A more general purpose breed is the Native American Indian dog, said to descend from the dog of choice of Plains Indians, who used it as a pack animal and pet. Perhaps the most general purpose of all American dogs is the Carolina dog, which roams wild in the swamps and woods of the Southeast. A type of pariah dog, a feral descendant of a once domesticated stock, a mutt, in other words, the tawny colored Carolina dog with its characteristic curved tail is thought by some to be a good approximation of the animal that accompanied the first people to enter North America ten thousand years ago.[7]

So hard is it to believe that Central American Indians transformed the thirty- to forty-pound Carolina dog into the six-pound Chihuahua that many dog fanciers speculate that today's smallest dog has more than a little genetic input from one of the various Chinese miniature dogs. But pre-Columbian art and graves testify to the presence of dogs similar to the Chihuahua long before contact between the Old and New World was regular. Close relatives of this Mexican breed are the Mexican hairless dog, or xoloitzcuintle, and the Inca hairless dog.

The Aztecs did not content themselves with shrinking dogs; they sacrificed them with the dead, used them in religious services, and ate them, as did the

Inca. According to Spanish accounts, before killing and eating a dog, the Aztec castrated it, and then fed it on corn to fatten it up. Not all Indians ate dog, nor did all Europeans disdain it. According to De Soto's chroniclers, "The Indians there [southeast United States] made him [DeSoto] service of three hundred dogs, for they observed that the Christians liked them and sought them to eat, but they are not eaten among the Indians."[8]

Canis domesticus was not the only animal to cross Beringia with *Homo sapiens*. The Indians also brought lice with them: *Pediculus humanus humanus* and *Pediculus humanus capitis*—body and head lice, respectively. Archaeologists have discovered lice mummified along with their human hosts, one nitpicker gathering a thousand head lice off one long-dead Peruvian. Lice were plentiful enough in ancient Mexico to have been put to curious use: "among the Aztecs before the advent of Cortez, is the tale cited from Torquemada. 'During the abode of Montezuma among the Spaniards, in the palace of his father, Alonzo de Ojeda one day espied . . . a number of small bags, tied up. He imagined at first that they were filled with gold dust, but on opening one of them what was his astonishment to find it quite full of Lice!' Cortez . . . then asked . . . for an explanation. He was told that the Mexicans had such a sense of duty to pay tribute to their ruler that the poorest, if they possessed nothing else to offer, daily cleaned their bodies and saved the lice. And when they had enough to fill a bag, they laid it at the feet of their king."[9]

Saving lice for a royal gift surprised the Europeans, but eating lice repelled them. Entomophagy was generally taken as a sure sign of savagery, and explorers regaled a fascinated and disgusted audience with tales of strange people eating strange things. Hudson Bay Company explorer Samuel Hearne recounted that a Chippewa, Matonabbee, "was so remarkably fond of them [lice] that he frequently set five or six of his strapping wives to work to de-louse their hairy caribou-skin shifts, the produce of which being always very considerable, he eagerly received with both hands, and licked them in as fast, and with as good a grace, as any European epicure would the mites in a cheese. He often assured me that such amusement was not only very pleasing, but that the objects of the search were very good; for which I gave him credit, telling him at the same time, that though I endeavoured to habituate myself to every other part of their diet, yet as I was but a sojourner among them, I had no inclination to accustom myself to such dainties as I could not procure in that part of the world where I was most inclined to reside."[10] More ominously, body lice harbor bacteria that cause typhus, one of the deadliest diseases known to humanity, epidemics of which, like the one that helped force Napoleon's retreat from Moscow, changed history.[11] Since lice were present in precontact America, perhaps typhus was too.

No one can yet tell. While a rash typically accompanies typhus, it leaves no telltale marks on the bones that archaeologists study. But some paleoparasitologists suspect that typhus epidemics periodically ravaged pre-Columbian America, similar to those in the Old World, and possibly killed up to 40 percent of those infected.[12]

Behind the debate of whether typhus infected pre-Columbian America is the politically volatile issue of just how edenic the precontact New World was. No one disputes the Amerind's unfortunate lack of immunity to Old World contagious diseases such as smallpox, measles, bubonic plague, and cholera. They destroyed entire peoples in repeated waves of killer epidemics that left the survivors demoralized, deracinated, and dependent. European and American explorers recount tales of large towns with impressive public buildings and hundreds of acres of fields lying silent, deserted, their inhabitants gone without a trace. That the Indian was helpless before these diseases means that they did not exist in the New World before 1492. Why not? Smallpox and measles, for example, probably crossed over to humans from their original animal hosts following animal domestication. Perhaps this crossover occurred *after* the Amerind ancestors left Siberia. Then, too, Old World epidemics are urban diseases, their ferocity dependent upon crowds of people. Even if the epidemics were around before the Siberians became Alaskans, the small hunter-gatherer bands inhabiting Beringia would have made poor reservoirs for hoard-hungry killer diseases. Beringia itself might have proved a potent prophylactic, thousands of years of its cold embrace freezing to death the diseases' hosts. If all of this is so, then 1492 might well have been the beginning of what one writer termed "the conquest of paradise."[13]

Pre-Columbians shared more than head and body lice. Careless lovers carried crab lice as well. Researchers combing through the pubic hair of a two-thousand-year-old Peruvian mummy in 1988 discovered *Pthirus pubis.*[14] Crab lice, so named because of their resemblance to miniature crabs, are the same as pubic lice, named after their residence of choice—pubic hair—although they're equally at home in unshaven armpits and nestled among facial hairs—beards, mustaches, eyelashes, and eyebrows. Their clawlike two front legs are adapted for clinging to hair, which means that infected prepubescent children commonly harbor them in their eyelashes and eyebrows. *Pthirus pubis* is most often spread by sexual contact, but it can be caught from contaminated clothing or bedding. Since adults can live only about forty-eight hours without feeding, who gave you yours is generally easily established. Crab lice live only on humans and, prior to the above discovery, were not known to have been present in pre-Columbian America.

Lice have spawned a number of insults, among the best known are nit-picking and lousy. People being people, we seem to assume it's *other* people who are metaphorically or literally lousy, so public service announcements almost invariably inform readers that "lice are cosmopolitan parasites of humans, occurring in all areas of the world and in all socio-economic classes."[15] Given the demeaning insults the privileged often hurl at the less privileged, it's a sweet sort of justice to learn from the Centers for Disease Control that "in the United States, African-Americans are rarely infested with head lice. This is believed to be due to the American louse's preference for the shape and width of the hair shaft of other races."[16] Perhaps the most repugnant metaphorical use of lice was that employed by soldiers in America's Indian wars, who justified murdering children by pointing out that "nits make lice." John Sevier — Revolutionary War hero, Indian fighter, first governor of Tennessee, whose statue stands in the U.S. Capitol Building and who also was a land thief and speculator, accused traitor, self-appointed governor of the secessionist state of Franklin that he illegally carved from Cherokee territory, and genocidal butcher whose name remains anathema among the Cherokee — is supposed to have coined the word *apropos*, a reference to his troops' practice of killing Cherokee men, women, and children, armed or unarmed, whether in insurrection or at peace.[17]

On January 29, 1863, Colonel Patrick Edward Connor led his army troops in a sunrise attack on the Shoshone Indians camped along the Bear River near what is now Preston, Idaho. What Connor called a battle others term a massacre: fourteen soldiers and an estimated 250 Indians died, 90 of who were women and children. Mormon leader Brigham Young recorded in his journal on February 7, 1863: "The soldiers in the late engagement with the Indians killed ninety squaws and children and wounded many other squaws; about fifty of the Indians escaped. Several squaws were killed because they would not submit quietly to be ravished, and other squaws were ravished in the agony of death. There were about 250 Indians killed in all." The governor reportedly had ordered Connor "to kill all the damned Indians," and Connor, who had during the previous year's campaign ordered his men "to destroy every male Indian whom you may encounter," this time replied to the governor, "nits make lice." For his efforts, Connor was made a U.S. Army general, and the Daughters of the Utah Pioneers later erected a monument praising the soldiers.[18]

But it is the politically ambitious Methodist minister and Union war hero, Colonel John Chivington, the "Fighting Parson," whom most people think of when they hear the phrase "Nits make lice." On November 29, 1864, just before he and seven hundred men under his command, many of them drunk, attacked the Cheyenne reservation at Sand Creek, southeast of Denver, Colorado,

Chivington berated the recalcitrant: "Damn any man who sympathizes with Indians," he said. "Kill and scalp all, big and little; nits make lice." They slaughtered two hundred Indians, mostly women and children. According to soldiers' later testimony, his men then mutilated the bodies, cutting open the pregnant women's wombs and taking men and women's genitalia to fashion into tobacco pouches and hatbands. Since Chivington had quit the army, a military investigation led nowhere; civil charges were never brought against him.[19]

"Nits make lice," having entered American folklore, has been placed, apparently erroneously, in the mouths of the Indian fighters Sheridan, Sherman, and Custer. People online have cited the phrase both in support of and in opposition to wholesale killing in response to 9/11. It appears as early as 1851 in *Tom Quick, the Indian Slayer and the Pioneers of Minisink and Wawarsink*, whose hero defends his killing of a defenseless Indian mother and her three children by muttering, "Nits make lice."[20]

Just because smallpox, measles, bubonic plague, and cholera were kept out of America does not mean that other tagalongs didn't sneak in. Lice did. Typhus may have. Inside early Americans were hundreds of organisms, many microscopic, some macroscopic, some helpful, some dangerous. The human fetus, growing in a largely sterile environment, is free of biotic contamination (except for the microbes that can pass through the placental wall). Upon entering the world, however, the newborn begins to acquire a panoply of resident life forms —some are necessary for life. For example, we and other mammals all carry within our intestines the bacterium *Escherichia coli*, which actually helps us digest our food. If borne without *E. coli*, we obtain them—and hundreds of other bacteria—by ingesting them with our food. These enterobacteriaceae live within our large intestine (enterobacteriaceae means intestinal bacteria), and, if you're around a newborn baby, you can roughly gauge the acquisition of intestinal flora by looking at his or her bowel movements, which will become increasingly dark and smelly as the baby acquires bacteria. While many strains of bacteria are harmless, some are not. Montezuma's revenge, the south-of-the-border version of traveler's diarrhea, is caused from ingesting bacteria, protozoa, or viruses that cause us—though possibly not the locals—contagious diarrhea. Depending upon virulence, the illness should run its course within a week. However, some strains of *E. coli* produce toxins that can kill, and one of these, *E. coli* O157:H7, is a homegrown American variant. This now-notorious undercooked hamburger bacterium, while not harming its cow host, causes bloody diarrhea and cramping in infected humans and can lead to kidney failure.[21]

Humans also carry larger creatures around in them, including tapeworms that can reach lengths of twenty feet. Early Americans carried with them several shorter worms, as archaeologists have discovered, finding in the five thousand-year-old mummified feces of South American Indians pinworm (*Enterobius vermicularis*), giant roundworm (*Ascaris lumbricoides*), and whipworm (*Trichuris trichiura*) eggs.[22] These three parasites, which today are the most common worms infecting humans, survived Beringia's deep freeze filter by hiding out inside their human hosts. Roundworm eggs found in pre-Columbian human fecal remains in Peru, Arizona, Tennessee, and Alaska suggest infection was widespread. According to the Centers for Disease Control, roundworms as long as a foot live within human intestines, daily producing up to two hundred thousand eggs that are dispersed in our feces. Accidentally swallowed, the eggs hatch, entering the bloodstream after penetrating the intestinal wall, and then make their way to the lungs, where they are coughed up, swallowed, and return to the small intestine to mature, mate, and start the process over again.[23] The human whipworm, *Trichuris trichiura*, has a similar life cycle, although it lives for several years attached to the wall of the large intestine. The females release up to ten thousand eggs daily, which are excreted with the feces, and, if subsequently ingested, hatch out into worms that migrate back to the large intestine and repeat the cycle.[24]

Although these two parasites are discomforting, the pinworm (*Enterobius vermicularis*) is worse—because it is visible. Adult pinworms live in the large intestine. After sex, the males die, and the females migrate out of the intestine onto the victim's anus, where each lays up to ten thousand eggs. Within hours, the eggs are ready to infect any human who accidentally swallows them, whereupon they hatch and, migrating to the large intestine, go about making a new generation of worms. The disgusting part of the cycle is the egg-laying moment; the human victim, his or her anus unbearably itchy, invariably scratches it, infecting fingers with pinworm eggs that are then spread to other people via direct contact or from shared bedding and clothing, while the anus, its skin broken from scratching, becomes infected. Adventurous pinworms have been known to emerge from the anus of female sufferers and migrate to the vagina, which they infest and irritate.[25]

People who suffered from pinworms as children no doubt remember the humiliation of today's examination method: a parent applied Scotch tape, sticky side down, to one's anus, hoping to catch eggs and worms for later examination by a medical professional. Since the females emerge early in the morning to lay eggs, the embarrassed child would be faced with baring his or her bottom—generally to mom—first thing in the morning.[26]

Native Americans faced with these internal parasites tried flushing them out with purgatives. South American tribes, which may have included the Inca, used the inner bark of the taheebo tree, or Pau d'Arco, and its close relatives to kill and expel intestinal worms. Modern science has confirmed taheebo's anthelminthic, antifungal, and anticarcinagenic properties, and Pau d'Arco tea and tablets are popular herbal items in the West. North American tribes employed pumpkin (*Curcurbito pepo*) seeds and black walnut (*Juglans nigra*) husks as anthelminthic purgatives, and Western herbalists offer both to customers.[27]

Plants hitched rides with Native Americans, who not only brought some with them from the Old World but also discovered, bred, and distributed many that were indigenous to the New World. Vegetables developed by Indians include maize, potatoes, and tomatoes—all three of which bear Amerind names, as do chocolate, vanilla, and tobacco. Many North American Indians relied on the three sisters—maize (*Zea mays*), squash (*Cucurbita* sp.), and beans (*Phaseolus vulgaris*)—when the Europeans arrived. But these vegetables are not indigenous to the United States; they come from farther south and only slowly made their way north.

North American tobacco (*Nicotiana rustica*) differs from *the* tobacco plant (*Nicotiana tabacum*), which is native to South and Central America. The latter, which happened to grow where Spain started her colonies, dominated the European market. English colonies in North America at first grew the indigenous *N. rustica*, which, although containing more nicotine than *N. tabacum*, makes for a harsher smoke. John Rolfe, Pocahontas's husband and a tobacco farmer, abandoned the native *N. rustica* in favor of the milder *N. tabacum*, and by 1619 tobacco was the principal cash crop of the Virginia colony. To this day the nonindigenous *N. tabacum* dominates American tobacco farms; our native *N. rustica*, known now as Turkish tobacco, grows in exile in Turkey, India, and Russia.

Two plants that pre-Columbian eastern North American Indians cultivated intrigue historians, who wonder how they got here. Most experts think that the common purslane (*Portulaca oleracea*) was a weed introduced by Europeans, and it is described as such in most guides, but it may have arrived here before Columbus. Archaeologists who in the 1970s discovered eighth-century seeds at Apple Creek in Illinois and fourteenth-century pollen in deposits in Crawford Lake, Ontario, suspected it likely that Native Americans carried the once popular potherb with them from Asia. Within historical times various tribes used purslane's succulent leaves and stems, fresh and dried, and its seeds as flour.[28]

How the bottle gourd (*Lagenaria siceraria*) got into Native American hands stirs controversy. Today it is distributed throughout the world's tropics, but with wild relatives in Africa, *L. siceraria* is thought to have originated there. While overland distribution in the Old World is possible, no one supposes that the warm-climate bottle gourd reached America via Beringia. Did an impervious skin allow seed-bearing gourds to float along west-trending currents from west Africa to Brazil, perhaps hundreds of thousands of years before humans arrived in South America? More interesting, did African fishing nets, with gourds attached, break loose and float over after humans reached South America, providing Americans with both seeds and floats? Or, most exciting of all, did African fishermen, blown out to sea, survive a sea crossing and, as prehistoric Robinson Crusoes, introduce gourds to America?[29] Behind these choices lies an anthropological debate: do shared cultural features reflect diffusion from a center of origin or independent discovery? How, that is, do we explain pyramids in both Egypt and Central America? Independent inventions? Cultural diffusion? While pyramids are the most obvious example, other, less striking parallels present even stronger arguments for casual contact. How is it that domesticated cotton grew in both the Old and New World long before 1492? Or that sweet potatoes grew in both South America and Polynesia? Or that cultures worldwide grew and used bottle gourds? Thor Heyerdahl, perhaps the most colorful of diffusionists, sailed the *Kon-Tiki* east from South America to Polynesia and later the *Ra* from Africa to America to demonstrate the possibility of pre-Columbian contacts between these peoples.

Although duller than other hypotheses, that bottle gourds floated over to the New World on their own remains the more probable explanation, according to most academics, barring actual proof of human contacts. Researchers have demonstrated that gourds can survive nearly a year immersed in salt water and still contain viable seeds. A similar accidental African transplant actually occurred in the nineteenth century when the cattle egret (*Bubulcus ibis*) colonized the New World. Indigenous to Africa, where it feeds upon insects stirred up by cattle, the egret was first recorded in British Guiana in the 1870s. Ornithologists theorize that the egret may have made the forty-hour Atlantic crossing numerous times before, but not until cattle farming downed much of eastern South America's forests did it find a suitable niche in the New World. Having found its niche, however, the bird dramatically expanded its range. Within seventy years it reached the United States, where it is now common on both coasts, and it has colonized much of the interior and penetrated as far north as Canada.[30]

However it got to the New World, the gourd proved extremely valuable. Both the leaves and fruits, when still young and tender, can be boiled or steamed. Tough and inedible, the mature gourds make containers, musical instruments, net floats, and ceremonial masks. Round-bellied gourds, which reminded more than one early people of a pregnant woman, led to the gourd's incorporation into creation myths and religious rituals. Some anthropologists think it the inspiration for clay pots and bowls. Certain tribes in northern South America (and Africa and New Guinea) use elongated varieties of gourd as a penis sheath. So important to primitive people was the gourd that there are those who argue that it may be the world's oldest cultivated plant—and that its cultivation was for cultic, not culinary, reasons.[31]

At least two modern American cultures maintain gourd uses that originated with Native Americans. A caffeine-rich tree native to South America, *Ilex paraguariensis*, is the source for maté, a tealike infusion especially popular in Argentina, where it is drunk from a special gourd called *cuias*, which are often elaborately decorated with designs incised into the gourd while it is still growing. More elaborate versions include sterling silver rims. Archaeological evidence attests to pre-Columbian use of *I. paraguariensis*, and early Spanish colonial accounts record native use of the infusion. Opinion is nearly unanimous that the Guarani Indians introduced maté to the Jesuits, who created large plantations of *I. paraguariensis*, using Indian labor to harvest the crop. While maté's popularity rose and fell with changing political and cultural fortunes (it was popularized as the drink of the gaucho), it has become the indigenous alternative to Asiatic and African caffeine sources, and interested Anglos can obtain *cuias* online for about twenty-five dollars.[32]

Closer to home, Florida Indians had gourds seven thousand years ago, as indicated from archaeological remains discovered near Cape Canaveral.[33] Indians carried gourds inland with them, archaeologists having discovered their remains at Mammoth Cave, Kentucky. But Native Americans' most famous use of gourds occurred in the southeastern United States, where they served as birdhouses for purple martins. Martins, *Progne subis*, normally nest in natural cavities in trees and rocks. But America's first great ornithologist, Alexander Wilson, described how Choctaw and Chickasaw Indians "cut off all the top branches from a sapling near their cabins, leaving the prongs a foot or two in length, on each of which they hang a gourd, or calabash, properly hollowed out for their convenience."[34] Old World settlers quickly imitated the Indians, since the martins ate quantities of noxious insects and frightened off crows and other crop predators. So pervasive have martin houses become that martins east of the Rockies rely almost exclusively on them for nesting sites, be they homegrown or store-bought gourds, plastic gourds, or houses that look like miniature mansions. Raised on poles to avoid predators, the houses generally hold twenty to thirty birds, though more ambitious projects can handle two hundred occupants.

Purple Martin
(Calabash)

A gourd used as a purple martin next. John J. Audubon, *The Birds of America* (New York, 1839–44).

Indeed, the Purple Martin Conservation Association believes that *all* eastern purple martins now depend on humans for housing and that they are "the tamest of all wild birds. Today, east of the Rockies, they are the only bird species totally dependent on humans for supplying them with nesting sites," and they are properly considered, not wild, but rather "semidomesticated."[35]

One of the first European accounts of gourds in North America is in Cabeza de Vaca's 1542 *Relacion*, which chronicles his incredible eight-year traverse of America from Florida to Mexico. During his time in Texas, de Vaca and his three companions became successful shamans, making their way from tribe to tribe and healing the sick and, according to de Vaca, even raising the dead. Gourds were a key instrument for shamans: "When we came near the houses all the inhabitants ran out with delight and great festivity to receive us. Among other things, two of their physicians gave us two gourds, and thenceforth we carried these with us, and added to our authority a token highly reverenced by Indians." De Vaca describes the gourds his party received from another tribe, "They brought us gourds bored with holes and having pebbles in them, an instrument for the most important occasions, produced only at the dance or to effect cures, and which none dare touch but those who own them. They say there is virtue in them, and because they do not grow in that country, they come from heaven; nor do they know where they are to be found, only that the rivers bring them in their floods."[36] Historians suspect that the latter account took place on the banks of today's Conchos River, a tributary of the Rio Grande in Big Bend country, the gourds floating down the Pecos and Rio Grande from upriver Pueblo Indian villages.

One of de Vaca's companions was the slave Estevan, who also performed as a shaman. After their return to Spanish Mexico, Estevan accompanied Spanish explorers headed north. Alone, ahead of the main party, he was killed by Indians. His companions, following directions Estevan had sent back before his death, came upon "Cíbola, which is situated on a plain at the skirt of a round hill. It has the appearance of a very beautiful town, the best I have seen in these parts. The houses are of the style that the Indians had described to me, all of stone, with stories and terraces, as well as I could see from a hill where I was able to view it. The city is bigger than Mexico City. At times, I was tempted to go on to the city itself, because I knew I risked only life, which I had offered to God on the day I started the journey. But, in the end, I was afraid to try it, realizing my danger and that if I died, I would not be able to make a report on this country, which to me appears the greatest and best of the discoveries I have made."[37]

Thus began the legend of the Seven Cities of Cibolo. Some say Estevan carried with him his shaman outfit, and that this is why he was killed; others, that his womanizing was his undoing. Nobody knows for sure. What we do know is that the Indians of the Cibolo region—the United States Southwest—still use gourds. The gourd dance, a staple of Indian powwows, is performed by members of tribal warrior societies such as the Kiowa Tia Piah Society, which dates back to the beginnings of the Kiowa nation.

An Entangled Bank

Roadside Weeds

> It is interesting to contemplate an entangled bank, clothed with many plants
> of many kinds, with birds singing on the bushes, with various insects flitting
> about, and with worms crawling through the damp earth, and to reflect that
> these elaborately constructed forms, so different from each other, and depend-
> ent on each other in so complex a manner, have all been produced by laws
> acting around us. . . . There is grandeur in this view of life, with its several
> powers, having been originally breathed by the Creator into a few forms or
> into one; and that, whilst this planet has gone cycling on according to the
> fixed law of gravity, from so simple a beginning endless forms most beautiful
> and most wonderful have been, and are being evolved.[1]

The "entangled bank" that concludes Darwin's *On the Origin of Species* has
become famous as a trope for natural selection. Given current religious opposition to Darwinism in America, that his only mention of *evolution* is here, at
the very end, in the same sentence, if not breath, with which he credits the
Creator with creation must surely entertain both Darwin and his Creator,
assuming either is interested in irony.

A strictly Darwinist view of things would make us and our effects upon the
world as subject to the "laws acting around us" as are other animals and the
plants. However, we tend to place those plants and animals inhabiting an
entangled bank, which are there thanks to human intervention, into categories
that are other than natural. So it is that any unkempt roadside reveals not only
natural selection but deliberate and accidental human selection as well. America's weedy places are literally living history, their various plant and animal en-
sembles the unwritten textbooks of the human transformation of this continent.

The wild carrot, for example, accompanied European settlers to the New
World. Cultivated in the Mediterranean region since ancient times, *Daucus
carota*'s familiar orange root is a far cry from its wild cousin's stubby, nearly

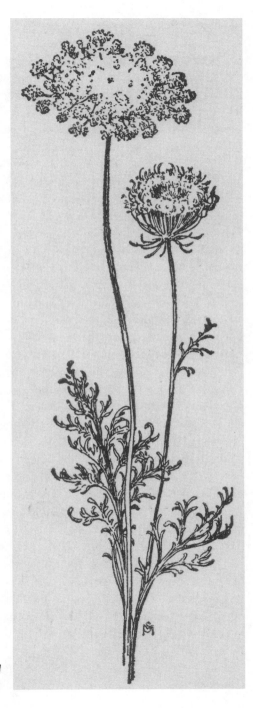

A wild carrot. Ada E. Georgia, *A Manual of Weeds* (New York, 1920).

inedible white root. Nevertheless, both cultivated and wild carrots are the same species and are often found growing close to each other. They offer a living lesson on the effects of genetic selection. Cut a cultivated carrot crossways and you'll see that the orange fleshy portion surrounds a paler, yellowish core. The core is woody and, left to grow for too long, turns as fibrous as a two-by-four. The thicker outer ring of orange is bark, encouraged by patient farmers to grow unnaturally thick and tender. Cut a wild carrot in two, and you'll see just how thick the original carrot's woody core was.

Thought to be native to Afghanistan and surrounding areas, the carrot long ago traveled east and west throughout Asia and Europe. Prehistoric Swiss lake-dwellers collected the seed, and four-thousand-year-old Egyptian paintings depict purple carrots, the vegetable's original color, which is still common in Asia and increasingly popular in American vegetable gardens. Patriotic Dutch gardeners are said to have bred orange carrots in honor of their royal family, the House of Orange. What is known for certain is that a century and a half ago the French gardening firm of Vilmorin and Andrieux gave us today's favorite cultivars following only four years of breeding wild carrots. Gardening enthusiast Philippe-Victoire de Vilmorin joined Louis XV's botanist Pierre d'Andrieux in 1743 in opening a gardening store that, generations later, commands worldwide attention as a leading seed company. The company's 1885 guide, *Le Jardin Potager* (*The Vegetable Garden*), still in print, is an organic gardening favorite.[2]

Within a hundred years of Columbus's landfall, the carrot grew wild in the New World. English sea captain Sir John Hawkins spotted it growing on Margarita Island, off Venezuela, in 1565. Both Jamestown and Plymouth colonies grew carrots, which soon escaped to become part of "wild" America. Today wild carrots, found throughout the United States, are listed as "noxious weeds" in several states. What the English call wild carrot, Americans curiously enough call Queen Anne's lace, though which Anne this is—Anne of Denmark and wife to James I of the King James Bible fame, or the later Anne Stuart, queen of England, or even the Queen of Heaven's mother, Saint Anne, patron saint of lacemakers—remains obscure. Legend has it that Anne, whichever one, pricked her finger while making lace. You can see the purple drop of blood in the heart of Queen Anne lace's large flower, which is, in fact, a collection of dozens of tiny flowers known as a compound umbel. But the *Oxford English Dictionary* cites the first use of the term *Queen Anne's lace* as 1894, over two hundred years after the last Queen Anne died, causing problems for those wishing to take seriously the origin of the name.[3]

Four years after Queen Anne died, John Parkinson, James I's apothecary and Charles I's botanist, wrote in his 1629 publication *Paradisi in Sole Paradisus*

Terrestris (Paradise, or Park, in Sun's Paradise, or Park, on Earth; an excruciating pun—park-in-sun's park on earth) that carrot leaves "in Autumne will turn to be of a fine red or purple (the beautie whereof allureth many Gentlewomen oftentimes to gather the leaves, and stick them in their hats . . . in stead of feathers.)," suggesting that early English colonists may have associated the plant with the royal court. Not that these headdresses were merely beautiful; the 1633 edition of John Gerard's *The Herball or Generall Historie of Plantes* notes that "the root boiled and eaten . . . procureth bodily lust. . . . seed drunke bringeth downe the desired sickness (contraceptive) . . . also good for the passions of the mother."[4]

Herbal enthusiasts make much of historian John Riddle's recent "rediscovery" of the carrot's contraceptive properties. Piqued by Appalachian women's use of carrot seeds as a "morning after" concoction, Riddle discovered that *D. carrota* has a long history of contraception use. Both the Greeks and Romans used it to induce menstruation and as a contraceptive and abortifacient. Modern Indian and Chinese eat the seed to reduce fertility, and studies on mice suggest the seeds actually do prevent conception.[5] A close relative of the carrot, giant fennel (*Ferula assafoetida*) was an even-more-powerful natural abortion-inducing plant. Known as *silphium* to the Greeks and Romans, today's giant fennel, or a now-extinct close cousin, provided the North African city-state of Cyrene so much money that it appeared on Cyrenian coins. Roman demand extirpated the plant in the vicinity of Cyrene, forcing the licentious to use less potent relatives such as fennel and carrot.[6]

Wider known is the carrot's ability to improve eyesight, thanks to the presence of beta-carotene, one of fifty known yellow to red plant pigments that are a natural sources of vitamin A. Discovered and named in 1831 by Heinrich Wilhelm Ferdinand Wackenroder, carotene, present in yellow and red vegetables and fruits as well as leafy green vegetables, is a major natural source of vitamin A for humans. It is vitamin A that improves night vision and helps prevent cataracts.[7] Carrot's effect on night vision even played a role in World War II. The Royal British Air Force's newly perfected and top-secret radar led to their downing an inordinate number of German Luftwaffe bombers at night. To disguise the role that radar played, the British announced that their success was due to their pilots' eating lots and lots and lots of carrots. Their most successful pilot, John Cunningham, was nicknamed Cat's Eyes because of his supposedly phenomenal night vision, when, in fact, he relied on coastal radar stations to pinpoint German bombers headed for Britain. The Germans fell for the deception, at least for a while, allowing the British to maintain a technological lead in radar development and air superiority in the Battle of Britain.[8]

To this day, our mothers tell us to eat our carrots to improve our eyesight—which they will, but not so much so as to make us ace fighter pilots.

Carrots' vision-building properties surfaced again in the world news when "golden rice" became available at the recent turn of the century. One to two million children worldwide die every year from vitamin A deficiency, and another five hundred thousand go blind. Since most of these unfortunates live in the Third World and eat rice, altruistic Swiss scientists spliced carrot genes responsible for producing beta-carotene into regular rice seed, creating a beta-carotene-enriched rice. Opponents to genetically modified (GM) foods faced a moral quandary: who could oppose stopping children from going blind, even if it meant the spread of "frankenfoods"? But deep-seated fears of genetic modifications won the day. GM opponents closed ranks against golden rice, claiming it alone was insufficient to meet vitamin A requirements, that more efficacious and less expensive preventatives already existed, and that the project was less altruistic than it was a public relations gimmick touting genetic engineering. "Grains of hope" became "grains of hype," "golden rice" became "fool's gold" and a genetic engineering "Trojan horse." No wonder the scientists who spent eight years developing the stuff lost their tempers. But they should have known that combining Monsanto, genetic engineering, and altruism in the same sentence would raise eyebrows. While ideologues on both sides debated angrily, public relations people in the besieged genetic engineering world, leaping on the rice as a golden opportunity to make their technology look good, overhyped the product. Yes, golden rice would alleviate vitamin A deficiencies; no, it alone would not end them—unless a child ate twenty to fifty bowls of it every day. Yes, the companies involved agreed to give poor farmers free seed; and, yes, they planned to make a bundle off sales elsewhere. Yes, the rice was safe (even if the beta-carotene genes did jump into other rices, that merely meant more beta-carotene to spread around); no, the rice had not yet been tested in the field. The upshot? As Gordon Conway of the Rockefeller Foundation, which sponsored some of the research, wrote in January 2001: "The public relations uses of golden rice have gone too far."[9] That was three years and one and a half million blind children ago.

Carrots are in trouble elsewhere as well. Growing wild throughout North America, *Daucus carota* has been repeatedly classed as a noxious weed; it is even illegal in Ohio. Invasive, it establishes itself in large monocultures in fields and pastures, outcompeting native plants and tainting the milk of cows that feed on it. Yet, there are those—lacemakers, quilters, painters, poets, herbalists, paper makers, florists, brides—who like it. Perhaps because of its suggestive shape, the carrot has long been associated with sexual matters. As discussed elsewhere, women have long used the seeds as a contraceptive. Men, on the other hand, have used the root as an aphrodisiac. The Roman emperor Caligula is said to have fed the entire Roman senate a feast of carrots in hope of starting an orgy. A more restrained use is American poet William Carlos Williams's famous comparison of a woman's body to a field of Queen Anne's lace:

> white as can be, with a purple mole
> at the center of each flower.
> Each flower is a hand's span
> of her whiteness. Wherever
> his hand has lain there is
> a tiny purple blemish. Each part
> is a blossom under his touch
> to which the fibres of her being
> stem one by one, each to its end,
> until the whole field is a
> white desire, empty, a single stem,
> a cluster, flower by flower,
> a pious wish to whiteness.[10]

A bouquet of Queen Anne's lace speaks of summer to many of us. Should you not have access to a field of wildflowers, you can, of course, buy Queen Anne's lace from a florist. Only what a florist calls Queen Anne's lace is, in fact, *Ammi majus*, also known as bishop's weed, a less invasive and smaller Queen Anne's look-alike.

Even more common than wild carrot is plantain, so underfoot everywhere that both Native Americans and New Zealand Maoris called it "white man's foot." Longfellow explains in *Hiawatha* that "Wheresoe-er they [the whites] tread, beneath them / Springs a flower unknown among us, / Springs the White-man's Foot in blossom." In America both *Plantago lanceolota*, English, or narrow-leafed, plantain, and *P. major*, common, or broad-leafed, plantain, crowd lawns everywhere, along with thirty-two lesser known affiliates, some native, some alien. Just to confuse matters, *P. major*, which Native Americans called both white man's and Englishman's foot, may be native to North America, no matter what the Indians thought.

Everyone agrees that *P. lanceolata* is alien to North America. But its companion in invasiveness, *P. major*, has roots more obscure. While most popular and many professional guides list common plantain as introduced, the U.S. Department of Agriculture's Plants Database calls *P. major* native. How could the Indians have been so wrong about the white man's foot? First of all, *P. major* does hail from Europe; no one questions that. Scientists have discovered its seeds in the stomachs of bog people sacrificed to the gods fifteen hundred years ago, and the Angles and Saxons knew it as *wegbrade* (waybread) or *wyrta modor* (mother of herbs), whose strength seems to come from its ability to withstand traffic:

> And, you, waybread, mother of herbs,
> open to the east, mighty within;
> carts rolled over you, women rode over you,
> over you brides cried out, bulls snorted over you.
> All you withstood then, and were crushed
> So you withstand poison and contagion
> and the loathsome one who travels through the land.[11]

Colonists brought *P. major* with them, both deliberately as a medicinal herb and inadvertently as a contaminant of animal hay, seed stores, and the soil often used to ballast ships. Thriving on the compacted soil of wayside verges and happiest growing in full sun, the English wegbrade was fruitful and multiplied.

Believers in *P. major*'s inherent right to citizenship cite extensive Indian use of the plant as proof of its American origin, although plenty of Johnnies-come-lately also made their way into the Native American pharmacology. They also point out that so common was common plantain in New England that Peter Kalm, Linnaean protégé and author of the 1753 book *Travels in North America*, thought it native.[12] Opponents, however, think that this ubiquity is the mark of an alien invader taking advantage of environmental disruption. Just to confuse matters more, Joseph Decaisne, an early-nineteenth-century director of Paris's Jardin des Plantes, determined that a plantain nearly identical to *P. major* was not only a distinct species, but was also native to North America. About the only way the average person can distinguish between the look-alikes, which grow in similar areas, is that *P. rugelii*, named by Decaisne after Ferdinand Rugel, a nineteenth-century American botanist, has leaves tinted red at their base. It occurs naturally only in the eastern half of the United States— although we're doing our accidental best to spread it.

This would be only a minor contretemps, except that the confusion puts nativists in a bind: to weed or not to weed. While the USDA lists common plantain as native, the National Park Service includes it on its online list of "Alien Plant Invaders of Natural Areas."[13] Ignoring the USDA, most of us pull, poison, and persecute plantain, although some among us actually pay for plantain plants. One Ohio nursery advertises three varieties of *P. major*: purple plantain, the "cultivated form of the weedy 'Cart-track Plant.' Noninvasive, this is

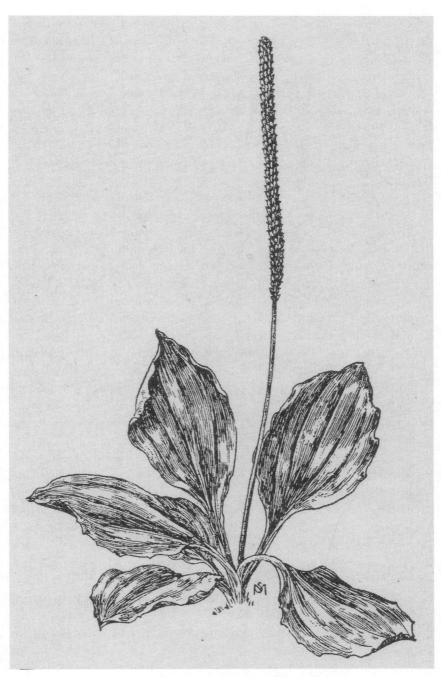

A common, or broad-leafed, plantain. Ada E. Georgia, *A Manual of Weeds* (New York, 1920).

a favorite color contrast plant for Hosta collectors; much used in British gardening" (and only $2.75 per plant); the "Absolutely charming 'Parsley Leaved Plantain' forming tight rosettes of elaborately frilled and cripsed leaves—small enough for a large trough; excellent between garden walk pavers. Very cute; very amusing; very over the top" (also $2.75); and *P. major rosularis*, "attractive dramatic spherical rosettes of leaflet bracts tightly packed, forming the ultimate 'Tussie Mussie'—very low growing; a favorite for kids looking for a new alien from Mars. A must if it would amuse you to explain (somewhat later) to your gardening friends that the plant they most want that is growing in outrageous hyper flounce along your pathways is (secretly) a gussied up plantain" ($3.00 each).[14]

Our forebears, however, hailed it as good for "pains in the guts, distillation of rhewm, fluxes, womens courses, spitting blood or bleeding at mouth or nose or of wounds, phtisick, consumption or ulcers in the lungs" and "tertian ague, dropsie and falling-sickness, toothach, pin and web in the eyes, pains in the ears, inflamations, burning or scalding, hollow ulcers, cankers, and sore mouth, or privy parts, piles," according to Nicholas Culpepper, whose 1652 *The English Physitian* remains in print today.[15] Born in 1616 to an ardent Puritan, Culpepper fled religious study at Cambridge for the arms of a rich heiress, who died en route to their elopement, leaving her lover heartbroken and broke. His apprenticeship to a London apothecary was cut short when Culpepper married a wealthy fifteen-year-old. He then set himself up as an apothecary, but the English Civil War intervened. Having joined with the Puritans, Culpepper was shot in the chest in 1643. With time on his hands, he set to writing his unauthorized 1649 *A Physicall Directory*. He threatened to break the apothecaries' lucrative pharmaceutical monopoly by putting the hitherto guarded recipes of these "bloodsuckers, true vampires," into the people's hands. As Culpepper himself pointed out: "I am writing for the press a translation of the physicians' medicine book from Latin into English so that all my fellow countrymen and apothecaries can understand what the doctors write on their bills. Hitherto they made medicine a secret conspiracy, writing prescriptions in mysterious Latin to hide ignorance and to impress upon the patient. They want to keep their book a secret, not for everybody to know."[16] Irate apothecaries, physicians, and Royalists retorted by associating Culpepper with radical Puritanism, treason, drunkenness, lechery, and lousy Latin: "The pharmacopoeia was done (very filthily) into English by one Nicholas Culpeper [*sic*] who commenced the several degrees of independency, Brownism, anabaptism; admitted himself of John Goodwin's school (of all ungodliness) in Coleman Street; after that he turned seeker, manifestarian, and now has arrived at the battlement of an absolute atheist, and by two years' drunken labour hath gallimawfried the apothecaries' book into nonsense, mixing every receipt therein with some scruples at least of rebellion or atheism, besides the danger of poisoning mens' bodies. And (to supply his drunkenness and lechery with a 30-shilling reward) endeavoured to bring into obloquy the famous Societies of Apothecaries and Chirurgeons."[17] Culpepper's run-in with the Societies of Apothecaries and Surgeons sounds like a seventeenth-century version of alternative medicine's clashes with today's American Medical Association, both centuries' adversaries hurling the same accusations of venality, incompetence, political unreliability, and religious nonsense at each other, with laypeople caught in the crossfire.

A *Physicall Directory* was but the beginning of Culpepper's assault on organized medicine. In 1651 his *Semeiotica Uranica, or An Astrological Judgement of Diseases* explained how to use astrology to diagnose disease. A year later he translated Galen's *Art of Physic* so, "that thou mayest understand . . . in a general way the manifest virtues of medicines . . . such as are obvious to the senses, especially to the taste and smell." In 1653 he published *The English Physitian*, in whose introduction he explained how "the admirable harmony of the creation is herein seen, in the influence of stars upon herbs and the body of man, how one part of the creation is subservient to another, and all for the use of man whereby the infinite power and wisdom of god in the creation appears." This was more easily seen if you bought several Culpepper books. He designed them to work in tandem, one following the other. Patients were therefore advised, "Consider what planet causeth the disease; that thou maist find in my semeiotia;" and "Consider by what planet the afflictd part of the bodie is governed; that my semeiotica will inform you in also." Having established the astrological causes of a disease, the patient then could turn to *The English Physitian*, where, "You have in this book the herbs for cure apropriated to the several diseases," and, "You may oppose diseases by herbs of the planet opposite to the planet that causeth them," or, alternatively, "There is a way to cure diseases somtimes by sympathy, and so every planet cures his own diseases." An understanding Culpepper advised the confused, "There was a small treatise of mine of humane vertues, printed at the latter end of my ephemeris for the yeer 1651. I suppose it would do much good to yong students to peruse that with this book."[18] No doubt Culpepper would have continued exposing medical malpractice and writing popular cure-alls, but he died in 1654, leaving his wife with seventy-nine unpublished manuscripts.

Culpepper's linking of astrology, disease, and herbal remedies still enjoys popularity with some. Not that mainstream medicine completely ignores *Plantago*. Brazilians use it to treat parasites, Vietnamese as a diuretic, and Bulgarians to control bronchitis. A Norwegian doctor's review in 2000 of plantain's medicinal properties reveals, "A range of biological activities has been found from plant extracts including wound healing activity, antiinflammatory, analgesic, antioxidant, weak antibiotic, immuno modulating and antiulcerogenic activity. Some of these effects may attribute to the use of this plant in folk medicine."[19]

But it is Americans who use more plantain than any other people—to quit smoking, to cure constipation, and to reduce heart disease. As one online herbal site explains, plantain contains "a remarkable glycoside of the monoterpene class (iridoid) called Aucubin. . . . Exact cause and effect relationships are not yet fully understood." Another site notes that "an extract of *P. major* is included as a mild sedative in a patented preparation for breaking the smoking habit."[20] One company sells one hundred, 500 milligram capsules of "whole dried *Plantago major* herb" for twenty bucks—roughly ten dollars an ounce for dried leaves you could pick right off your lawn. If you don't fertilize, it will be organic as well. Plantain comes into its own as constipation cure. The seeds, high in fiber and mucilage, are consumed after being ground into powder and mixed with water. Once in the intestines, the fiber absorbs liquid and swells, the resulting mass causing involuntary muscle contractions leading to a bowel movement, which, thanks to the mucilage, is relatively painless.[21] Several species of plantain are good at this job, but the champs are Spanish psyllium, or fleawort, *Plantago psyllium*, and Indian or blood plantago, *Plantago ovata*. Both are major crops in India, which exports most of the harvests to the United States, where nearly nine thousand tons of seed are imported each year, 60 percent of which winds up in over-the-counter laxatives such as Fiberall and Metamucil.[22] Aging astronaut John Glenn even took some into outer space with him.[23] Of course, if you're too embarrassed to buy bulk laxatives, you can always gather plantain seeds from your backyard, steep them in a teaspoon of hot water, and drink this mixture down before going to bed. *Plantago ovata* is native to Texas, the Southwest, and California; *P. psyllium*, an introduced alien, grows throughout New England, the "old" Northwest, the West Coast, and in some Middle Atlantic states. While not as effective in treating constipation, *P. lanceolota* and *P. major* grow pretty much everywhere; herbalists swear by them.[24] Kellogg's cereals once swore by plantain's cholesterol-lowering ability. In the late 1990s the U.S. Food and Drug Administration allowed Kellogg's to advertise its cereals that contained ground *P. psyllium* seed husks as lowering the risk of coronary heart disease after studies indicated not only that such soluble fibers lowered blood cholesterol levels as effectively as did reducing fat intake, but also that consumers found it easier to eat more fiber than less fat. Although Kellogg's initial product line failed to take off, enthusiasts foresee supermarkets filled with psyllium-fortified products.[25]

Nearly as ubiquitous as both wild carrot and plantain is amaranth, which is both a garden flower and a weed. So widespread are the various amaranths that scientists continue to debate just where many of them originated. Asian amaranths, bred as potherbs to be cooked and eaten like spinach, have larger leaves than their American cousins, which were bred for their seed heads. Originally grown as food, both Asian and American amaranths have also made it into our gardens, where their showy leaves and showier seed heads have garnered popular names such as love-lies-bleeding, red cockscomb, and velvet flower.

Several species of amaranth were important crops for pre-Columbians, from the Incas in South America to the Aztecs in Mexico and the Pueblo in the southwest United States. High-altitude Peruvian peasants still plant *Amaranthus caudatus* and *A. hybridis,* and Andeans eat the leaves like spinach and boil, roast, and grind the tiny black seeds, which also provide a red dye for coloring corn dishes.[26] Both the Aztec and Southwest American Indians also ate amaranth, having inherited several cultivated species, including *A. cruentus, A. powellii,* and *A. hypochondriacus* from the Mayans. Archaeologists have discovered amaranth and corn pollen in large numbers in Pueblo ruins in New Mexico, revealing that pre-Columbians in the Rio Grande watershed cultivated amaranth. Farther south in Mexico, however, amaranth was even more important. Every year the Aztec capital Tenochtitlán received as tribute 8.1 million kilograms of *huauhtli,* or pure amaranth seed or seed mixtures predominantly of amaranth. So important was huauhtli to the Aztecs that they named an amaranth seed-eating bird *uauhtotl,* the *huauhtli* bird (*tototl*). They drank *uauhatolli,* a drink (*atole*) of water mixed with huauhtli and ate *huauquillamalmaliztli,* a dough stuffed with huauhtli leaves.[27]

This is known thanks to the *Codex Mendoza,* a sixteenth-century Aztec tribute record that English priest and travel writer Samuel Purchas enthusiastically describes as "the choisest of my jewels, ... a historie, yea a politicke, ethike, ecclesiastike, oeconomike history, with just distinctions of times, places, acts, and arts," all rendered in pictures. In came into Purchas's hands after a most convoluted history: The Spanish governor of Mexico obtained the *Codex* from Indians and had it translated into Spanish a mere ten days before the fleet sailed for Spain, only to see the French seize the ship carrying the *Codex*. It was then given to the French king's geographer, from whose estate Richard Hakluyt, then chaplain to the English ambassador, bought it and had it translated into English in order to publish it. But no one willing to pay the price of printing the accompanying pictographs. Purchas inherited it along with Hakluyt's other papers and published it in *Hakluytus Posthumus, or Purchas His Pilgrimes* as "The history of the Mexican nation, described in pictures by the Mexican author explained in the Mexican language; which exposition translated into Spanish, and thence into English, together with the said picture-historie, are here presented."[28] Purchas's version repeats over and over the amount of "guautli, which is the seed of Blethos" required from various provinces; guautli being Purchas's rendering of huauhtli.[29]

Purchas is perhaps best known today for his description of Kubla Khan's palace, Xanadu: "In Xamdu did Cublai Can build a stately Palace, encompassing sixteene miles of plaine ground with a wall, wherein are fertile Meddowes, pleasant Springs, delightfull Streames, and all sorts of beasts of chase and game, and in the middest thereof a sumptuous house of pleasure," which Samuel Taylor Coleridge used to open his much-anthologized poem, "Kubla Khan":

> In Xanadu did Kubla Khan
> A stately pleasure-dome decree:
> Where Alph, the sacred river, ran
> Through caverns measureless to man
> Down to a sunless sea.
> So twice five miles of fertile ground
> With walls and towers were girdled round:
> And here were gardens bright with sinuous rills
> Where blossomed many an incense-bearing tree;
> And here were forests ancient as the hills,
> Enfolding sunny spots of greenery."

Coleridge loved reading Purchas, whose best-known travel accounts are *Purchas his Pilgrimage* (1613), *Purchas his Pilgrimes* (1619), and *Hakluytus Posthumus, or Purchas His Pilgrimes* (1625), this last based on Elizabethan geographer Richard Hakluyt's unpublished notes.

But for those interested in pre-Columbian Mexican uses of amaranth, Purchas's excerpts from Spanish accounts of the conquest of Mexico are more important than Coleridge's "Kubla Khan." And it is to the Jesuit priest Josephus Acosta that Purchas turned for his information. Acosta's *Historia Natural y Moral de las Indias* (1590), written following seventeen years in Spanish America, is not only a fascinating repository of Native American customs but also is an influential book. John Locke cites it in his development of the social contract theory of government, and it contains the first known argument for a Bering Strait passage by Indians from the Old to the New World. Locke's theory, as Thomas Jefferson would later summarize it, "that governments derive their just powers from the consent of the governed," cites a number of authorities, including Acosta:

And if Josephus Acosta's word may be taken, he tells us that in many parts of America there was no government at all. "There are great and apparent conjectures," says he, "that these men [speaking of those of Peru] for a long time had neither kings nor commonwealths, but lived in troops, as they do this day in Florida—the Cheriquanas, those of Brazil, and many other nations, which have no certain kings, but, as occasion is offered in peace or war, they choose their captains as they please. . . . " These men, it is evident, were actually free; and whatever superiority some politicians now would place in any of them, they themselves claimed it not; but, by consent, were all equal, till, by the same consent, they set rulers over themselves. So that their politic societies all began from a voluntary union, and the mutual agreement of men freely acting in the choice of their governors and forms of government.[30]

The origin of Native Americans obsessed Europeans of Acosta's time, who tried to account for their origin within terms acceptable to a biblical view of history. Since Noah's flood eradicated everyone except Noah's immediate family, where had the Indians come from? Did they descend from Babylonians lucky enough to escape both the water and God's omniscient eye? Had they crossed over when Plato's Atlantis was still dry? Were they the lost tribes of Israel, a theory that remained popular for hundreds of years, intriguing both Thomas Jefferson and Mormon prophet Joseph Smith? But Acosta's solution was simpler: the Indians had walked. "I conjecture . . . that the new world, which we call Indies, is not altogether severed and disjoyned from the other world; and to speake my opinion, I have long beleeved that the one and the other world are joyned and continued one with another in some part, or at the least are very neere. And yet to this day there is no certaine knowledge of the contrary. For towards the Articke or Northerne Pole all the longitude of the earth is not discovered, and many hold that above Florida the land runnes out very large towards the north, and as they say joynes with the Scithike or German Sea. . . . Some peopling the lands they found, and others seeking for newe, in time they came to inhabite and people the Indies, with so many nations."[31]

All of which is fascinating, but really of little import to the truly significant matter at hand, the pre-Columbian uses of what we call weeds. Acosta's stories about the New World includes a chapter on "In what manner the devill hath laboured in Mexico to counterfait the feast of the holy sacrament used in the Popish church." According to Acosta, "The Mexicanes in the moneth of May, made their principall feast to their god Vitzilputzli, and two dayes before this feast the virgins whereof I have spoken (the which were shut up and secluded in the same temple, and were as it were religious women) did mingle a quantitie of the seede of beetes with roasted mays, and then they did mould it with honey, making an idoll of that paste, in bignesse like to that of wood, putting in stead of eyes, graines of greene glasse, of blue, or white; and for teeth, graines of mays."[32] Purchas's "beetes" are our amaranth, which is still known by the common name wild beet thanks to the superficial resemblance of various species' leaves to beet leaves, which were and still are substituted for each other. "Mays" is, of course, our maize.

Royally dressed, the idol was carried in a procession that ended with it being placed on the top of a temple pyramid, where women brought "pieces of paste compounded of beetes, and roasted mays, . . . of the fashion of great bones. . . . They called these morsels of paste, the flesh and bones of Vitzliputzli. . . . and the priests and superiors of the temple tooke the idoll of paste, . . . and made many pieces, as well of the idoll it selfe as of the Tronchons which were consecrated, and then they gave them to the communion, beginning with the greater, and continuing unto the rest, both men, women, and little children; who received it with such teares, feare, and reverence, as it was an admirable thing, saying, that the did eate the flesh and bones of God, wherewith they were grieved."[33]

Bernardino de Sahagun echoes Acosta's account in *Historia General de las Cosas de la Nueva España* (A General History of the Things of New Spain, 1570), which counsels readers, "if you know of anything among these natives relating to this subject of idolatry, immediately inform the temporal or spiritual authorities so that it may be quickly remedied. . . . Anyone who does not persecute this sin and its perpetrators by legitimate and meritorious means shall not be considered a good Christian," which is a glancing reference to the Spanish's outlawing amaranths as a crop.[34]

While Father Acosta's position was that "the gospell of our Lord Jesus Christ thrust out all these superstitions, giving them the right foode of life, which unites their soules to God," Protestant cleric Purchas thought otherwise, supposing that Acosta's accounts revealed, not the triumph of right-minded Christianity over devilish pagan imitations of Christianity, but rather the only-to-be-expected affinities between the devil's pagan and Catholic followers. In his marginal comment, Purchas opined, "The devill liking that unchristian, antichristian prodigious opinion of transubstantiation, and the consequents, elevation, adoration, reservation, Corpus Christi mad solemnities and idolatrous processions, with rites beyond any former paganisme, in disgrace of the true Sacrament, falsely calling this their Idoll an unbloudy sacrifice, which hath cost so many thousands their bloud in fire and otherwise (the Papists at once disputing of Christs naturall body and despiting and renting his mysticall body) hath found nothing fitter to transport into the Indies, nothing more contrarie to sense, reason, religion, humanitie, or wherein more to triumph over mankinde in all these, then this brutish and bloudy solemnitie, here described."[35] Whatever the spiritual sources of New World religious rituals, that they relied on native plants is plain. Acosta's beet, maize, and honey paste were called *tzoalli,* the Aztec word for statue, and if the authorities thought they were rid of tzoalli, they were wrong, because tzoalli lives today as *alegria,* a Mexican delicacy that uses a paste of amaranth seed and sugarcane syrup.[36]

Repelled by its religious use, the Spanish nevertheless admired amaranthus's showy seed heads and took them back to Europe with them. The grain amaranths, A. *hypochondriacus* and A. *caudatus,* thus made the transition from crop to garden flower. To this day most Westerners know them as prince's feather and love-lies-bleeding, annuals with showy flowers. The flowers are actually seed heads, or inflorescences, which Native Americans selected millennia ago for their food value.

The English word *amaranth* appeared as early as 1548, but the flowers were known in Spanish as *bledo* and *papagayo;* in French, *discipline des religieuses* (nuns' whip), *fleur de jalousie* (flower of jealousy), and *queue de renard* (Reynard's tail, Reynard being the fox of French folklore); and other English common names include love-lies-bleeding, cockscomb, prince's feather, flower gentle, velure floramor, velvet flower, and Joseph's coat. So quickly did amaranth become established in European herbal use that Culpepper wrote in his *Complete Herball* manuscript, "The flowers, dried and beaten into powder, stop the terms in women, and so do almost all other red things. . . . The flowers stop all fluxes of blood; whether in man or woman, bleeding either at the nose or wound. There is also a sort of Amaranthus that bears a white flower, which stops the whites in women, and the running of the reins in men, and is a most gallant antivenereal, and a singular remedy for the French pox."[37]

Although newly discovered as American flowers, the plant was named amaranth because of its association with European flowers that the ancients called "the immortal amaranth," from the Greek *amarantos* (unfading). Many classicists and floral historians think the classical amaranth is the flower that today is called everlasting, *Helichrysum orientale,* an evergreen still popular in Europe, especially as a commemorative flower for All Saints' Day, November 1. Ironically, since the ancient Greeks also decorated their tombs with amaranth, today's Christians are continuing a twenty-five-hundred-year-old pagan ceremony, using a flower whose common name confuses it with the notorious Aztec amaranth.

But God is tolerant, because the amaranth grows not only in the Old and New World, but also in heaven, where angels use it to decorate their hair and crown their heads, as Milton explains in *Paradise Lost:*

Immortal Amarant, a Flow'r which once
In Paradise, fast by the Tree of Life,
Began to bloom; but soon for man's offence
To Heav'n removed, where first it grew, there grows,
And flow'rs aloft, shading the Fount of Life,
But where the river of Bliss through midst of Heav'n
Rolls o'er Elysian Flow'rs her Amber stream;
With these that never fade the Spirits elect
Bind their resplendent locks inwreath'd with beams.[38]

Milton's amaranth combines classical tales of flowery apotheoses and Church Fathers' fanciful interpretations of 1 Peter 5:4: "crown of glory that fadeth not away." Third-century Clement of Alexandria's heavenly wreath is perhaps the first development of the idea that "we must have no communion with demons. Nor must we crown the living image of God after the manner of dead idols. For the fair crown of amaranth is laid up for those who have lived well. This flower the earth is not able to bear; heaven alone is competent to produce it."[39] In Greek, Clement's "fair crown of amaranth" (*ho kalos tou amarantinou stephanos*) even more clearly derives from 1 Peter 5:4, "*ton amarantinon tes doxes stephanon*," where *stephanos* is Greek for crown and *amarantin* for incorruptible.[40] Nor is Milton's "amarant" a misspelling; he's copying the Greek. The English and botanical "amaranth" is a misspelling; the final syllable of the correctly spelled "amarant" having picked up an "h" from a false etymological association with "anthos" (flower).

Since most English poets until the twentieth century enjoyed a classical education, it is difficult to know at times whether they are referring to Milton, 1 Peter, or classical literature when, like Shelley, they write of "the amaranth bower" of eternity, or, like Coleridge, they smell apocalypse in the French Revolution:

The sapphire-blazing gates of Paradise
Are thrown wide open, and thence voyage forth
Detachments wild of seraph-warbled airs,
And odors snatch'd from beds of amaranth,

. . . .

Seize on my young anticipating heart
When that blest future rushes on my view!
For in his own and in his Father's might
The SAVIOUR comes!

Wordsworth's more plebeian vision of the flower, while using classical imagery, eschews the Christian for the pagan:

> YOU call it, "Love lies bleeding," — so you may,
> Though the red Flower, not prostrate, only droops,
> . . . A flower how rich in sadness!
> . . . So drooped Adonis bathed in sanguine dew
> Of his death-wound, . . .
> While Venus in a passion of despair
> . . . suffered, as Immortals sometimes do;
> But pangs more lasting far, "that" Lover knew
> Who . . .
> His own dejection, downcast Flower! could share
> With thine, and gave the mournful name which thou wilt ever bear.

The amaranth in your flower garden, then, enjoys the imprimatur of pagan Greek and bloody Aztec, pious Christian and enthusiastic revolutionary, spurned lover and diseased debauch. While the USDA considers A. *hybridus* native, odds are that the roots of that shockingly bright red to purple loves-lies-bleeding flanking your driveway come from Mexico by way of Spain. In any case, should you not be partial to the gaudy amaranth, the odds are that a less gaudy variety of A. *hybridus* lurks in the tangled bank at the edge of the road.

Certainly the amaranth growing around Sidney, Nebraska, comes from South America and Mexico. Sidney is center of the American amaranth crop, which is grown in an attempt to introduce to the American palate the staple crop of ancient Meso-America. Searching for foods to supplement an increasingly uniform diet, Michigan nutritionist John Robinson discovered some forty years ago farmers growing eight-foot-tall amaranth plants in fields around the ancient Inca capital of Cuzco, Peru. Ignored by conventional food companies, Robinson turned to organic and alternative farming experts at the Rodale Research Center, whose field trials proved amaranth's worth, something indigenous farmers had long known. Three times as fibrous as wheat and with five times as much iron, amaranth has become a darling of the health food sector and an attractive alternative for people allergic to wheat. However, many "amaranth" products may contain less than 20 percent amaranth, studies having shown that no one notices a difference in taste or texture in wheat products that have only this amount of amaranth. Although as many as five manufacturers — Health Valley Natural Foods, Arrow Mills, Walnut Acres, Nu-World Amaranth, and American Amaranth, Inc. — market forty to fifty amaranth products, promoters caution, "the markets are still very small. . . . A farmer entering the market with grain from several hundred acres of amaranth could cause a surplus and drastically lower prices."[41]

Nebraskans prefer planting A. *cruentus* and A. *hypochondriacus*, which the Mayans domesticated so long ago that they are no longer invasive. Not so their many cousins, native and alien, growing alongside them. The USDA lists fourteen species of amaranth as established in the wild in the United States, including the Incan crop plant, A. *hypochondriacus*. Most notorious, however, is A. *retroflexus*. Called variously redroot or green amaranth and pigweed, the annual A. *retroflexus* flowers in the fall, producing from one hundred thousand to two hundred thousand seeds per inflorescence, and each seed potentially is viable for forty years. Growing nearly everywhere, A. *retroflexus* is one of those weeds that can provoke bar fights between nativists and alienists, who are divided on to the plant's patrimony. The USDA considers A. *retroflexus* an alien that can be both noxious and invasive, and nativists have declared war on it. But, as with plantain, others disagree. Swiss researcher Hans-Martin Buerki argues that A. *retroflexus* is actually a native American, even if it acts like an alien, and that Linnaeus of all people is responsible for the confusion. The same Peter Kalm who identified common plantain as American sent Linnaeus samples of A. *retroflexus*. In addition to preserving his own specimens, Linnaeus also shipped seed, including that of A. *retroflexus*, to various European botanical gardens. By 1800 the American expatriate was a common weed in Europe, from whence it passed into Africa and Asia. Today it has established itself throughout the temperate world.[42]

Odds are, no matter what entangled bank Darwin observed or that you view, many of the inhabitants will reflect as much the touch of humanity as the laws of nature. If only you could determine whether we or the Creator put them there.

House Pests

Some of Those Who Share Your Quarters

House pests, like the houses they plague, are almost all imports to America. Few, if any, are accurately named either popularly or scientifically as to country of origin, although the warm, humid environments they like point to a tropical birthplace for these cosmopolitan creatures. Not that country of origin has stopped us from slurring other nations; the misnamed American cockroach (*Periplaneta americana*), German cockroach (*Blattella germanica*), and Oriental cockroach (*Blatta orientalis*) probably came from Africa. Even professionals get emotional over cockroaches: "One of the filthiest of all insects is the cockroach, which secretes a foul liquid from its scent glands, an obnoxious saliva from its mouth, and leaves its excreta wherever it travels."[1]

The one-and-a-half-inch-long American cockroach, also called the water bug, flying water bug, and palmetto bug, arrived here aboard early explorers' ships. Many entomologists think it was probably this cockroach that John Smith described in 1624 as plaguing Virginian colonists, "A certaine India bug, called by the Spaniards a cacarootch, the which creeping into chests they eat and defile with their ill-sented dung," since its fecal droppings are among the largest and most offensive of our cockroaches'. Happiest in warm, damp, dark places, such as your kitchen cabinets and basement, the American cockroach also throngs in unimaginable numbers in our city sewers, which, in addition to heating ducts and tunnels, provide artificially tropical conditions in the north. Down South, where it can live outdoors, *Periplaneta americana* is called the palmetto bug and is so pervasive that some entomologists think it might, in fact, be native—although most think neither this species nor the other forty-six genera found in America are indigenous. Cockroaches are seldom found indoors except after heavy rains or during migration—when thousands can infest your yard and house, over five thousand having been trapped in a single sewer manhole. It is our largest and fastest roach, and even if you don't see it, you're likely to notice the cast skins and large fecal droppings.[2]

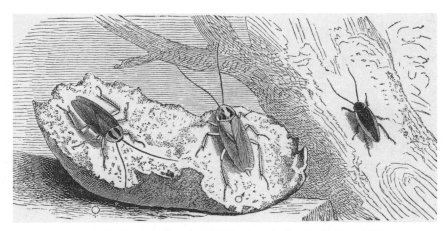

German cockroaches and an Oriental cockroach. John S. Kingsley, ed., *The Riverside Natural History* (Boston, 1888).

Like other cockroaches, the American has three life stages: egg, nymph, and adult. Adult females lay one egg case, or ootheca, a month for nearly a year, each case containing about sixteen eggs. Wingless, immature nymphs hatch from the cases in six to eight weeks, and take from six months to a year to mature, shedding their skins as many as fourteen times and gradually growing ever-longer wings. A final skin shedding results in an adult, which can live another year. Newly molted cockroaches are white, giving rise to fascinating, but erroneous, stories about colonies of albino cockroaches, but their color gradually darkens. The American cockroach eats almost anything organic, although it has a penchant for sweets and, according to some, alcohol—half-empty beer bottles often containing one or more blissfully drowned cockroaches. Bottles coated with sweet residue or filled with a sweet liquid at the bottom make effective roach traps; commercial versions were manufactured during the Victorian era, and homemade traps are still used in poorer countries and by enterprising, would-be scientists following the cockroach-collecting suggestion on the popular kid's science program *Newton's Apple*.[3]

Primarily an aesthetic and social blight, the American cockroach can also spread disease, living in sewers but happily penetrating our houses. Cockroaches can carry fifty different human pathogens, including bacteria, viruses, fungi, protozoa, and worms, and spread diseases such as pneumonia, salmonella, and typhoid.[4] While several wasps that lay their eggs in American cockroach ootheca have been discovered, with the young feeding on the cockroach eggs as they develop, most cockroach control in America relies on preventing cockroachs from entering our buildings, or poisoning them once they gain entry. Up north their tender, tropical nature can be used against them; at least one major university controls their populations by turning the heat off during winter vacation.

In sheer numbers, however, the German cockroach (*Blattella germanica*) is our worst cockroach pest. Found worldwide, the German cockroach's spread seems limited solely by colder temperatures. Central heating, which became widespread in New York City at the same time the Croton Reservoir was opened, in 1842, led not only to apartment and brownstone infestations, but also the misnomer Croton bug, with many New Yorkers mistakenly thinking the bugs emerged from the newly built water tunnels. The first reference to Croton bugs in the *New York Times* is an 1852 Costar's ad guaranteeing elimination of "rats, mice, cockroaches, Croton bugs, bugs, ants, bedbugs, etc," suggesting the misnomer had become common knowledge within ten years. Prior to the completion of the reservoir, water was in short supply on Manhattan Island, as were German cockroaches, which, like all their kin, need warmth, water, darkness,

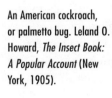
An American cockroach, or palmetto bug. Leland O. Howard, *The Insect Book: A Popular Account* (New York, 1905).

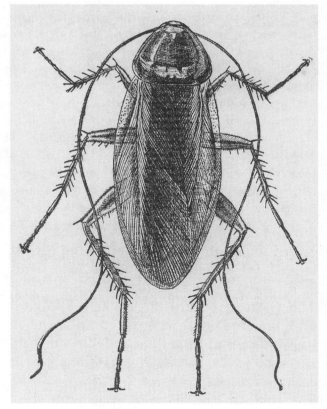

and food. The new water system not only supplied New Yorkers with cheap and abundant water, it also provided the cockroach with warm water pipes that were dank, dark conduits from apartment kitchen to apartment kitchen. So common were Croton bugs that their name became a euphemism in William Randolph Hearst's stump speech during his 1906 bid to become the Democratic gubernatorial candidate: "The Independence League and the Democratic Party are housecleaning and out of every dark and filthy corner come political cockroaches and corporation Croton bugs and wary old rats of Wall Street that swarm into the Republican establishment next door. We are housecleaning in order to make them go. And they go because they hate the bright light of publicity and the pure air of honesty."[5] Hearst's attempt to exterminate political vermin was no more successful than more plebeian attempts to exterminate insect vermin; he lost the election.

To a certain class of New Yorker, Croton bugs represented the end of fashionable society. "Never in all New York's history has such a plague of vermin visited us," wrote "an Apartment Dweller" in 1921 about "our water roaches—the Croton bug infection is the tactful way that the exterminators put it. . . . Like the flapper problem and prohibition, we can lay it on the war." An exterminator "makes it clear that our eighteen months of war were gain days for the insects. The housekeeper was interested in war and war work. The woman accustomed to two and three servants came down to one—and that one she did not oversee. Spring cleanings were passed over superficially. Slack housekeeping prevailed on every crosstown street in New York. High wages tempted women out of the home into industry. The business woman, who had her own apartment, made Red Cross bandages after working hours, instead of cleaning up closets. Meantime the bugs were multiplying." After the war, "with the two years of inflated wages, the servant problem became even more stringent." Liberated women and slovenly servants were not the only cause of roach infestations. Meddling health officials outlawed the use of cyanide gas to kill bugs in buildings after several residents died. "A cheap method had been worked out, and was used by all the exterminators for exterminating all the vermin within range —yes, and their eggs with them to the third and fourth generation. The room was made airtight and cyanide gas was released by an operator in a gas mask. . . . Ah well, somebody is always taking the joy out of life. The gas that was fatal to insects was fatal also to humans." After two or three fatalities, the board of health restricted the use of cyanide gas.[6]

Cyanide gas is the notorious gas used by the Nazis to exterminate humans, but it was—and still is—a widely used fumigant. Enthusiastic pre–World War II accounts of its efficiency sound ghoulish today: "The vapours given off by decomposition in contact with air kill the insects and animals which breathe it in a few minutes. Its action is the same in whichever way it be introduced into the body, by digestion, respiration, or introduced into the blood through a wound. A drop of hydrocyanic acid placed on the eye of a dog causes it to die in a few seconds of a dreadful death. . . . One gram of potassium cyanide was placed in a 250 cubic centimeter flask. . . . A butterfly died in four minutes; a dragon fly in ten minutes; an earwig in ten minutes; a plant louse is annihilated in less than two minutes; a stag beetle in four minutes; and a grasshopper in less than two minutes." Indeed, Zyklon-B was first used at Auschwitz as its manufacturers originally intended—as an insecticide. But its potential to kill humans led to Auschwitz ordering nineteen tons of the poison in 1942 and 1943.[7]

Like other cockroaches' metamorphosis, the German's is termed incomplete, there being only three stages—egg, nymph, and adult—rather than the four—including a cocoon—found in completely metamorphosing insects, such as butterflies. The German cockroach is especially fecund, egg to adult taking one hundred days, considerably less than that of the American, and accounting for the German's reputation as a stubbornly invasive animal. While the American cockroach female deposits her ootheca next to or even on a food source, the German female carries her ootheca attached to her abdomen until it is nearly ready to hatch. Not only is the German prolific; it is insolent as well, accused of actually feeding off and biting our dirty human faces while we sleep. German cockroaches have also been accused of causing human allergies, and some medical experts suspect many so-called food allergies are allergies to cockroach-contaminated foods. Even worse, cockroaches such as the German have been implicated in the spread of diseases such as diarrhea, dysentery, cholera, leprosy, plague, typhoid fever, polio, and SARS.[8]

The inch-long Oriental cockroach (*Blatta orientalis*), the third most common cockroach pest in America, plagues most of the South, Midwest, and Northwest. Its sixteen-egg ootheca takes one and a half to three months to develop; the hatching nymphs take one year to mature; and adults can live up to half a year, with reproduction taking place year round. Cold-sensitive like other roaches, the Oriental nevertheless prefers living outside, although cold and overcrowding can drive it inside, often in huge numbers.[9] Its East Coast nickname, shad roach, derives from the simultaneous and coincidental spring arrival of shad fish in the rivers and the appearance of large numbers of *B. orientalis*. European nicknames reflect ethnic divisions, the bug generally being named after one's neighbors, northern Germans calling it Schwabe, Schwabians calling it Prussian, Germans to the east calling it Russe, Germans to the west calling it Französe, while Nova Scotians call it Yankee settler.[10]

Entomologists might quibble over just which species is running across our kitchen counters, but most of us don't care. All cockroaches are *the* cockroach, and *the* cockroach is reprehensible. As long ago as the time of ancient Greece, the cockroach was the butt of jokes. In 421 B.C.E., Aristophanes had his idealistic Trygaeus mount to heaven on a giant dung beetle because the beetle could eat Trygaeus's excrement and thus less provisions would be needed for the ambitious voyage. Modern cockroachology begins with Gregor Samsa's unfortunate metamorphosis in Kafka's novel, Gregor having, after a night of troublesome dreams, woken to find himself transformed into a giant beetle. While purists debate whether or not Gregor was, in fact, a cockroach, popular opinion has it that he was. Don Marquis's Archy, definitely a cockroach, also wrote an autobiography, beginning as a column in a 1916 New York *Evening Sun*. Politics flavors the words of Chicano activists such as Oscar Acosta, who celebrate their "cockroach people's" stubborn survivability, while William S. Burroughs's *Naked Lunch* exposes the cockroach within. The French know that if you "have the cockroach," or "*avoir le cafard*," you're depressed, with the term being an argot for the blues. How a cockroach came to mean depressed nobody really knows, though there are those who suspect the term, first made popular by the French Army, may ultimately come from the Arabic *kafir*, infidel, via Spanish and Portuguese. The most famous cockroach, though, is undoubtedly Mexico's national lyric "La Cucaracha." Today's mariachi band and children's favorite, the song was popular with both sides during the 1910–20 Mexican Revolution, and historians have traced its origins back to Spain. The most infamous passage is perhaps:

> La cucaracha, la cucaracha
> Ya no puede caminar
> Porque no tiene, porque le falta
> Marijuana que fumar.
>
> (The cockroach, the cockroach
> Now he can't go traveling
> Because he doesn't have, because he lacks
> Marijuana to smoke.)

Urban legend claims some people literally have the cockroach. One story reveals someone licking envelopes that were infected with cockroach eggs. They cut their tongue, and one of the eggs hatched and grew, until oral surgery liberated it. Another legend tells of a girl's gums that were infected with roach eggs from a dirty Taco Bell taco.[11] Then there are you and me, people who inadvertently eat cockroaches every day. Health experts know that our homes, restaurants, and industrial food-processing plants are rife with cockroaches, whose shed skins, corpses, feces, and body parts contaminate a wide variety of food products. So widespread and unavoidable is cockroach contamination that the Food and Drug Administration has had to set allowable levels of contamination in foods such as chocolate.

Almost, but not quite, as disgusting as the cockroach is the rat and its tag-along fleas and associated diseases, none of which, naturally, is native to America. The rat is actually two rats: the black (*Rattus rattus*) and the brown (*Rattus norvegicus*). The brown, also known as the Norwegian (thanks to Linnaeus who so named it as a slur against his Swedish nation's historical enemy), barn, house, sewer, and wharf rat, is both a pest and pet, as well as a laboratory animal. The black rat, or ship, roof, and climbing rat, is nobody's friend, except maybe Willard's. As their common names suggest, the two animals live in close association with people, though they tend to divide their territories, the more aerial black rat living upstairs while the brown rat lives downstairs. However, since either species can live high or low, you can't really be sure which one you're looking at in the wild. The only indication besides habitat is the black rat's longer tail. Both animals are human commensals, living in close association with us. Like so many other commensal pests, both rats show evolutionary adaptations for living around humans. Some experts have even suggested that they

A black rat. John S. Kingsley, ed., *The Riverside Natural History* (Boston, 1888).

A brown rat. John S. Kingsley, ed., *The Riverside Natural History* (Boston, 1888).

should be considered at least partly, albeit accidentally, domesticated. Along with humans, they are perhaps the most widespread vertebrates on earth.

This doesn't make most of us like them. Humans have loathed rats for as long as they have plagued us—and plague us they have and do, literally. Both scientists and historians suspect it was the rat that lay behind the fourteenth century's Black Death, a plague that killed 30 percent of all Europeans in a matter of years and so disrupted society that it hastened the collapse of feudalism and the rise of the Renaissance, Reformation, and capitalism. Not bad for a rat. As its adherents—and there are some—point out in the rat's defense, sick fleas were the plague's actual cause. And, although there are few if any who rush to the flea's defense, a bacterium, *Yersinia pestis*, sickened the fleas that the rat merely carried into the proximity of humans.

No matter what you blame, bacterium, flea, or rat, all three now live in the United States, whose western states represent one of the world's largest repositories of bubonic plague, which is endemic in our Western wild rodents, including rock squirrels, prairie dogs, ground squirrels, and chipmunks. Every year ten to fifteen Americans contract the plague, generally from handling infected wild animals or from a dog or cat that contracted the disease when chasing infected rodents. Fortunately for these victims, they typically contract bubonic plague, a form that infects the lymph glands in armpits, necks, and groin areas and swells into small, hard bumps, or *buboes*, as the Italians called them, which gave rise to the term *bubonic plague*. More virulent and contagious is pneumonic plague, which infects the respiratory system and can result from either the eventual spread of the bubonic form into the blood and respiratory systems or from inhaling plague bacteria sprayed out by someone with pneumonic plague. One in two of those who contract pneumonic plague dies from the disease, which government officials fear makes it a weapon of choice for bioterrorists. History reveals that the plague has been used in the past as a weapon. Tartars besieging the Crimean port of Caffa in 1346 lobbed corpses of plague victims into the city in order to infect the Genoese inhabitants, who fled to Italy, carrying with them the seeds of the Black Death.[12]

Friends of the brown rat point out that the black rat is generally supposed to have been the primary rat responsible for the bubonic plague, which surfaces with deadly regularity throughout history. The plague's probable homeland, central Asia, facilitated the disease's spread throughout the Old World, infected fleas and rats following both conquering armies and peaceful merchants east into China and west into Europe and Africa. Always present, the plague sometimes breaks out in limited epidemics. Some people think that the destruction of Sennacharib's army before the gates of Jerusalem was one such example, although biblical descriptions are too brief to be certain. Far more destructive are pandemics, when plague sweeps through large areas, killing millions. The first known spread was from Egypt throughout the Roman Empire while Justinian was emperor, killing millions of people, including tens of thousands in Byzantium. The resulting social chaos, many think, hastened the fall of the empire.

The most infamous pandemic was Europe's Black Death, which ravaged the continent from 1346 through 1361 and killed an estimated fifty million people. An apocalyptic sense of doom set in, desperate people killing thousands of suspected agents such as Jews, witches and heretics. Troupes of flagellants beat themselves as they wandered from town to town, spreading both their gospel of the end times and, inadvertently, the plague itself. Art, turned introspective, gave rise to spectacular depictions of the crucified Christ as a fellow sufferer and to the danse macabre, a dancing, skeletal Death leading representatives of every social class into the grave. Social institutions followed their leaders, feudalism's economic and the Church's spiritual foundations both having been undermined. Out of the chaos, some historians believe, rose a new world order — ours.

A three-hundred-year sleep ended with the 1665 Great Plague of London, which killed one hundred thousand inhabitants in one year and inspired Daniel Defoe's *Journal of the Plague Year*, whose graphic descriptions haunt any who read them. Defoe's fictive narrator describes the rising number of dead in the weekly plague bills, and the healthy and the sick being shut up together in houses where "the door was marked with a red cross, a padlock on the outside . . . and a watchman set to keep the door, according to public order." While "Lord have mercy upon us" was ordered to be written above the cross, the Lord showed little mercy, Defoe recounting, "the most dismal shrieks and outcries of the poor people, terrified and even frighted to death by the sight of the condition of their dearest relations, and by the terror of being imprisoned as they were." Death carts prowled the nighttime streets, dumping with indifference their loads into mass graves, the corpses "wrapt up in linen sheets, some in rags, some little other than naked, or so loose that what covering they had fell from them in the shooting out of the cart, and they fell quite naked among the rest." The dying even cooperated in their ignominious end; "people that were infected and near their end, and delirious also, would run to those pits, wrapt in blankets or rugs, and throw themselves in, and, as they said, bury themselves."[13]

What caused the plague remained obscure, a contagious corruption of the air being the favored explanation: "The calamity was spread by infection; that is to say, by some certain steams or fumes, which the physicians call effluvia, by the breath, or by the sweat, or by the stench of the sores of the sick persons, or some other way, perhaps, beyond even the reach of the physicians themselves." The only preventive, then, was to counteract the foul air with healthful odors. "Some advised to make a very strong smoke in the room where the window or door was to be opened, with rozen and pitch, brimstone or gunpowder and the like." Another preferred "holding garlic and rue in his mouth, and smoking tobacco. . . . His wife's remedy was washing her head in vinegar and sprinkling her head-clothes so with vinegar as to keep them always moist." The religious practiced a variety of methods, so that "the whole church was like a smelling-bottle; in one corner it was all perfumes; in another, aromatics, balsamics, and variety of drugs and herbs; in another, salts and spirits." But everyone agreed that dogs and cats "capable of carrying the effluvia or infectious streams of bodies infected even in their furs and hair" must be killed, and so upwards of two hundred and fifty thousand were put to death. Defoe records that some thought that the plague "might be distinguished by the party's breathing upon a piece of glass, where, the breath condensing, there might living creatures be seen by a microscope, of strange, monstrous, and frightful shapes, such as dragons, snakes, serpents, and devils, horrible to behold. But this I very much question the truth of, and we had no microscopes at that time, as I remember, to make the experiment with."[14] Which is a shame, for if they had, they might have detected the killer, *Yersinia pestis.*

As it is, Y. *pestis* surfaced two hundred years later in Asia, in a third pandemic that spread rapidly thanks to steamship travel. Plague-threatened Hong Kong saw two research scientists scrambling in 1894 to be the first to identify the culprit, the favored and famous Japanese, Shibasaburo Kitasato, and his French rival and underdog, Alexandre Yersin. Both men discovered the bacillus in the buboes of corpses nearly simultaneously, but the more famous Kitasato published first and got the credit. Only later did science realize Kitasato had misidentified the bacillus. Yersin, who also discovered a vaccine for plague, was awarded primacy, and his name was attached to the bacillus. In 1898 another Frenchman, Paul Louis Simond, working in Bombay, proved that rats carried the bacillus and suggested infected fleas were the cause.[15]

But the plague is not the only reason to dislike rats. Everyone has no doubt heard a McRat or Kentucky Fried Rat story about a hapless consumer who bites down on a piece of chicken or hamburger only to discover that it's a rat. In fact, few if any of these tales are true, although the ones about rats in your toilet are. Sewer rats have been known to gain access to houses by swimming and climbing up through the toilets, and roof rats by coming down through the vent pipes. Not that everyone hates rats. There are those among us who actually keep them as pets. And laboratory scientists have their lab rats. Both lab and pet rats are domesticated versions of the brown rat, which first drew breeders' attention as a byproduct of dog fights. The English bred a small dog called a feist to catch rats. Rat-baiting was a popular sport in the nineteenth century, and dog fanciers would bet on how many rats a feist could kill in a certain amount of time. Henry Mayhew described one such fight in 1851: "The moment the dog was 'free,' he became quiet in a most business-like manner, and rushed at the rats, burying his nose in the mound till he brought out one in his mouth. In a short time a dozen rats with wetted necks were lying bleeding on the floor, and the white paint of the pit became grained with blood. In a little time the terrier had a rat hanging to his nose, which, despite his tossing, still held on. He dashed up against the sides, leaving a patch of blood as if a strawberry had been smashed there."[16] Immigrants brought the feist to America, where it continued to be a barnyard ally of the farmer and developed into a squirrel-hunting dog as well. The noun *feist* and its variant *fice* became southern terms for any small mongrel dog, and *feisty* became an adjective. The feist became better known as merely a rat terrier, with popular legend incorrectly crediting Teddy Roosevelt with coining the term. Terriers, of which there are numerous breeds, derive their name from the French *terrier*, or ground, having been bred to burrow after game. Curiously, the word *feist* is related to *fart*, meaning to break wind.

Rat fights required lots of rats, and supplying the sporting houses provided income for the poor, who rounded up both black and brown rats by the hundreds. One London establishment required three hundred to seven hundred rats a week. Nor did rat catchers necessarily kill all they caught; some began breeding the ones that caught their fancy, and so pet rats arose. One such fancier was Jack Black, Queen Victoria's rat and mole catcher, a professional with an ornate outfit and a cart decorated with painted rats to advertise his trade. "I used to wear a costume of white leather breeches, and a green coat and scarlet waistkit, and a gold band round my hat, and a belt across my shoulder. I used to make a first-rate appearance, such as was becoming the uniform of the Queen's rat-ketcher." Black had bred his rats for color: "I have 'em fawn and white, black and white, brown and white, red and white, blue-black and white, black-white and red. . . . They got very tame, and you could do anythink with them. I've sold many to ladies for keeping in squirrel cages." One such lady was *Peter Rabbit*'s Beatrix Potter, who dedicated her 1908 book, *The Roly-Poly Pudding*, to her pet rat, Sammy, "the intelligent pink-eyed representative of a persecuted (but irrepressible) race. An affectionate little friend and most accomplished thief!"[17]

Rat fanciers such as Black and Potter laid the groundwork for the twentieth century's development of the laboratory rat, which, along with the fruit fly and mice, constitutes one of the most famous laboratory animals. But it was Philadelphia's Wistar Institute that developed "genetically homogeneous rats as a living analog to pure chemicals" for biological research, breeding in the first three decades of the twentieth century the premier lab rat in the world—so prestigious and lucrative that over half of all lab rats in the world are examples of the institute's copyrighted albino research rat, the Wistarat. The institute's name remembers early-nineteenth-century Philadelphian anatomist Caspar Wistar, whose intellectual soirees—"Wistar parties"—were as famous as his lectures, which were accompanied by both wooden and papier-mâché models and wax-injected and dried-out human body parts. An amateur paleontologist, botanist, and friend of Thomas Jefferson, Wistar undertook to educate Meriwether Lewis about what he might expect to encounter while exploring the newly acquired territories of the Louisiana Purchase. It is after Wistar whom Nuttall chose to name the misspelled wisteria.[18]

Research labs also employ a relative of the rat, the smaller house mouse. After Mendel's genetic research and discoveries, scientists raced to prove his laws applied equally to animals and plants. But wild animals were too variable to demonstrate the genetic variation seen in garden peas. Biology needed a laboratory animal, and the house mouse (*Mus musculus*) proved ideal. The Chinese and Japanese had been breeding mice for millennia, developing variously colored ones as well as strains that danced, jumped, and climbed. European fanciers followed the Asian lead, and by 1900 there were dozens of strains available for people who wanted pets. Not only were these pets colorful, they also had been bred to be docile, fertile, and accepting of close confinement and human contact—traits that would make them ideal laboratory animals. Harvard researcher William Castle realized this while also recognizing that their various coat colors were analogues to Mendel's peas. Needing a ready supply of mice, Castle turned in 1902 to nearly Granby, Massachusetts, where retired schoolteacher Abbie Lathrop had switched from farming chickens to raising mice. Lathrop had planned to supply the pet or fancy mouse trade, but Castle's lab and others provided her a readier source of money. Her colonies had begun with only two mice, but would grow to house eleven thousand. But even her fancy mice were not the genetically pure specimens biological research demanded. One of Castle's students, Clarence C. Little, set out to make the perfect lab mouse by mating brothers and sisters for twenty successive generations until he had nearly identical clones. Little's first successful mouse, DBA (after its coat color—dilute, brown, and nonagouti), which appeared in 1909 and is still around today, came from Lathrop's mice. Indeed, almost all of the

Two mice. John S. Kingsley, ed., *The Riverside Natural History* (Boston, 1888).

estimated twenty-five million lab mice in the world today can trace their lineages back to Lathrop's Massachusetts farm. Little set up the Jackson Institute in Bar Harbor, Maine, in 1929 to continue his genetic experiments. It was JAX, as the institute is known in professional circles, that wound up providing, first to America and then to the world, research-quality mice bred for specific genetic traits—obesity, blindness, albinism, alcoholism, whatever. Variety nicknames for JAX mice, such as claw paw, deaf waddler, flailer, greasy, loop tail, and twitcher, suggest a New England version of the island of Dr. Moreau, and few people really want to know what happens to the nearly two million JAX mice sold each year.[19]

Mus musculus's association with humanity probably dates from the Neolithic invention of agriculture some ten thousand years ago, when farmers in China, India, and the Fertile Crescent inadvertently provided the mouse with a ready supply of food and shelter. Geneticists recognize four *M. musculus* subgroups, whose worldwide distribution reflects their varied associations with people. One, which today dominates most of Asia, spread eastward out of China; another spread north out of Southeast Asia, mixing with the Chinese strain in Japan to form what is perhaps the mouse's most restricted subspecies; another reigns in the Indian subcontinent, where it originated, while a fourth claims western Europe, from which it spread to dominate the Americas, sub-Saharan Africa, and Australia. All known house mice in North America derive from European populations, with the exception of a small group in California, which came east to America with Asian immigrants.[20]

M. musculus, Rattus rattus, and *R. norvegicus* all arrived in the Americas by stowing aboard ships from the Old World. Today they can be found in homes in every state and Canada and Mexico, both as uninvited pests and as pets. In the South, where I live, they live outside in warmer weather, coming indoors in winter—which is when we set our mousetraps or lay out poison for them. The poison is Warfarin, an anticoagulant that when ingested, causes the mice to bleed to death. Warfarin's discoverer, Karl Paul Link, was a biochemist at the University of Wisconsin working with other scientists to solve the problem of why moldy sweet clover made cattle bleed to death. While some researchers were trying to breed a nonlethal clover, Link was researching the chemistry behind moldy clover's lethality, which turned out to be its transformation of a naturally occurring ingredient, coumarin, into dicoumarol, an anticoagulant. When cattle ate too much of this, they bled. Link's 1940 discovery was patented the following year as a human anticoagulant. In 1946 Link also discovered that a more powerful compound related to dicoumarol would kill rodents. Link worked for the Wisconsin Alumni Research Foundation, and they held the patent for Warfarin, named by marrying their acronym with the ending sylla-bles of coumarin. Launched in 1948, Warfarin was the means in 1951 that a sailor used in a suicide attempt. When his overdose failed to kill him, intrigued doctors discovered that the mouse and rat poison Warfarin was an excellent human anticoagulant. Marketed as such in 1954, it became well known after President Eisenhower took it after suffering a heart attack. Unfortunately, Warfarin-resistant rodents, including both brown and black rats and house mice, quickly developed, and exterminators had to search for new poisons.[21]

It Seemed a Good Idea at the Time

The Well-Intentioned Ecological Disaster

Who are the greatest villains in America's long history of alien invasion? Columbus heads many a symbolic list, since he is credited with being the first European to land in the New World. That, of course, lets the Vikings off the hook, although the effects of their invasion, admittedly, were limited. But Columbus, though a fitting symbolic figure, actually didn't touch America per se. Those who purposefully did it to us, aided and abetted invaders, came later. And, while one can debate who is the most notorious, anyone's list of unwanted deliberate introductions would no doubt include kudzu, carp, and starlings. Conveniently, all three can thank very specific people for their widespread introductions into the United States.

The legendary invader of the American South, kudzu (*Pueraria lobata*) appears to have first been introduced to America as a birthday present from Japan, presented at the 1876 Philadelphia Centennial Exhibition via the Japanese Pavilion. The pavilion included a garden, in which the "kuzu" vine was featured. Eight years later, the New Orleans Exposition included the same exhibit, and southerners began to plant what they came to call "porch vine," a sort of super-wisteria whose grape-scented blossoms and dense shade seemed a panacea in pre-air-conditioning days. Philadelphia's Fairmont Park stands where the 1876 Centennial Exhibition stood, and enthusiasts of things Japanese can visit Shofu-so, a modern replica of a seventeenth-century villa with a tea house and a traditional garden that includes imported bamboos, pines, azaleas, a stone pagoda, and koi fish but no kudzu.[1]

Not, apparently, that the Japanese were entirely to blame for the vine's introduction. No less than a U.S. marshal has been fingered as culpable. President Lincoln sent Thomas Hogg, Jr., to Japan in 1862, where he served both as marshal and as an adviser in setting up a Japanese customs service. Son of a prominent British horticulturist and an ardent Republican himself, Hogg also apparently advised the Japanese on what plants to bring over to their pavilion.

In addition, he sent numerous species home to interested horticulturists, and he is remembered today in the name of a multicolored hosta, Thomas Hogg.[2]

Estimates vary widely on the number of acres in the United States that are covered with kudzu, but one commonly cited number is seven million. With up to one plant per square foot and vine entanglements that can reach six feet in depth, that's a lot of kudzu. The vine, which can run along the ground, sprouting roots and thus cloning itself every so often, or climb trees, telephone poles, houses, whatever, can actually grow a foot a day. Its species name, *lobata*, refers to its trifoliate leaves, while the genus name, *Puerari*, commemorates a Swiss botanist who had nothing to do with the plant. Often hidden by profuse leaves, wisteria-like racemes of delicately scented flowers bloom in the summer, producing pod-covered seeds. The roots can dig as deep as twelve feet, and they form enormous tubers that can weigh more than two hundred pounds. Fond of mild winters and humid summers, kudzu has established itself from Florida to New York and Massachusetts and from the East Coast to as far west as Nebraska. But Alabama, Georgia, and Mississippi are its epicenter, thanks in part to climate and even more to the U.S. government and kudzu enthusiasts.[3]

The vine may have remained a little-noted shade plant but for dreamers bent on saving the family farm and stopping erosion. One of the legends of American horticulture, David Fairchild, was a plant explorer for the U.S. Department of Agriculture. His enviable job was to travel the world in search of new plants suitable for growing in America. Fairchild "discovered" kudzu while on a trip to Japan in 1902, and he enthusiastically promoted it. The Japanese use the entire plant, making hay out of the leaves, weaving grass cloth out of the stem fibers, and peeling, pounding, and soaking the tuberous roots to make starch for candy and noodles. Diced roots thicken soups. The young leaves and shoots can be eaten raw, boiled, fried, pickled, or sautéed, and the flowers can be pickled or cooked. And kudzu allegedly cures alcoholism, as well. Reason enough to import the vine, which in America would be touted as cheap fodder. Fairchild joined the USDA in 1889 as a twenty-year-old botanist. Within ten years he helped to create the Office of Foreign Seed and Plant Introduction, which he would head for twenty-four years. He hobnobbed with the rich and the powerful, marrying Alexander Graham Bell's daughter and retiring to Miami, where in 1938 a rich friend founded and named in his honor the eighty-three-acre Fairchild Tropical Garden, a showcase for tropical plants that includes hundreds of different kinds of palms and cycads. Fairchild also wrote several books, including *The World Was My Garden*, an autobiographical account of his life as a plant collector, which is still in print. Instrumental in introducing us to avocados, bamboos, mangoes, nectarines, and pistachios, he is perhaps best remembered for his role in planting Washington, D.C.'s famous flowering cherry trees. Eliza Ruhamah Scidmore, who had witnessed Japan's famous sakura, returned determined that America enjoy a similar ritual. She first proposed in 1885 that flowering cherry trees be planted on the recently reclaimed Potomac waterfront, but officialdom ignored her until she obtained the support of President Taft's wife in 1909. For several years prior to 1909, Fairchild had himself promoted the idea of a boulevard of flowering cherry trees, following his success in growing them on his Chevy Chase property. With Mrs. Taft's support the project flourished, and in 1910 two thousand trees arrived in Washington — only to be burned because they were infested with bugs. Two years later, on Valentine's Day, three thousand healthy trees left Japan for America. In 1934 Washington held its first Cherry Blossom Festival.[4]

Even before Fairchild, homegrown kudzu enthusiasts had sprouted in the South. The most notorious of these were Charlie and Lillie Pleas of Chipley, Florida, whose fame is enshrined on a Florida roadside historical marker: "Kudzu, brought to this country from Asia as an ornamental, was developed near here in the early part of the Twentieth Century and given to the world as a soil-saving, high-protein forage plant by Mr. and Mrs. C. E. Pleas. The fast-growing, deep-rooted leguminous vine has been widely grown in the United States as a drought-resisting, erosion-controlling plant that compares with alfalfa in pasture and hay-making values." Legend has it that the Pleas' kudzu conversion was serendipitous. Charlie is said to have seen his cattle eating an errant vine, which he may or may not have planted to shield his garbage cans from view. Whatever the details of his moment of revelation, Pleas became a believer. In 1907 he tended a patch of kudzu at the Jamestown, Virginia, tricentennial celebration. In 1925 he published *Kudzu — Coming Forage of the South*, and he and his wife sold mail-order plants nationwide from their Glen Arbor Nursery. For fifty years Pleas preached the kudzu gospel, and so great was his fame that Fairchild remembered, "I wanted so badly to talk with Pleas that I dragged him out of his bathtub one night as I was traveling through, to tell me about his experiments at Chipley." Pleas died a believer, but Fairchild's enthusiasm for kudzu waned as he saw "the picture of how the vine climbed over a precious White Barked Pine . . . from China and which was growing in my yard at 'In the Woods,' near Washington. After trying for years to establish it and succeeding, I spent years of unsuccessful effort to eradicate it. It was only after we sold 'In the Woods' and the new owner pastured his cow in the yard and kept it browsed down, that is disappeared."[5]

That cow is one reason the kudzu-farming revolution fizzled. Despite the vine's reputation for strangling slow calves and children, it's actually easier to overgraze than grass. Hogs can take out a kudzu patch in no time, rooting out the tubers and leaving the rest to wither and die come winter. And too much of the vine is, well, vine—woody runners that are hard to eat and harder to harvest. Impoverished southern farmers may have embraced kudzu in the Depression as a low-cost, poor-land, poor-man's miracle crop, its leguminous properties enriching the land similar to clover, but the richer, post–World War II farmer wanted higher-yield feed crops—fescue and Bermuda grass, exotics that required fertilizing, mowing, and attention. Before the siren of African grasses seduced him, the poor southerner had planted hundreds of thousands of acres in kudzu, following the advice of promoters such as Channing Cope of Georgia. Cope's bully pulpit was the *Atlanta Constitution,* from which "the father of kudzu" preached that "Cotton isn't king here anymore; kudzu is king!" He gave birth to the American Kudzu Club in 1943 and wrote *The Front Porch Farmer* in 1949, which informed farmers that the vine "works while you sleep." Kudzu beauty queens and dances proliferated, and, if you believe the believers, two hundred thousand were converted.[6]

Among the enlightened was Uncle Sam, in the guise of the Soil Conservation Service agents such as "Kudzu" Bailey of South Carolina, who touted the miracle vine as an erosion control device and paid eight Depression-era dollars an acre to plant it on some 1.2 million Piedmont acres. The green revolution might have devoured the entire nation except that kudzu doesn't behave well in America. Although also imported into South America and Australia, kudzu is a pest only in the southern United States. The American variety, while spreading like kudzu, doesn't set seed well. Which means that Japan became the major supplier of kudzu seed to the United States in the 1930s; with the advent of war government agents scoured the American South looking for viable seed to close the kudzu gap. By the 1950s, however, disenchantment had set in: the Department of Agriculture quit planting it, highway departments and railroad companies quit using it except where nothing else would work, and in 1998 Congress declared it a noxious weed.[7]

Kudzu kills by blanketing whatever it grows on in a smothering welter of leaves and vines. Anyone driving the back roads of the South is familiar with apocalyptic-looking forests strangled by kudzu, scenes that have given rise to stories of killer kudzu, like these lines from poet James Dickey: "Green, mindless, unkillable ghosts. / In Georgia, the legend says / That you must close your windows // At night to keep it out of the house. / The glass is tinged with green, even so." Impressive though these vine-drowned trees seem, the kudzu entangling them has had sixty years to do its deed, suggesting kudzu's "mile-a-minute" reputation is exaggerated. Kudzu can be contained; the Great Smokey Mountains

National Park has eradicated it from within its borders, for example. And more American forest is blanketed in Japanese honeysuckle than in kudzu, but the former, while having destroyed more acreage, isn't as photogenic.

Kudzu has a grip on our imagination. Dickey's poem typifies the scaremongers, but there are just as many people who are convinced that there is something we can use the vine for. Those who would redeem the vine promote kudzu as a "tree-free" paper. Anyone who's tried to tear a kudzu vine in two knows you can't. The same fibers that prevent your ripping apart kudzu vines makes them an ideal source for pulp paper. Others are studying kudzu's alleged ability to cure alcoholism, cancer, obesity, and bone loss. Kudzu has its popular-culture admirers as well: an Atlantan nicknamed his racecar "Kudzu," a country music group released "Under the Kudzu," and Doug Marlette won a Pulitzer Prize with his cartoon strip "Kudzu." Kudzu has crept into the language itself, being a corruption of its Japanese name *kuzo*. At first an alien noun, kudzu insinuated itself into mainstream parlance as a simile: "spreading like kudzu" spread—like kudzu—far beyond the borders of the vine itself. From simile to verb was a short leap. You can kudzu someone, be kudzued yourself by a pushier rival, and as you read this, kudzu is kudzuing America.

The carp is another immigrant helped along by Uncle Sam. Most fishermen and environmentalists regard its widespread introduction into our waters as a disaster caused almost single-handedly by Spencer C. Baird. Baird became assistant secretary of the Smithsonian Institution in Washington, D.C., in 1850 and secretary in 1878. He also served as director of the National Museum, founded the marine biological station at Wood's Hole, Massachusetts, and became in 1871 the first U.S. commissioner of fisheries, in charge of rebuilding the nation's fishing industry. He did this in part by building fish farms for native and imported fish, including *Cyprinus carpio*, the carp. An Old World fish bred both as a pet—koi are carp—and as food, the carp is prized as a sport fish in Europe. Nor was Baird the first to think of importing it into America. Henry Robinson imported French carp into Newburgh, New York, in the 1830s, raising dozens of fish and releasing them into the nearby Hudson River, hoping to begin a commercial fishery. But Baird would later declare carp from the Hudson to be mongrel fish, not the pure-bred common carp he was importing from Germany. German carp also had been brought to California in 1872 by Sonoma resident J. A. Poppe, who distributed them to several states as a food fish.[8] But it was Baird who engineered the nationwide introduction of carp, following an 1874 Fish Commission report on "Fishes Especially Worthy of Cultivation," which preferred carp "because it is a vegetable feeder, and although not disdaining animal matters can live on vegetation alone and can attain large

A carp (top), along with a mirror-carp, goldfish, and barbel. John S. Kingsley, ed., *The Riverside Natural History* (Boston, 1888).

weight kept in small ponds and tanks." Three hundred and forty-five German carp were imported into Baltimore and then Washington, D.C., where they were raised in a lake near the Washington Monument that became known popularly as the National Carp Pond when opened to the public in 1878. It closed in 1906. By 1879 the Fish Commission was distributing fingerlings throughout the states. In 1882 it distributed 143,000 fish; in 1883, 260,000; all told, between 1879 and 1896, the commission shipped 2.4 million carp throughout the United States, Canada, and Mexico. By the early 1900s carp was a recognized farm crop; in the decade following World War II, thirty-six million pounds were harvested.[9]

Despite the dreams of promoters such as the Duke of Argyll, who prophesied that the carp would become "among the most prized of our fresh fish," the boom eventually fizzled. Commercial ocean fishing supplanted freshwater farming, especially as consumer concerns over polluted waters increased. Carp farming largely disappeared, while fishing for wild carp never really caught on, feral carp being too erratic tasting. While farmed carp's taste could be controlled with careful management, wild carp were liable to taste "muddy" if they grew in ponds or in slow-moving rivers. Promoters had been aware of this problem all along. Baird's carp farmer, Rudolph Hessel, even wrote that "in many places it [the river carp] is more highly appreciated than the pond carp, probably because the river water does not impart to it the moldy taste which is sometimes found with the carp inhabiting ponds situated in marshy localities and morasses which have not a sufficient supply of fresh water." Optimism prevailed, however, with Hessel noting, "The carp thrives best in those parts of the Danube where the water is the least clear, at the influx of the muddy water of its tributaries," and feeds on "the offal from kitchens, slaughter-houses, breweries, and the sewers" of riverside cities. He supposed that the fish would "thrive excellently" in the even muddier Mississippi and "probably nearly all American rivers."[10] Which it did and does, now being established in every state but Alaska.

The common or king carp comes in several strains, ranging from short, deep-bodied Galician fish to longer, thicker-bodied French and Bohemian fish, and from fully scaled "common" carp to nearly scaleless "leather" carp, and the in-between "mirror" carp, which is further divided into subvarieties based on the pattern formed by the scales it does possess. Colored common carp, or koi, occasionally escape into the wild, but probably contribute relatively little to the gene pool. Your goldfish, *Carassius auratus*, while a relative, is not a carp. You can tell the two apart because common carp have catfish-like barbells around their mouths, while goldfish do not. The Romans were probably the first people to farm carp instead of merely capturing them in the wild. They brought live fish from the Danube to the Italian peninsula and thereby introducing them into Western Europe. The fish spread slowly, though, as we know from their absence in early monastic fishing documents. No one knows who first brought carp into England, although the old couplet is almost certainly wrong in maintaining that "Hops and Turkies, Carps and Beer / Came into England all in a year." Halfway around the world, Asians were also farming carp, with one Japanese strain developing striking color variations. These are Nishikigoi, or koi—swimming flowers, variegated red, orange, yellow, blue, and white—which have recently become quite fashionable in the West. Few American anglers would agree with Izaak Walton, seventeenth-century author of *The Compleat Angler*, that "the carp is the queen of rivers, a stately, a good, and a very subtil fish," despite the efforts of organizations such as the Carp Anglers Group, which promotes the carp as "what may be the largest and most game fish in your local waters" and provides pictures of awesome forty-plus-pound fish caught throughout America. Noncarp anglers deplore the animal as a muddy-tasting trash fish that destroys the environment and drives out native fish. Carp can devastate underwater vegetation, especially during spawning season when several avid males will aggressively pursue a gravid female. They also have been implicated in reducing the numbers of other fish. But they're here to stay, and what kid having hooked a forty-pounder would think them a mistake?[11]

Eugene Schieffelin's starling disaster more than matches Baird's piscine faux pas and Hogg's kudzu calamity, especially when you consider that Schieffelin's environmental disaster didn't have the backing of the entire U.S. government. Schieffelin was a founding member of the American Acclimatization Society, chartered by the state of New York to encourage "the introduction and acclimatization of foreign birds, animals, vegetables, etc, having in many cases special regard to their value as antidotes to the ravages of insects, diseases in grain, etc."[12] Born of the hubris of Enlightenment optimism, nineteenth-century acclimatization societies looked back to a French model, the Societe Zoologique d'Acclimatation, which continues today as La Societe Nationale de Protection de la Nature et d'Acclimatation de France.

The American Acclimatization Society was cutting-edge biology then. Their ambitious but never-realized plans included an entire park in New York City set aside for "a permanent, systematic and comprehensive collection of living animals, birds, fishes, and plants, and to make this the central point from which to spread around those varieties of the animal and vegetable kingdoms suitable for the varying climates of our country."[13] In addition to utility, the society also supported aesthetics, striving "to render still more attractive this great city to its citizens and strangers alike," a sentiment that motivated others throughout America. Cincinnati, Ohio, and Portland, Oregon, attracted particular attention in the *New York Times*, which opined that "one of the most disinterested movements that has been recently chronicled is one which has for its object the importation of German singing-birds, and birds whose habits render them useful in the destruction of insects." The paper noted the Cincinnati Society of Acclimatization's 1873 and 1874 importation of nearly three thousand birds in individual wooden cages in an attempt to fill Ohio's woods and fields with the blackbird, thrush, golden finch, green bird, bull finch, redbreast, starling, skylark, green finch, goldfinch, knot pecker, wagtail, magpie, hedge sparrow, titmouse, nightingale, redtail, German quail, and fence sparrow. Across the

A European starling and a Sardinian starling. John S. Kingsley, ed., *The Riverside Natural History* (Boston, 1888).

continent in Oregon, a similar public-minded Society for the Importation of German Song Birds sought to bring both the same European and other East Coast American birds to the Northwest. Although the newspaper noted that the Cincinnati "songsters imported last year are also returning" and that "large numbers of the descendants of the first lot imported [into Oregon] have come back from their winter migration," only one species, the starling, established sustained breeding populations.[14]

Starlings were released in Cincinnati in 1873 and in Portland, Oregon, in 1889 or 1892. The Portland papers noting that "among those which have been acclimated, and have increased and spread over the country, may be mentioned starlings, which nest yearly in many places about the city, on high buildings and church steeples." Curiously, however, it is Eugene Schieffelin's 1890 starlings that have achieved infamy. Kim Todd imagines a sixty-four-year-old Schieffelin staggering through the snow with eighty starlings in cages on March 6, 1890, the birds ironically spending their first free night perched on the ledges of the American Museum of Natural History. "From the 80 starlings that Schieffelin set free in 1890, and the 40 more he added in 1891, the number in North America has grown to two hundred million." Perhaps. What makes these 1890 birds' infamy even more odd is that they were not the Acclimatization Society's first. The November 15, 1877, *Times* records that "last July the Acclimatization Society freed in the [Central] Park some starlings and Japanese finches." Whether these survived is, of course, a matter for speculation—but it seems certain that Schieffelin was involved in importing starlings at least thirteen years before he is generally credited with the activity and that his 1890 starlings were neither the first nor the only starlings to establish themselves in America.[15]

Whoever introduced them, *Sturnus vulgaris* are to most everybody, *avis non gratis*, being dirty, noisy, gregarious, and aggressive, their million-member flocks destroying farmers' fruit crops, fouling our city sidewalks, and driving out such favorites as native bluebirds. They are the dominant bird in my city neighborhood, roosting in large flocks in trees and attics. One pair hammered their way through a half-inch facia board to set up residence in my garret, their quarrelsome and greedy squadrons so disgusted me that I gave up feeding birds. T. C. Boyle describes their Hitchcock-like horror in his short story about Schieffelin's 1890 mistake: "They come like apocalypse, like all ten plagues rolled in one, beating across the sky with an insidious drone, their voices harsh and metallic, cursing the land. Ten million strong, a flock that blots out the huge pale sinking sun, they descend into the trees with a protracted explosion of wings, black underfeathers swirling down like a corrupt snow, . . . ten million tiny cardiovascular systems generating a sirocco of heat, ten million digestive tracts processing seeds, nuts, berries, animal feed, and streaking the tree trunks with chalky excrement. Where before there had been leafspill, lichened rocks, sunlit paths beneath the trees, now there are foot-deep carpets of bird shit."[16] They made it here thanks to Schieffelin's desire to populate America with every bird mentioned in Shakespeare. He seems to have started with the first part of *Henry IV*, in which Hotspur remarks in act 1, "I'll have a starling shall be taught to speak," starlings then being popular pets that, like parrots, could be taught to speak.

Despised though the starling may be, it does have his admirers. The 1911 *Encyclopedia Britannica* effuses, "A more engaging bird scarcely exists, for its familiarity during some months of the year gives opportunities for observing its ways that few others afford, while its varied song, its sprightly gestures, its glossy plumage, and, above all, its character as an insecticide which last makes it the friend of the agriculturist and the grazier render it an almost universal favorite," while the Web site www.starlings.net is "devoted to the European starling and those who adore it."[17] Mozart recorded in his diary in May of 1784 the purchase of a starling that whistled notes from one of his own works, the Piano Concerto in G Major (K. 453). Since the piece had never been performed in public, either the bird copied Mozart or Mozart copied the bird, or both copied a similar-sounding folk tune. Biographers still debate the point, according to biologist and psychologist Meredith West, who thinks the bird copied the master. When his pet died, Mozart wrote a requiem for it: "A little fool lies here / Whom I held dear— / A starling in the prime / Of his brief time." A week later Mozart composed what his catalogers have titled "A Musical Joke" (K. 522), an "awkward, unproportioned, and illogical piecing together of uninspired material" that West thinks, rather than a sendup of a hypothetical amateur composer, is Mozart's remembered transcription of his departed starling's song. Like all starling compositions, it would have been to human ears "awkward, unproportioned, and illogical." Musical opinion is still out on the thesis.[18]

Nineteenth-century English literary allusions to starlings are generally as a pet and mimic, such as Robert Louis Stevenson's mention in *Kidnapped* of one bird that could whistle "The North Countrie." But the most developed image was one of poignant imprisonment, the bird having been taught to say, "I cannot get out." Both Jane Austen in *Mansfield Park* and Charles Dickens in *Bleak House* mention this tradition, which appears to have arisen from Laurence Sterne's *A Sentimental Journey*. Yorrick—Sterne—meditating on the infamous Bastille, supposes much of its terror imagined: "As for the Bastile; the terror is in the word.—Make the most of it you can, said I to myself, the Bastile is but another word for a tower." But then he hears:

> A voice which I took to be of a child, which complained "it could not get out."—I look'd up and down the passage, and seeing neither man, woman, nor child, I went out without farther attention. In my return back through the passage, I heard the same words repeated twice over; and, looking up, I saw it was a starling hung in a little cage.—"I can't get out,—I can't get out," said the starling. I stood looking at the bird: and to every person who came through the passage it ran fluttering to the side towards which they approach'd it, with the same lamentation of its captivity. "I can't get out," said the starling.—God help thee! said I, but I'll let thee out, cost what it will; so I turned

about the cage to get to the door: it was twisted and double twisted so fast with wire, there was no getting it open without pulling the cage to pieces.—I took both hands to it.

The bird flew to the place where I was attempting his deliverance, and thrusting his head through the trellis pressed his breast against it as if impatient.—I fear, poor creature! said I, I cannot set thee at liberty.—"No," said the starling,—"I can't get out—I can't get out," said the starling.

I vow I never had my affections more tenderly awakened; nor do I remember an incident in my life, where the dissipated spirits, to which my reason had been a bubble, were so suddenly call'd home. Mechanical as the notes were, yet so true in tune to nature were they chanted, that in one moment they overthrew all my systematic reasonings upon the Bastile; and I heavily walked upstairs, unsaying every word I had said in going down them.

Sterne later explains the bird's life. Caught as a fledgling on the cliffs of Dover and taught to speak English, it was left in Paris, "but his little song for liberty being in an unknown language at Paris, the bird had little or no store set by him." Sterne's oblique criticism of French politics becomes more pointed when he crosses with the bird the Channel back into England, where first Lords and then Commons adopted him. "But as all these wanted to GET IN, and my bird wanted to GET OUT, he had almost as little store set by him in London as in Paris. It is impossible but many of my readers must have heard of him; and if any by mere chance have ever seen him, I beg leave to inform them, that that bird was my bird, or some vile copy set up to represent him."[19]

Shakespearean songster, symbol of oppression, ecological terrorist—*Sturnus vulgaris*, the European starling, is as American as the rest of us, and no less controversial a figure. Give him a chance; if you can overlook his loud and gregarious ways, he's not that bad looking a bird, with his clerical gait and black frock and green silk waistcoat.

Misplaced Americans

As Rootless as the Humans Who Invited Them In

Humans are not the only species to have immigrated on their own into the United States. A number of our more visible fauna come from elsewhere, many under their own steam. Some are indigenous to the United States and have greatly expanded their native ranges, becoming pests in their new homes and raising interesting questions as to just what is native. Although some of my great-aunts, glorying in their colonial roots, looked down their noses at fellow citizens whose roots lay more shallow, Native Americans must consider such two-hundred-year differences picayune. Nevertheless, my Johnny-come-lately family, it turns out, has been here longer than the iconic coyote has occupied its current range, and many whose family passed through Ellis Island are more American than that scourge of the South, the boll weevil. Texans might claim the armadillo as a native, but it's been there less time than have the Anglos who stole the place from the Mexicans, and, ignoring Horace Greeley's advice, the Colorado potato bug, which at least is aptly named, being indigenous to that state, bucked national tendencies and migrated east—but not until the nineteenth century.

About the coyote, no one is neutral: varmit or victim, North America's native dog has been inspiring fierce debates ever since humans first encountered it. Folklorists classify Native American stories of coyotes as "trickster" tales, frequently salacious stories of dubious morality, often involving deceit and duplicity. In short the coyote was wily long before Warner Brothers. Credited with providing humanity with fire, the coyote also introduced death.

Although Spanish chroniclers knew and described the coyote in the sixteenth century, most Americans first heard of it thanks to Lewis and Clark, who were fascinated with what they termed a "prairie wolf" and spent several weeks trying to kill one—testimony enough to the coyote's wiliness. In May 1805, Clark wrote of "the small wolf or burrowing-dog of the prairies which is found in almost all the open plains. It is of an intermediate size between the fox and dog, very delicately formed, fleet and active. . . . These wolves generally associate in bands of ten or twelve, and are rarely if ever seen alone, not being able singly to attack a deer or antelope. They live and rear their young in burrows, which they fix near some pass or spot much frequented by game, and sally out in a body against any animal which they think they can overpower; but on the slightest alarm retreat to their burrows, making a noise exactly like that of a small dog."[2] During Major Stephen Long's 1819–20 expedition to the Rocky Mountains, trained scientists for the first time encountered the marvels that Lewis and Clark had described in their journals. It was expedition biologist Thomas Say who gave the prairie wolf its scientific name, *Canis latrans*, or barking dog, because "their bark is much more distinctly like that of the domestic dog, than of any other animal; in fact the first two or three notes could not be distinguished from the bark of a small terrier, but these notes are succeeded by a lengthened scream." The only canine other than the domestic dog that habitually barks, the prairie wolf was a novelty to American explorers of the Louisiana Purchase but was well known to the Spanish farther south, who transformed the Nahuatl name, *coyotl*, into coyote. As with so much in the American West, the Spanish term *coyote* vanquished the English *prairie wolf*, although Americans still can't decide whether it has two or three syllables, competing dictionaries preferring conflicting pronunciations.[3]

Today coyotes range from Alaska to Costa Rica, from California to New-foundland and Florida—thanks almost entirely to European colonization. In 1500 the animal was limited basically to Mexico and the Great Plains. But the extermination of the grizzly bear, mountain lion, and wolf removed the coy-ote's primary natural competitors and predators, while cattle and sheep proved easier game than larger elk and bison. The coyote expanded its range, reach-ing into Canada by the 1850s, where it continued northward to Alaska and then turned east. By the 1920s it was in New York, and it had populated all of New England by 1970. Crossing the Mississippi, it spread throughout the South-east as well, turned north, and joined forces in Virginia with its northern com-patriots. By the end of the twentieth century, the coyote occupied all of North America.[4]

Despite human resistance.

Ranchers everywhere considered the coyote a varmit, and hundreds of thou-sands of coyotes were shot, poisoned, gassed, and trapped throughout their ex-panding range, to widespread public approval. With both public and private bounties on its head, a pelt worth several dollars on its back, and a population having cull rates of up to 70 percent, the coyote may have seemed doomed. But two hundred years of concerted human effort merely resulted in a wilier, more widespread coyote population. Not that we didn't put a lot of thought into killing coyotes. Between the world wars, a patchwork of local and state efforts received a boost from the federal government's Animal Damage Control program, which underwrote predator extermination. Popular with ranchers, the various devices used to kill Wile E. Coyote read like perverse Acme Corporation inventions. Sodium fluoroacetate, or Compound 1080, first developed in Nazi Germany, and so potent that the Environmental Protection Agency reports seven drops will kill a one-hundred-and-fifty-pound person, was widely used to poison bait meat, killing not only coyotes, but also, inadvertently, dogs, wolves, foxes, eagles, rodents, vultures, condors, and people. Incapable of exterminating coyotes, Compound 1080 did hasten the near extinction of the black-footed ferret, the California condor, and the red wolf—all three now the objects of Uncle Sam rescue programs. So devastating and dangerous was Compound 1080's indiscriminate use that it was banned in 1972, only to come back thirteen years later in a restricted guise, thanks to rancher lobbying. Today ranchers can get livestock protection collars, ingenious Velcro collars with rubber bladders containing enough Compound 1080 to kill two to six people and, with luck, one coyote when it bites into one fastened around the neck of a calf or lamb.[5] Then there's the "humane coyote getter," a gun shell containing sodium cyanide that when triggered shoots a fatal dose into the mouth of the curious varmit. "Cancelled in 1972 [by the Environmental Protection Agency] due to the incidence of human injuries and the occasional killing of domestic dogs," the "humane coyote getter" gave way to a spring-loaded M-44, which should be used only with antidote kits and "not be placed in areas likely to cause adverse impacts on humans and endangered species."[6] Public wildlife officials, of course, closely supervise the use of such devices. The only catch is who supervises the supervisors. A 1991 Fish and Wildlife Service sting operation suggested that one supervisor needed adult supervision, since he was selling Compound 1080 under the table to ranchers eager to circumvent legal restrictions. On eight-ounce can of Compound 1080 cost one thousand dollars on the black market, contributing nicely to the agent's "retirement fund," while killing varmints that killed forty-dollar lambs.[7] Then there's Compound 1080's attractiveness as a terrorist weapon, it being relatively cheap, extremely lethal, and without an antidote.

You would think that with all the hoopla regarding the coyote as varmit that nobody would deliberately aid the animal's spread. But that's exactly what hunters did in the Southeast. Released into enclosures sometimes hundreds of acres in size, feral coyotes from Texas provided jaded Floridians something novel to shoot as long ago as the 1920s. Escapes were inevitable, and today the coyote ranges freely throughout Florida. But some people still enjoy hunting them in enclosures, where they provide an attractive alternative to foxes. In 1994 members of one group bought and released into their 320-acre fox pen animals they said they thought were Florida coyotes. This wouldn't have been so bad, except that these coyotes had rabies, which they then gave to a dog. The Centers for Disease Control (CDC) in Atlanta were called in and determined that the rabies the dog had was a Texas variant that was endemic to coyotes, not a Florida variety. Seven dogs died, twenty-nine people were treated as a precaution, and the CDC in terms described as "depopulation of the free-ranging carnivores within the enclosed foxpen" killed "thirty-two coyotes, five raccoons, two gray foxes, two bobcats and one cat." Shaking their fingers, the CDC pointed out that middle Atlantic and northeastern rabies came from southern raccoons brought north in the 1970s to be hunted and warned that "in addition to rabies, public health risks associated with wildlife translocation include zoonotic infections such as plague, hantavirus pulmonary syndrome, brucellosis, echinococcosis, Lyme disease, Rocky Mountain spotted fever, ehrlichiosis, and tularemia." Which should make you think twice about bringing that Texas coyote back home with you.[8]

Not that you would want to if you had read Mark Twain's description of the beast in *Roughing It:* "The cayote is a long, slim, sick and sorry-looking skeleton, with a gray wolf-skin stretched over it, a tolerably bushy tail that forever sags down with a despairing expression of forsakenness and misery, a furtive and evil eye, and a long, sharp face, with slightly lifted lip and exposed teeth. He has a general slinking expression all over. The cayote is a living, breathing allegory of Want. He is *always* hungry. He is always poor, out of luck and friendless. The meanest creatures despise him, and even the fleas would desert him for a velocipede."[9] Some say this lies behind Wile E. Coyote, the creation of Warner Brothers' cartoonist Chuck Jones. The cartoon character made his debut—along with Road Runner and Acme Products—in 1949 in "Fast and Furryous." Like a manic version of Keats's narrator in "Ode on a Grecian Urn," we want to console Wile E.: "never, never canst thou catch him / —though winning near the goal. / . . . forever wilt thou lose, and he be safe."

But the nature camp has its version of the coyote as well. A defiant Ernest Thompson Seton yippy-yied in his 1913 "The Coyote's Song" that "I'm the voice of all the Wildest West, the Patti of the Plains; / I'm a wild Wagnerian opera of diabolic strains; / I'm a roaring, ranting orchestra with lunatics becrammed; / I'm a vocalized tornado—I'm the shrieking of the damned." Eighty years later an angrier Terry Tempest Williams wrote, "Driving toward Malheur Lake in the Great Basin of southeastern Oregon, I saw a coyote. I stopped the car, opened the door, and walked toward him. It was another crucifixion in the

West, a hide hung on a barbed-wire fence with the wrangler's prayer: Cows are sacred. Sheep, too. No trespassing allowed. The furred skin was torn with ragged edges, evidence that it had been pulled away from the dog-body by an angry hand and a dull knife. My eyes returned to Jesus Coyote, stiff on his cross, savior of our American rangelands. We can try to kill all that is native, string it up by its hind legs for all to see, but spirit howls and wildness endures."[10] I'd like to believe this. Only, of course, the coyotes that I see here in Virginia are no more native than am I. We're both here because the wilderness is gone and the word *native* nearly meaningless. The alien sheep we eat were here before the both of us.

Considered an authentic Texan, the nine-banded armadillo is actually a recent migrant to the Lone Star state, having been first recorded there in 1849, when Audubon in his *Quadrupeds of North America* painted and described what he said "resembles a small pig saddled with the shell of a turtle." It was common north of the Rio Grande and ranged even farther inland. Since then the animal has expanded north and east explosively, becoming a well-known member of the fauna of Oklahoma, Arkansas, Mississippi, Louisiana, Alabama, Florida, and Georgia and beginning to move even farther north into Kansas, Missouri, and South Carolina.

An armadillo. John S. Kingsley, ed., *The Riverside Natural History* (Boston, 1888).

European settlement lies behind this ecological explosion, which is but the tail end of a migration that began three million years ago. *Dasypus novemcinctus* is the northernmost member of the armadillo family, most of whose twenty species live in South America. The emergence of the Panamanian land bridge linking South and North America initiated the Great American Exchange, with animals from both continents expanding their ranges, such as opossums and armadillos heading north. At least three relatives of *D. novemcinctus* beat humans to North America: *D. bellus*, a true armadillo about twice as big as ours, and two giant cousins, the six-foot-long, two-thousand-pound glyptodon, *Glyptotherium texanum*, and the smaller, five-hundred-pound pampathere, *Holmesina septentrionalis*. The glyptodon appears to have been restricted to warmer regions such as Texas, Florida, and South Carolina, but both its cousins ranged as far north as Kansas and North Carolina. Indeed, some biologists suspect that today's nine-banded armadillo population expansion can be explained partly as its filling a niche left vacant by *D. bellus*'s extinction. This may be poetic justice, since all three extinctions may have been thanks to humans, part of the North American megafauna that disappeared at the same time that humans first appeared in North America.[11]

In any case, our armadillo lagged behind its relatives, crossing the Rio Grande only after European agricultural practices had made the landscape more attractive. The Rio Grande, like all large rivers, provides a natural barrier to animal expansion, especially for such poor swimmers as the armadillo. And, for those armadillos that did make it across, the frequently burned-over Native Americans' Texas was inhospitable. Suppression of fire and the introduction of cattle extended the shrubby environment favored by the armadillo, which, once across the Rio, flourished. While its spread east to the Atlantic coast was probably inevitable— with the only sizeable barrier, the Mississippi River, conveniently crossed by bridges—humans both deliberately and inadvertently sped its dispersal. Train-hopping armadillos hitched free rides on cattle trains heading east, and Floridians imported them in the 1920s. Cocoa, Hileah, and Titusville, Florida, all vie for having been the first East Coast home to armadillos, Cocoa crediting escapees from a local zoo, Hileah a Marine recruit homesick for Texas, and Titusville a wrecked circus truck.[12]

Only cold weather and drought stop the armadillo. The Rocky Mountains' rain shadow throughout the High Plains halted the armadillo's westward trek, although if humans helped it along to California, it could easily range northward into Canada on the Pacific Coast. Its continuing advance north on the East Coast will probably come to halt somewhere in Pennsylvania, where the winters are too cold for it and the snow cover prevents it from finding food, which is mainly insects but can be nearly anything. Disliked for digging up Texas lawns while looking for grubs, the armadillo is reputed to be a gravedigger as well, the loose soil of freshly dug graves apparently to its liking, since it is given to digging tunnels more than ten feet long that can be home to both other armadillos and animals such as opossums, cottontail rabbits, cotton rats, skunks, and burrowing owls.[13]

A Texas icon, the armadillo is a pet, dinner, a table lamp, a lab animal, and a health threat. Although easily housebroken and happy to eat dried pet food, the armadillo often proves a handful, since it is incurably nocturnal and possesses scent glands that produce smells noxious to human noses—which may help explain why that homesick Marine in Florida let his go. The Indians of Mexico have long eaten armadillo, and Americans took up the habit once there were enough animals north of the Rio Grande to make it worthwhile. The Depression increased its palatability, and the armadillo became known as Hoover hog. A Texas A&M professor produced two thousand cans of armadillo meat, and game wardens offered recipes. Today armadillo appears in both chilies and barbecues throughout the Southeast.[14]

But many Americans' first hands-on experience with armadillo was thanks to Charles Apelt, a German immigrant to central Texas, who decided that armadillo shells made great baskets. By 1900 the Apelt Armadillo Company was selling both live armadillos and armadillo-shell baskets. By 1920 Apelt employed fifty men to hunt wild armadillos and prepare their shells, which he turned into baskets, wall ornaments, and lamps. Though by far the largest and best known of the Texas armadillo basketmakers, with sales worldwide, Apelt had local competition. Camp though they may be, the baskets were popular: one dealer sold more than forty thousand in the six years prior to World War I. Unfortunately the Apelt Armadillo Company closed its doors in 1971.[15]

Apelt had not only been selling armadillos to you and me, he also had been supplying researchers. It turns out that the nine-banded armadillo can have fewer or more than nine bands, and enterprising Texas zoologists, having counted the bands on 1,768 armadillo baskets, managed to write three papers on heredity in armadillos. Live armadillos also attracted researchers. One of the few mammals routinely to give birth to genetically identical babies, armadillos almost always give birth to quadruplets from the same fertilized egg—making them perfect laboratory animals for genetic experiments.

But leprosy is what propelled the armadillo to medical fame. Leprosy is an Old World disease notorious for face disfigurement and nerve damage that leads to loss of appendages. Although today it is thought to be perhaps the least infectious of contagious diseases, historically leprosy was greatly feared, primarily for the horrible disfigurements that accompany it. Victims were almost invariably driven into exile by their own families. Twenty-four hundred years ago, a Hindu wrote, "Let him, whose body is covered with pustules like the bubbles of foul air that rise from the marsh and burst as they come to the surface, hide and live in isolation on a dunghill, with pariah dogs and other filthy beasts. Let us drive him from our village with stones and cover him, who is himself a living excrement, with ordure. May the immortal rivers reject his corpse," and God commands in Leviticus that "the leper in whom the plague is, his clothes shall be rent, and the hair of his head shall go loose, and he shall cover his upper lip, and shall cry, Unclean, unclean. All the days wherein the plague is in him he shall be unclean; he is unclean: he shall dwell alone; without the camp shall his dwelling be."[16] The Bible assumes physical uncleanliness stems from spiritual uncleanliness; worshiping incorrectly, King Uzziah is stricken with leprosy. But biblical leprosy probably wasn't our leprosy; its symptoms differ, and most historians suspect Alexander the Great's troops brought the disease back to Europe from India in the fourth century B.C.E., long after Leviticus was written.

Norwegian doctor Armauer Hansen's 1873 discovery of *Mycobacterium leprae*, the bacterium that causes leprosy, opened a door to more enlightened views toward its victims as well as the hope for treatment, if not a cure. The nineteenth century's preferred treatment, hydnocarpus oil, a skin ointment derived from the leprosy oil tree (*Hydnocarpus wightiana*), long used in India for relief of skin diseases, was replaced by 1950 with an antibacterial sulfa drug, dapsone, which remains a major drug for treating what has come to be known as Hansen's Disease (HD). Unable to grow the HD bacterium outside of a mammal, researchers despaired of ever having large enough cultures to do sufficient research to find a cure. Learning that HD bacilli grow best under cool conditions and realizing that armadillos maintain a body temperature several degrees lower than most mammals, biologists Wally Kirchheimer and Eleanor Storrs inoculated them with *M. leprae*; not only did armadillos contract HD, they proved more susceptible than humans. Overnight armadillos became the preferred research animal for HD, and they remain the major source for *M. leprae* bacilli for research and medical use. Optimism that armadillos might provide a vaccine for HD faded, however, and the disease still plagues millions.

Using wild armadillos for her initial research, Storrs made the controversial discovery that some of the animals already had HD. She and Kirchheimer disagreed over this and other issues, and a scientific slugfest ensued; at stake were not only reputations, but also millions in research grants and possible fame as the conqueror of leprosy. Storrs's discovery was independently corroborated, and the later discovery of infected animals in Texas and Mississippi muted charges that her laboratory was itself the source of infection. To this day no one has successfully proven how American armadillos contracted leprosy; the assumption is that the source was leprous humans or tainted medical wastes. HD is endemic along the Texas Gulf Coast, and some people there regularly handle armadillos. Since, however, HD can take years to manifest its presence in humans, it is rare that doctors ever discover the initial source of infection.[17] Texas, however, remains a place where nonnative armadillos infect nonnative humans with a nonnative bacillus.

Four-footed beasts are not the only creatures to have occupied America, thanks to the intervention of humanity. Six-legged insects have also jumped at the chance to expand their ranges. Two so notorious that they have entered American folklore are the Colorado potato bug and the boll weevil. While the potato beetle is, at least, a native of the West, the boll weevil is as much an immigrant as any human, its ancestors having arrived in the United States only in the nineteenth century.

The first white man known to have described the potato beetle, *Leptinotarsa decemlineata*, was Thomas Nuttall, an English immigrant to the United States. One of the premier field naturalists in American history, Nuttall discovered countless new species of plants and animals throughout the United States, resulting from early explorations in Philadelphia and the Chesapeake Bay area, the Great Lakes, the Plains, and the Rockies. His published accounts of his journeys landed him a job at Harvard, from which he resigned in order to continue prospecting for new species. So it was that his former student Richard Henry Dana, who had himself dropped out in order to go sailing, found Nuttall walking the beach at San Diego: "I had left him quietly seated in the chair of Botany and Ornithology, in Harvard University; and the next I saw of him, was strolling about San Diego beach, in a sailor's pea-jacket, with a wide straw hat, and barefooted, with his trowsers roiled up to his knees, picking up stones and shells. He had travelled overland to the North-west Coast, and come down in a small vessel to Monterey. There he learned that there was a ship at the leeward, about to sail for Boston; and, taking passage in the *Pilgrim*, which was then at Monterey, he came slowly down, visiting the intermediate ports, and examining the trees, plants, earths, birds, etc., and joined us at San Diego shortly before we sailed."[18]

It was twenty-five years earlier, though, that Nuttall became the first to describe the potato bug, which he discovered while exploring in the footsteps of Lewis and Clark. Having been dispatched to the Great Lakes to collect plant and animal specimens, he was at the headquarters of John Jacob Astor's American Fur Company on Mackinac Island in Lake Superior when he got wind of

Potato bugs (left and right) and potato bug larva (center). John S. Kingsley, ed., *The Riverside Natural History* (Boston, 1888).

the company's plans for a trip following Lewis and Clark's 1804 traverse of the continent; never one to turn down a chance for adventure, Nuttall traveled to St. Louis, joined up, and in 1811 floated up the Missouri as far as the Mandan Villages of North Dakota, made famous in George Catlin's 1833 paintings. Among those on board was Sacagawea, the famous female interpreter on the Lewis and Clark expedition, who had left civilization to return to the wilderness. Upon his return to St. Louis, the impending War of 1812 prompted Nuttall to flee America for England, and it wasn't until 1818 that he published his *Genera of North American Plants and a Catalogue of the Species to the Year 1817.*[19]

But it was the equally famous Thomas Say who gained credit for the first scientific description of the beetle in his *1824 American Entomology, or Descriptions of the Insects of North America.* Say accompanied Major Stephen H. Long's 1819–20 expedition up the Mississippi and its tributaries to the Rocky Mountains. It was during this trip that Say first scientifically described the coyote and the Colorado potato bug—two of the literally thousands of species he was first to describe. In addition to collecting new species on this expedition, Say also led exploring parties, including one into Kansas, where Pawnees robbed them of their horses and possessions and forced them back. Say and his companions noted the increasingly arid conditions of the Plains as they traveled westward, and his observations reinforced the popular notion that in the West lay the "Great American Desert," a sandy desert to rival the Sahara.

Both Say and Nuttall noted the potato bug's association with the buffalo bur, *Solanum rostratum.* A member of the nightshade family—and hence kin to the potato, much to farmers' dismay—the buffalo bur is native to Mexico and the American Great Plains, where it was associated with the disturbed soils of buffalo wallows. Now found throughout the contiguous United States as well as in Europe and Australia, the annual plant is classed as both noxious and invasive, thriving on overgrazed pastures and paddocks and finding its way into grass, feed, and garden seeds; store-bought "tomato" plants have revealed themselves to be, in actuality, buffalo bur.[20]

First associated with potatoes west of Omaha, Nebraska, in 1859, the potato bug soon became a national threat, often described in distinctly military terms: "In 1861, the potato bugs, which had already acquired a taste for the cultivated tuber, invaded Iowa. During 1864 and 1865 they crossed the Mississippi River. In March 1871, they swarmed on the wing in the streets of St. Louis and the following Summer saw the Detroit River literally alive with them. At the same time myriad of potato bugs were crossing Lake Erie on ships, boards, and other floating objects. By 1873 the advance guard of the vast army had appeared on the Atlantic seaboard, and the ocean beaches were thickly covered with them. At some places in Connecticut they were washed ashore in such numbers as to poison the air. Railway trains were stopped by them. They accomplished their march across the continent at the rate of fifty to ninety miles a year."[21]

This is a remarkably accurate description of the spread, despite its "alien invasion" aspects. Early debate as to whether the potato bug came east by nibbling on potatoes that pioneers planted or by following its native food source and potato relative, the buffalo burr, has settled down, with most scientists agreeing that the bug first followed the buffalo bur east, with the bur itself hitching rides on buffalo and cattle backs. Only later did it develop a more refined, Eastern palate that preferred the domesticated potato. Biologists specializing in plant and animal invasions have termed *Leptinotarsa decemlineata* "a model for studies of invasion dynamics." Typical of invasive species, faced with no predators and an untapped supply of food, its first appearance can be overwhelming, as the preceding paragraph illustrates. This sudden eruption is often followed by an equally mysterious population collapse, brought on by the Malthusian forces of war, disease, and starvation, thanks to increased predation, crowded quarters, and a disappearing food source—which can surprise humans as well: "There are all the way from forty to fifty tons of Paris green lying uncalled for in the warehouses of the wholesale drug houses of the city this Summer. The reason for this monumental display of idleness is that there are no potato bugs this summer. This is only comparatively true. There are a few potato bugs, but the number has been small."[22]

The nineteenth century's response was no different than our reaction to similar invasions today. Dismay at the initial onslaught gave way to optimism when farmers discovered Paris green killed the potato bug. Paris green, or copper acetoarsenite, was invented in 1814 in Schweinfurt, Germany, as a coloring agent. It rapidly became one of the most popular dyes in the business, with one American firm manufacturing four hundred thousand pounds of it in 1872.

It colored everything from tickets to boxes and wallpaper to dresses, as one over-wrought reporter told readers, "You frequently go to balls with enough arsenic in your dress to kill off every partner you dance with during the evening; and you do, undoubtedly, cause that next day's sickness and headache from which you and others suffer. . . . You went about the room distributing arsenic as you waltzed; you poisoned yourself, and you poisoned the others." Only a quarter of an ounce could kill, and kill it did, poisoning workers by the score, who died of "arsenic pock" and lung disease. Paris green was also a cheap and easy means of murder or suicide: five cents worth of the easily available powder would kill an adult. Nearly all references to the substance in nineteenth-century *New York Times* pieces are to murders or suicides, the latter being so common that one reporter termed Paris green, "that panacea of the ills of love-sick servant maids." So deadly was it that its manufacturer thought it should be banned except as an agricultural poison. Though its English beneficiary, William Mor-ris, who used it in his wallpapers, pooh-poohed the timid in 1885: "As to the arsenic scare, a greater folly is hardly possible to imagine: the doctors were being bitten by witch fever. . . . Of course it is proving too much to prove that the Nicholsons [his customers] were poisoned by wall-papers; for if they were a great number of people would be in the same plight and we should be sure to hear of it."[23] Finally banned within the United States in the second half of the twentieth century, copper acetoarsenite remains an insecticide, molluscicide, wood preservative, and dye in other countries. And, throughout the second half of the nineteenth century, it was the preferred, indeed only effective, insecti-cide against the potato bug. Pointing out serious consequences for the environ-ment, the *Times* blamed Paris green runoff from potato and tobacco fields for "millions of fish and fowl dying" in the Connecticut River in August 1878.[24]

The potato bug's spread frightened Europe as much or more than it did America. Both England and Germany enforced—unsuccessfully—customs inspections to prevent the bug's importation. Anticipating alarmists of today, both nations feared terrorists would use the potato bug as a biological weapon. The *Times* informed readers that "it is now gravely announced in an English newspaper that an Irish agent has been sent to America to lay in a stock of Col-orado beetles, which are to be secretly let loose in the fields of fair England." And when a German immigrant to Savannah, Georgia, sent his father in Prus-sia a barrel of potatoes, "German officials seized the potatoes and searched his father's house and put him under police surveillance, the innocent Georgia roots being magnified into a socialist plot to introduce the Colorado potato bug into the empire." At the same time that the government sought to exclude the bugs, others thought them attractive; a horrified British Privy Council begged whoever in Manchester had been given a gift of the bugs and cautioned the person "not to let them escape from the garden" and to contact local authorities immediately. "Unfortunately, there is no act of Parliament forbidding a person to keep any kind of insect for which he may have a fancy."[25] The English may have made a pet of the potato bug, but American southerners made it a pet name. Few southerners do not know at least one "tater bug." The bug's hump-backed shape also gave rise to Americans' calling the similarly shaped Neapolitan or Old World mandolin the "tater bug mandolin."

Another six-legged transplant, *Anthonomus grandis grandis* was, as the song has it, "just lookin' for a home" when it crossed the Rio Grande from Mexico into Texas sometime in the late 1800s. For more than two thousand years, the snout-nosed beetle had eaten its way through the Mexican Valley, but not until 1840 did Western science take note of it. Corpus Christi druggist Charles W. DeRyee is thought to have been the first to note its immigration into America in an October 3, 1894, letter to the United States Department of Agriculture: "The 'Top' crop of cotton of this section has been very much damaged and in some cases almost entirely destroyed by a peculiar weevil or bug, which by some means destroys the squares and small bolls. Our farmers can combat the cotton worm but are at a loss to know what to do to overcome this pest. They probably deposit their eggs in the square and their larvae enter the boll as soon as sufficiently formed and are out of reach of the poison. Will you kindly, for the benefit of our farmers, let me know what this pest is and send me any literature that may be available which will enlighten and benefit our farming people. I will send you by mail today a lot of these bugs put up in a small vial." The USDA identified DeRyee's then-little-known bug as *Anthonomus grandis*, the boll weevil, and informed DeRyee that it was "a most undesirable addition to the enemies of the cotton plant, and there is imminent danger that it may spread into other portions of the Cotton Belt."[26] Spread it did, through Texas and reaching Louisiana in 1903, then into Arkansas, Mississippi, Alabama, Tennessee, both of the Carolinas, and Virginia. Within thirty years of crossing the Rio Grande, the weevil had infested 85 percent of America's Cotton Belt, munching a broader path of devastation than Sherman ever dreamed, at an estimated cost of 15 billion dollars, a loss of 175 million dollars a year to farmers alone, with the horror years of 1920 to 1923 each costing 400 million dollars and in 1950 a record 750 million dollars. The bug's impact upon arriving was both precipitous and overwhelming: Mississippi, for example, produced 191,790 bales of cotton worth 11 million dollars in 1907; in 1912 the state produced only thirty thousand bales worth 3.5 million dollars.[27] The boll weevil, however, was simply following its nose from cotton field to cotton field. So it is that an immigrant insect, eating an immigrant plant, transformed the way of life of immigrant humans throughout the South and entered American folklore as a subversive symbol of passive social resistance.

The boll weevil's provender is cotton, which, curiously enough, is native to both the Old and New World. Its pre-Columbian presence in America has supplied many a diffusionist with yet another example of how American culture supposedly derives from Old World adventurers boldly seeking new worlds to colonize or unfortunate fisherfolk blown out to sea; Thor Heyerdahl remains the best known of these, and his crossing of the Atlantic in the papyrus *Ra* boat was intended to show the plausibility of his theory that American cotton, pyramids, and reed boats in Lake Titicaca all came from Egypt. The Mormons, believing that Jews colonized the Americas, point to many of the same parallels as support. But plain Jane scientists merely suppose the two cottons to be an unexplained anomaly. Whether Old World or New, cotton is definitely not native to the United States, so there was no reason for the boll weevil to head north prior to cotton taking over southern agriculture. And cotton might never have become king had Eli Whitney not invented his cotton gin to remove the seeds from the cotton fiber. As anyone who has tried to do this by hand knows, it simply ain't possible to do a decent job. Whitney's engine freed cotton of its last technological obstacle. Andrew Jackson chased off the remaining Native Americans from the Deep South, and the white South became fabulously wealthy. Similar to today's repressive oil regimes, optimistic southerners assumed a dependent Europe would be a willy-nilly ally with King Cotton if northern abolitionists made too much of a ruckus over slavery, only to find themselves alone in 1861. After the war the same southerners turned their newly freed slaves and hapless poor whites into sharecroppers and continued their recalcitrance toward social change.

But what neither Lincoln nor Sherman could achieve, A. *grandis* did. Reading Faulkner, Caldwell, and Mitchell, you would think scalliwags and carpetbaggers had done the South in. No doubt they tried mightily. But a quarter-inch-long bug laid the groundwork for the Snopes's triumph over the Satorises by giving reluctant southern farmers no choice but to change. Ingenious schemes devised to defeat the boll weevil litter the history of southern agriculture. Perhaps the simplest—and probably fictive—device was a mail-order killer guaranteed to work. Suckers who bought it received two pieces of wood with the instructions: place weevil between boards and crush. A desperate 1903 Texas legislature authorized a fifty-thousand-dollar reward for whoever discovered an effective preventive for boll weevils. Despite a secret poison compound, castor beans, Paris green, cannibalistic Guatemalan ants, birds, and a variety of machines, no one got the money.[28] County agriculture agents became popular for the first time thanks to their efforts to control the weevil and to introduce new crops and farming techniques. Although nothing stopped the weevil, cotton farmers still tried fighting the pest—largely with pesticides, so that cotton today consumes an estimated 25 percent of all pesticides used in the United States, some of which are highly toxic. In 1916 calcium arsenate was discovered to kill weevils, and for forty years it remained the farmer's mainstay, often shaken by hand over plants—which resulted in workers suffering arsenic poisoning. The postwar miracle pesticide DDT ended the risk of arsenic poisoning, but it was supplanted by today's favorite, methyl parathion, an organophosphate insecticide invented in the 1950s, which, unfortunately, is toxic to much more than boll weevils and is a suspected carcinogen. Nevertheless, the Environmental Protection Agency (EPA) estimates that American farmers apply three to four million pounds of methyl parathion every year to everything from alfalfa and almonds to walnuts, wheat, and sweet potatoes—and cotton. Although the EPA convinced manufacturers voluntarily to cancel use of methyl parathion in 1999 on a variety of food items, mainly orchard crops, thereafter concluding the level of insecticide in our diet was acceptably low, the agency also warned that methyl parathion remained a problem to workers exposed to it and to wildlife in general and to birds, aquatic invertebrates, and honey bees in particular and that the extent of its pollution of American waters was simply unknown. Although its use persists indoors (such use is illegal in the United States), methyl parathion rapidly degrades outside. You would think that spraying cotton plants with the stuff wouldn't really affect human health that much since all we do with cotton is wear it. However, once the fiber is separated from the seed, we process the seeds for cottonseed oil, half a million tons of which winds up every year in everything from salad dressings to snacks, while beef and dairy cattle eat three million tons of the seeds. No one except healthy food advocates seems to care; government testing for contamination levels is sporadic at best.[29]

Cotton enthusiasts maintain that this is as it should be, given their high hopes for the eradication of the boll weevil. The National Boll Weevil Eradication Program, an innovative integrated pest-management program started by the USDA in the 1970s that combines changed planting practices, insecticides, postharvest plant destruction, and pheromone baiting, has led to 4.5 million acres of cotton fields in the Southeast, Arizona, and California being declared weevil-free. That still leaves a lot of cotton yet to be saved, but advocates point out that liberated fields now use 40 to 90 percent less pesticides than before. That much of this pesticide reduction stems from "Bt cotton," genetically engineered plants containing insect toxins that come from the soil bacteria *Bacillus thuringiensis*, or *Bt*, has, of course, merely raised concerns among those opposed to genetic engineering and the skepticism of those familiar with the "pesticide treadmill." While any new pesticide—be it arsenic, methyl parathion, or *Bt*—initially works wonders, killing off insects with no resistance, it eventually works less and less effectively, as resistant insects have more and more resistant offspring, until a day comes when the pesticide simply doesn't work any longer—and we invent a new one. Concerned scientists wonder what we will replace *Bt* cotton with and what effect *Bt* crops have on nontargeted insects, since *Bt* kills almost any insect that ingests it.[30]

But the boll weevil, having entered into both American soil and popular culture, ignores this contretemps. What other ecological disaster, for example, has garnered itself as grand a statue as Enterprise, Alabama's 13.5-foot-tall monument to the boll weevil? When the weevil devastated Coffee County's cotton crop in 1915, a local visionary convinced a farmer to plant peanuts the next year. When C. W. Baston paid his debts off and banked a profit thanks to his eight-thousand-bushel peanut crop, the rest of the county deposed King Cotton and elected peanut their cash crop. On December 11, 1919, a grateful Enterprise dedicated a three-thousand-dollar Italian marble statue in honor of the boll weevil's role in diversifying local farming. For thirty years the statue was only a good-looking woman in a revealing gown, but in 1949 local artist Luther Baker achieved artistic immortality when he made a boll weevil for her to hold above her head. Baker's bug and its successors were stolen; today a security camera watches over the enterprising bug and his lady friend.[31] Not that others hadn't noticed that King Cotton's deposition had actually improved things in the Deep South. In 1910 the *New York Times* ran a full-page spread titled, "Why the Deadly Boll Weevil, Bringing Revolution with Him, Is Called the 'Prosperity Bug.'"

Cotton brought the weevil to the South, and music introduced it to the rest of America. Most of us know "The Boll Weevil" song better than we do the weevil. As with all folk music, various versions exist, but in nearly all of them the itinerate weevil, in cahoots with the local merchant, outwits a hapless farmer and steals his home:

> The merchant, he got half the cotton
> The weevil got the rest;
> They didn't leave the farmer's wife
> But one old cotton dress:
> Just lookin' for a home, just lookin' for a home.

Bankruptcies were common during the boll weevil's ravagings, and social historians credit it with helping fuel southern blacks' great migration northward and southern whites' similar hegira to textile towns in the southern Piedmont. As "The Boll Weevil" recounts:

> The farmer says to the merchant
> We ain't but only one bale
> An' before we give you that'n
> We'll fight and go to jail.
> We'll have a home, we'll have a home.

Although the weevil itself was no respecter of social conventions, the song could not ignore the South's racial divide, so that, in some versions, its narrator concludes:

> An' if anybody should ask you
> Who it was that made this song
> Just tell 'em 'twas a big buck niggah
> With a pair o' blue ducks on.
> Ain't got no home, ain't got no home.

Gone Fishin'

An Unnatural Pastime

Nothing could be more typical of a lazy summer's day—An American youth is headed toward his favorite fishing hole armed with a cane pole and a can of worms. Yet few scenes have more nonnative elements in them than this one. The kid, the pole, the fish, the worm, the pond—all are nonindigenous.

Not itself plant or animal, the pond is often an artifact of civilization. Although the United States has an estimated 41.6 million acres of ponds, lakes, and reservoirs, these are not dispersed uniformly throughout the nation. Guam, for example, has only one 27-acre reservoir, and Hawaii reports only 2,100 acres of small lakes, while Alaska possesses 12,780,000 acres, California 1,600,000 acres, Florida 2,000,000 acres, Louisiana 1,000,000 acres, Minnesota 3,200,000 acres, Oklahoma 1,000,000 acres, and Texas 3,000,000 acres. Much of this, however, is artificial. Virginia, where I live, for example, has nearly 150,000 acres of lakes, and the land is dotted with farms ponds—all but two of which are man-made. The only lakes in Virginia that predate Europeans are Lake Drummond in the Great Dismal Swamp and Mountain Lake in the Valley and Ridge Province. So it is in many mid-Atlantic states. Farther north the glaciers left behind thousands of lakes and ponds scattered throughout the northern tier of states, as the numbers reveal: Maine reporting 980,000 acres of lakes, Minnesota 3,200,00, New Hampshire 70,000, New York 790,000, North Dakota 660,000, and Wisconsin 982,000. While the "Land of a Thousand Lakes" still merits its name, many smaller wetlands, especially in the Plains states, have disappeared. Farther south the swampy bays of the south Atlantic states have also largely disappeared beneath the plow, while the catfish ponds of the Mississippi watershed are, as often as not, artificial impoundments. Natural bodies of water are scarce in the drier regions of the nation, although man-made lakes may be numerous. Texas, for example, boasts 3,000,000 acres of lakes. The West Coast has plenty of lakes, but these are not uniformly scattered throughout the states and many are artificial. Southern Californians, for example, may be surprised to learn that their state has 1,672,000 acres of lakes, more than forty-six other states have. Nobody knows how many farm ponds America has. The federal Soil Conservation Service helped build more than 2 million farm ponds from 1945 to 1975, mostly in the South and Midwest. Virginia is estimated to have 50,000 small ponds, while Mississippi claims to have 280,000. Iowa estimates that it gains 1,000 new ponds every year. The old fishing hole, then, may well be as nonnative as our fisherman's worm.[1]

The preferred fishing worm is the night crawler, *Lumbricus terrestris*, an earthworm. And warm, wet weather at night brings them crawling out in droves. I once lived in a damp basement that looked out into an even damper yard. One night after a rain, I looked out my front window and, slightly horrified, saw the ground heaving with earthworms. They were enormous, eight, ten glistening inches long, one end anchored in the ground, the other weaving and snaking and worming through the grass and dirt and air. The next morning, I examined the ground. I easily could see their holes because every one was stuffed with leaves and stem ends they had dragged down with them. The entire side lawn was studded with what looked like miniature withered bouquets.

Darwin reports a German study that calculated 53,767 worms per acre. That is a lot of worms. If you thought fishermen simply went out into the back-yard and looked under a rock or log for worms, you're strictly an amateur. Worms are a big business and too important to be left to kids on Saturday morning. Down South in the Florida panhandle, for instance, they scare them up by "worm grunting," using vibrations to drive worms out of the ground. Nobody's quite sure why worms dislike vibrations, but they do, popping out by the dozens when grunters pound a stake in the ground and make it sing by rubbing it with metal. You can try the same trick at home with a pitchfork; drive its tines into the ground and play it like a bass fiddle. In England people claim birds have learned to forage along the edges of major highways for worms driven out by heavy trucks. To collect worms, some people electroshock the ground, and others douse a likely spot with acid—vinegar if you're a fisherman, formalin if you're a scientist bent on broadening our knowledge. Not that the worm you call up is necessarily a night crawler. The one most likely to be called up in the Florida panhandle, for instance, is *Diplocardia mississippiensis*, and its diminishing numbers has caused a ruckus in Apalachicola National Forest, where locals harvest them for fishing. When feeding, *D. mississippiensis* concentrates calcium in its casts, or excrements, enriching the panhandle's calcium-poor soil to such a degree that some experts think the number of worms may influence how many eggs the red-cockaded woodpecker lays. Because the red-cockaded woodpecker is an endangered species, the worm's numbers need to be carefully monitored.

The Forest Service issues worm-gathering permits and taxes the harvest—to the outrage of locals who for years have been gathering worms for free.[2]

But *the* fishing worm is, as many a bait store window proclaims, "Live Canadian Night Crawlers." That's our old friend, *L. terrestris*. In Ontario it's a million-dollar business; golf courses and the like are rented out at night to wormers, who scoop up 2.5 billion worms a year by the bucketful. Canada cornered the market on night crawlers thanks to the Ice Age. Half a million years ago, a mile-high wall of ice came south, gouging out the Great Lakes, depositing Long Island, and eradicating every earthworm north of the Ohio River. When the ice retreated ten thousand years ago, it left half a continent barren of trees, birds, grasses, flowers, snakes, rats, wolves, caribou, and earthworms. Worms travel slowly, some twenty feet a year in scientific worm races. Do a little math, and you find out that the native American worms could have only made their way forty miles north of their starting point. Nature cheats, though, letting careless robins drop their dinner, and the American worms almost made it, stopping somewhere around the forty-ninth parallel. Europeans with their apple trees and fellow-traveling worms beat them to Canada. Without competition *L. terrestris* has been fruitful and multiplied and multiplied and multiplied. Or so the story goes. *Lumbricus terrestris* certainly did well in Canada. But nobody knows for certain that pockets of *L. terrestris* didn't survive glaciation. Worm Watch Canada has enlisted schoolkids to survey their backyards for worms, in hopes of discovering just what kind of worms actually lurk in the Canadian soil and where they came from.[3]

Lumbricus terrestris is a hermaphrodite, having both male and female reproductive organs. But he does not have sex with herself; rather, they enjoy the Tiresian pleasures of being male and female at the same time. Their male pores, through which they pass sperm down a seminal groove, are located on the fifteenth segment. The muscles of this groove contract in sequence, passing the sperm like a football from segment to segment until it reaches the partner's clitellum. The clitellum is the saddle-shaped, often lighter-colored part of a night crawler. From here, the sperm travels towards the head of the other worm, where it is taken up and stored for later use. During copulation this area becomes covered with mucus. After copulation this mucus hardens and is shed like a sweater, over the worm's head. As it passes along, this hardened mucus sac, or cocoon, picks up sperm and then eggs, which unite outside the worm in the cocoon. Of course, while worm number one is shedding his sperm, she's also lathering up her clitellum and readying her ova for discharge.

The female pores resemble male pores externally and are located on segment fourteen, directly in front of the male pores. Unlike human females, earthworms consistently produce multiple eggs, flooding out of ovaries and then down and out the oviducts. Although she may release as many as twenty eggs, only one or two will eventually hatch from the cocoon. Like humans, they are sexually active year-round, although, again like humans, they slow down when it's too hot or too cold, or they're too old. A single worm can construct as many as a hundred cocoons a year, each cocoon taking sixteen weeks to hatch, and each hatched worm then taking nine months to reach full size.

Unlike other earthworms, night crawlers do it on the surface. So you can watch them, though the action, because they are cold-blooded, is not exactly heated. Two worms, apparently locating each other by glandular secretion, will lie head to head with their clitella touching. Each clitellum has a series of glandular thickenings on the belly side that may be useful in helping the worms stick to each other while copulating. That's all you'll see for up to an hour: two worms, simply lying there, each getting slightly sticky, each oblivious to sight and sound. Then it's all over; with a sigh, each worm rolls over and heads for bed.

You won't see even this much if you pick the wrong worm. Many worm species are parthenogenic, breeding without sex. Lots of northern hemisphere worms are parthenogenic, others are strictly hermaphroditic, and some can go either way. Sex is supposed to scramble genes and so increase survival odds in a changing environment. So why parthenogensis? Some scientists think it developed after the Ice Age, when worms simply couldn't find partners as easily. Whatever the reason it developed, develop it did, and now there are entire species of once happily hermaphroditic worms that have no need for their male equipment, which has atrophied. Virgin birth invariably results in female offspring. The female equipment is obviously necessary to give birth; since the male is not, the offspring are always female.

Of course, sex isn't all there is to being an earthworm. There's eating: decaying plant matter, live protozoa, rotifers, nematodes, bacteria, fungi, decomposing animals both small and large. A night crawler can consume 30 percent of its body weight in food each day. Granted, that's not much if it only weighs, say, a gram. But, proportionally, it's as if a human were to eat fifty pounds of food a day. You can see some of this food if you hold a worm up to the light. That dark blob running down its insides is mostly its digestive system. Darwin found them discriminating, if unrefined, diners. His worms preferred vegetable leaves (celery, cabbage, and carrot especially) to tree leaves and preferred those leaves high in sugar (maple especially) to those high in tannin (oak, beech, and conifers). Above all else, they liked moist manure.[4]

Worms eat by swallowing bits of food matter and digesting it in a crop and gizzard system. Like chickens they swallow tiny stones they then store in their gizzards to use as millstones. Worms don't just swallow nutritious stuff; like many a kid, they eat dirt. In fact, Aristotle called them the "intestines of the earth," suggesting that they went about digesting the planet. And they do. Worms pass enough dirt through their bodies to cover an average acre with two-tenths of an inch of "castings" a year. You can see these castings scattered around worm burrows, and some species use them to build towers and hills. Like human waste, worm casts add up: an acre of dirt two-tenths of an inch thick is eighteen tons of worm waste a year. But we're lucky; along the Nile worm bowels move a thousand tons of waste per acre per year. In South Africa the stuff piles up so fast farmers use bulldozers to scrape it away!

Every gardener knows manure is good, and here's the lowly earthworm dumping eighteen tons an acre gratis. Ever since Darwin, the worm's been considered the gardener's friend, turning and enriching the soil. Darwin also pointed out the archaeologist's debt to the worm: two-tenths of an inch a year means an inch every five years, a foot every sixty years. Archaeologists can dig up their treasures because worms have buried them. The downside is that the same worms can undermine stones and walls. Darwin saw their handiwork in the toppled stones of Stonehenge. Golf course and lawn fanatics dislike piled-up worm casts, which are not only ugly to some but might also deflect the ball. Equally troublesome are the moles that worms attract. These burrowing maniacs actually store worms for leaner days; they keep them from crawling away by biting off their heads.

If a mole were to leave a worm for long enough, he'd come back to find it had grown a new head and crawled away. Everyone knows worms can regenerate themselves if cut, although both ends can't pull off the trick. A worm needs its middle in order to regenerate; take off too much, and it dies. You can often spot regenerated tails and heads by their lighter color and slimmer proportions. But regrowth doesn't always work just right. Sometimes a head grows where a tail should have and vice versa. Not to be outdone by nature, scientists have played Dr. Frankenstein with worms. Sewing severed worms together, science has discovered that two-tailed worms outlive two-headed worms. We now know you can splice the head of one worm to the tail of another, and they'll live. It works even when you sew one on sideways. Not content with merely slicing worms up, science has also gassed, poisoned, and electrocuted them—and discovered that worms don't like to be gassed, poisoned, or electrocuted.

Unlike you or me, an earthworm can breathe while it eats. It hasn't any lungs: it's small enough to get enough oxygen by diffusion through its skin. Like ours, its blood is red. You can see the circulatory system in young worms not yet darkened by age. Like many lower animals, its nervous system's main line runs along its belly, not its back as in humans. No worm is an Einstein, although experimentation has shown that you can teach a worm to avoid electric shocks. And contrary to fishermen's belief, that worm on a hook is writhing, not wiggling; worms produce the same chemicals when impaled on a hook as higher animals do when subjected to physical pain.

Earthworms eat their way through the soil by swallowing dirt and then excreting it. They can also push it aside with their heads. Night crawlers can thus build burrows that sink up to two to three feet deep, escaping the rigors of winter cold and summer drought. Many think worms are, in part, yucky because of their slime. That slime is really mucus that the worm secretes to keep itself moist and to provide a cushion against hard objects. You can see how important keeping moist is for a worm after picking up a sidewalk worm carcass. A few hours after death, a worm is a dried up piece of leather. The mucus coat helps protect an animal that is 80 percent water. The worm's *bauplan* is simple: a tube within a tube. There's the outside mucus-coated body wall and the inside digestive tract. Between the two is the coelum, a fluid- and organ-filled cavity. It's this stuff you get all over your fingers when you stick a fishhook through a worm. A worm is thus a thin tube of flesh surrounded by and encasing dirt—which pretty much describes you and me.

Find a good-sized worm and run your fingers along its body from head to tail, and you'll feel little pricks. Those are its setae, bristlelike structures that are moveable. These help a worm travel—and stay put. You can watch how effective their traction is by observing birds trying to pull worms out of their burrows. Often, to the delight of cartoonists, they fail, thanks to the worm's setae, which are gripping the sides of the burrow. Worms move by contracting and relaxing muscles in the body wall.

That fish our young angler is after is liable to be exotic as well. The federal government lists 647 species as being either exotic or having been transplanted outside their native range, which is 39 percent of all fish species within the United States. Florida is worst off, with 82 percent of its fish species originally foreign to the United States. The modes of introduction are various, but, often as not, it's the government, well-intentioned individuals, or industry. The aquarium industry alone can claim to have introduced twenty-seven nonindigenous fish to America, the most notorious of which is undoubtedly the piranha.

Unhappily for horror movie fans, almost all sightings are of single individuals undoubtedly released by guilty aquarium owners. The U.S. Geological Survey notes that the tropical fish will have a hard time surviving in most of the continental United States, although there's always southern Florida and California, as well as your local nuclear power plant's warm water to worry about.[5]

Less notorious but actually more troublesome are bass and trout. A mainstay of the fishing industry, the smallmouth bass (*Micropterus dolomieu*) now lives in every state except Alaska, far beyond its original home in the headwaters of the Mississippi, Ohio, and Tennessee rivers. It has been implicated in the decline of native fish in Arizona, the Columbia River basin, and the Potomac River and in the decline of frogs and salamanders in California. In Texas it threatens the native Guadalupe bass through hybridization.[6] The largemouth bass (*Micropterus salmoides*) originally lived in the St. Lawrence River, the Great Lakes, the Mississippi River basin, and the Gulf Coast drainage basins and along the East Coast south of Virginia. But it is now found within all contiguous forty-eight states, where it has been charged with contributing to the decline or even extinction of native fish that it preys on. Like the smallmouth, it's also accused of eating too many California frogs and salamanders.[7] But try telling this to a kid who's just caught one on a pole.

It's not just your local farm pond that's stocked with largemouth. So-called sportfishing and trophy ponds also stock largemouth that have been specially reared. Special ponds are cleared of all but breeding-size largemouth, whose spawn are caught and transferred to nursery ponds, where they grow large feeding on zooplankton that has itself been encouraged by overfertilizing the water until it's green. These larger fingerlings are then removed to yet another pond, where they are trained to take artificial food and rapidly grow to a large size. Incidentally, they are habituated to taking the bait the paying customer uses to catch them.[8]

The place for bass information is BASS, the Bass Anglers Sportsman Society, which sponsors the annual invitational Bass Masters Classic, a three-day, five-fish-a-day tournament won by the person who catches the heaviest fish. A one-ounce difference separated first and second place one year, a significant difference when first place has meant more than a million dollars in promos and other benefits. A sweet dream for the estimated twenty-eight million freshwater American anglers who spend nearly seventy-five billion dollars each year on the one that got away. Fishing for those dollars are hundreds of boat, motor, rod, reel, lure, and line manufacturers as well as the local fishing supply store and the kid selling red worms. So pervasive is bass fishing that even nonfishers recognize the profile of a bass boat, and the Bass Masters Classic is shown on television.

Cousins, large and smallmouth bass are best told apart by their mouths, the largemouth's extending back under the eye, the smallmouth's ending where the eye begins. Both are fun to catch and good to eat, explaining their popularity in fish-stocking projects. But the first major redistribution of bass was inadvertent. The Great Lakes, created by glaciers during the last Ice Age, drain into the St. Lawrence River and Atlantic Ocean. However, Niagara Falls served as a barrier to the mingling of salt and freshwater plants and animals—until the Erie and Welland canals were built in the 1820s. Linking the Hudson to the Great Lakes, the 1825 Erie Canal provided a ready route for settlers heading west and produce heading east. The 1829 Welland Canal, circumventing Niagara Falls, provided an even more direct link to the sea. But people were not the only creatures to benefit from the opening up of a new frontier. Bass, formerly confined to the interior drainages of the American continent, easily passed into the Hudson River watershed along with midwestern barges bound for New York City. Less likeable animals passed the other way as well. Most notorious of all was the sea lamprey, a primitive, jawless parasitic fish that latches hold of its prey and eats it. A native of the Atlantic Ocean, the lamprey colonized the lakes via the Welland Canal. Invasion continues today, with the infamous European zebra mussel having first been spotted in North America in 1988. Since then it has spread rapidly throughout several watersheds, clogging pipes and threatening overstressed ecosystems. More than canals helped the mussel along, however. Scientists think that its planktonic young got here in ballast water taken from the Black Sea that later was discharged into the Great Lakes before ships were loaded with cargo—probably midwestern wheat bound for the Soviet Union. Such ballast discharge has only recently become a recognized problem, both in the United States and elsewhere. The speed with which today's large ships carrying millions of gallons of water teeming with microscopic life forms can cross oceans guarantees contamination, despite efforts to require the discharge of such ballast waters far out to sea. But ballast discharge has been providing America with immigrants for a long time; weed experts think that English colonial ships laden with dirt that they dumped in our port cities provided many weeds free passage to the New World. As I discuss in "Out of Africa," grass bedding dumped in our southern ports provided African plants access to this continent.

No one objected to the basses' eastward movement, however. Both fish spawn in the late spring to early summer, after the males have excavated small nests in the sand or gravel of lake or river bottoms. After hatching, the males guard the fry for up to a month, until they are large enough to live independently.

They then disperse, which is just as well, both species being cannibalistic when crowded. When grown, both large and smallmouth bass prefer feeding on smaller fish, but they both will devour whatever comes their way, from insects to amphibians to worms.

Trout are better known in literary circles than bass thanks to the cachet of fly-fishing. When speaking of trout in most of America, you generally are talking about rainbow, brook, or brown trout. Both the rainbow and brook trout are native Americans; the rainbow (*Oncorhynchus mykiss*) was originally confined to the coastal rivers of the West Coast where, in its seagoing form, it is called steelhead. The brook trout (*Salvelinus fontinalis*) is native to eastern Canada and the northeastern United States, west to Minnesota and south in the Appalachians to Georgia. The brown trout (*Salmo trutta*) is a European import. But all three have been moved about wherever conditions might support them. They are wildly popular with both anglers and diners. In 2003 trout farmers rang up 66.4 million dollars in sales of fish and eggs, while state and federal fish hatcheries gave away an estimated 61 million dollars the same year. Commercial farmers sold an estimated 58 million fish, while the government raised and gave away another 118 million. Government fish, intended primarily for restocking, are smaller than the commercial fish that are intended for eating. Two-thirds of America's commercial trout production takes place in Idaho's Snake River Valley, where abundant, cold, flowing water makes for ideal trout farming. Nearly all of these are rainbow trout destined for stores and restaurants.[9]

As we have seen, such redistributions can wreak havoc on native ecosystems. The rainbow has received its share of criticism, hybridizing with rarer, native species, bringing with it communicable diseases, outcompeting established native species, and preying sometimes on rare species, including the brook trout.[10] The European brown trout also threatens native fish populations. Unlike the rainbow, however, the brown does not maintain itself without restocking, so that its continued presence is entirely due to continued human intervention, often by government agencies.[11] Despite being the mainstay of today's trout farms, the rainbow initially was unpopular. In 1882 the *New York Times* reported that critics at the American Fish-Cultural Association damned it, saying, "The rainbow trout would drive out the native brook trout as the Norway rat has driven out the native rat, and the English sparrow the native bird," and reporting that fishermen refusing to keep it, fish pond owners regretting stocking it, and fish eaters panning its taste.[12] The brown trout, being of European extraction, won favor with fish fanciers in New York; however, the 1885 *Times* reported it as "successfully acclimatized in America. . . . [and] an important addition to American waters."[13]

What bass boats are to bass, fly rods are to trout. Generations of literary anglers have taught us to appreciate the distinction between bait fishermen and anglers, the one a reprobate and the other a saint. Hemingway, for example, had Jake Barnes in *The Sun Also Rises* use worms; his fly-fishing companion not only outfishes him but also calls him a lazy bum. Nick Adams in Hemingway's "Big Two-Hearted River: Part II" uses a fly rod but baits it with grasshoppers— and for him, "the fishing would be tragic." But it is Norman Maclean's *A River Runs through It* that makes the distinction most clear, beginning as it does with the great sentence: "In our family, there was no clear line between religion and fly fishing." Learning to "cast Presbyterian-style," Maclean fuses the spiritual, aesthetic, and practical in a story where redemption is found on a river. For Maclean's Presbyterian minister father, the dean of literary fishermen, Izaak Walton, "is not a respectable writer. He was an Episcopalian and a bait fisherman."[14]

Although a transcendentalist and a bait fisherman, Thoreau too mused on the spiritual side of fishing when he wrote in *Walden*, "Time is but the stream I go a-fishing in. . . . I would drink deeper; fish in the sky, whose bottom is pebbly with stars." Such musings befit the grown angler, but our young American has more in common, I think, with the decidedly unphilosophical boy Thoreau: "Formerly I had come to this pond adventurously, from time to time, in dark summer nights, with a companion, and making a fire close to the water's edge, which we thought attracted the fishes, we caught pouts with a bunch of worms strung on a thread; and when we had done, far in the night, threw the burning brands high into the air like skyrockets, which, coming down into the pond, were quenched with a loud hissing, and we were suddenly groping in total darkness." Thoreau's pout is a thoroughly American catfish; no one had yet thought to stock Walden Pond with bass and rainbow trout, as it is today. The grown Thoreau fishes the same night waters, catching different fish:

> Sometimes, after staying in a village parlor till the family had all retired, I
> have returned to the woods, and, partly with a view to the next day's dinner,
> spent the hours of midnight fishing from a boat by moonlight, serenaded by
> owls and foxes, and hearing, from time to time, the creaking note of some
> unknown bird close at hand. These experiences were very memorable and
> valuable to me,—anchored in forty feet of water, and twenty or thirty rods
> from the shore, surrounded sometimes by thousands of small perch and shin-
> ers, dimpling the surface with their tails in the moonlight, and communicat-
> ing by a long flaxen line with mysterious nocturnal fishes which had their

dwelling forty feet below, or sometimes dragging sixty feet of line about the pond as I drifted in the gentle night breeze, now and then feeling a slight vibration along it, indicative of some life prowling about its extremity, of dull uncertain blundering purpose there, and slow to make up its mind. At length you slowly raise, pulling hand over hand, some horned pout squeaking and squirming to the upper air. It was very queer, especially in dark nights, when your thoughts had wandered to vast and cosmogonal themes in other spheres, to feel this faint jerk, which came to interrupt your dreams and link you to Nature again. It seemed as if I might next cast my line upward into the air, as well as downward into this element, which was scarcely more dense. Thus I caught two fishes as it were with one hook.[15]

Thoreau appears to have used a handline, not a pole, or rod, as Maclean's father insisted upon calling it. "Always it was to be called a rod. If someone called it a pole, my father looked at him as a sergeant in the United States Marines would look at a recruit who had just called a rifle a gun." Maclean's father's rod was eight and a half feet long, weighed four and a half ounces, and "was made of split bamboo cane from the far-off Bay of Tonkin."[16] Almost all store-bought poles—rods—are foreign. Fishing pole bamboo, or golden bamboo, *Phyllostachys aurea*, originates in China, where forests of it and other kinds of bamboo provide fast-growing material for dozens of objects ranging from scaffolding to mats. Its rival for fishing poles in America is our native cane, *Arundinaria gigantea*, which grows nearly as high and once upon a time formed extensive canebrakes in the South, which entered into American lore. Davy Crockett rode through one on his way to the Alamo: "The reeds, the same as are used in the northern states as fishing rods, had grown to the height of about twenty feet and were so slender, that having no support directly over the path, they drooped a little inward, and intermingled their tops, forming a complete covering overhead. . . . The largest brake is that which lines the banks of Cane Creek, and is seventy miles in length, with scarcely a tree to be seen the whole distance. The reeds are eaten by cattle and horses in the winter when the prairies yield little or no other food."[17] The haunt of bear, wolf, panther, and the most feared of all, the canebrake rattler, *Crotalus horridus*, so camouflaged as to be invisible until stepped on, the canebrake was a remnant wilderness. Black, red, and white hunted in it, and John Lawson describes in his 1709 *New Voyage to Carolina*, "Indians firing the Canes Swamps, which drives out the game, then taking their particular stands, kill great quantities of both bear, deer, turkies, and what wild creatures the parts afford."[18] To abolitionists the canebrake symbolized slavery's worst oppressions. Having been sold down the river, Harriet Beecher Stowe's Uncle Tom daydreams: "He seemed to see familiar faces of comrades who had grown up with him from infancy; he saw his busy wife, bustling in her preparations for his evening meals; he heard the merry laugh of his boys at their play, and the chirrup of the baby at his knee; and then, with a start, all faded, and he saw again the canebrakes and cypresses and gliding plantations, and heard again the creaking and groaning of the machinery, all telling him too plainly that all that phase of life had gone by forever."[19] Sojourner Truth, too, evoked it in her condemnation of slavery: "Beneath a burning southern sun have we toiled, in the canebrake and the rice swamp, urged on by the merciless driver's lash, earning millions of money; and so highly were we valued there, that should one poor wretch venture to escape from this hell of slavery, no exertion of man or trained blood-hound was spared to seize and return him to his field of unrequited labor."[20] But people lived in canebrake country. Leftover Indians and runaway slaves hid out in their immensities, and poor whites were relegated there by the wealthy, so that canebrake became an insult, a canebrake preacher, for example, being an itinerant, off-brand sort of Protestant. Canebrakers, considered trash by many, could become heroes, and Walt Disney's Davy Crockett is celebrated as "the Canebrake Congressman."

Cane has been extirpated throughout much of its native range, both through habitat destruction and overgrazing, so that canebreaks are now considered critically endangered ecosystems, although the cane itself is not in danger.[21] Porcher noted that "the canes attain a great height and size on our river courses, and are a characteristic growth; they once grew luxuriantly throughout the upper country of South Carolina and Georgia, whence the names of the creeks and rivers, but have been almost entirely consumed by animals." Describing it, Lawson wrote, "Of canes and reeds we have many sorts. The hollow reed, or cane, such as angling-rods are made of, and weavers use, we have great plenty of, though none to the northward of James-River in Virginia. They always grow in branches and low ground. Their leaves endure the winter, in which season our cattle eat them greedily. We have them (towards the heads of our rivers) so large, that one joint will hold above a pint of liquor."[22] Where still found, it remains "one of the most valuable native forages in the Coastal Plain region of Virginia and North Carolina," according to the U.S. Forest Service.[23]

Cane was not, however, bamboo to Lawson, who writes, "The small bamboo is next, which is a certain vine, like the rest of these species, growing in low land. They seldom, with us, grow thicker than a man's little finger, and are very tough. Their root is a round ball, which the indians boil as we do garden-roots, and eat them." This is *Smilax laurifolia*, an evergreen and often thorny vine that forms impenetrable thickets in our lowlands from New Jersey to

Florida. Why anyone would call *Smilax* bamboo is puzzling, because the vine in no way resembles the grass. But it is still known as such, and it and its close relatives are still eaten in the South and Caribbean.

Bamboo is, of course, famous as a tree grass, and some species, for example timber bamboos, can grow one hundred feet tall. Fishing pole bamboo, which grows up to thirty feet high and an inch and a half in diameter, survives below freezing temperatures and is found in many states. Unfortunately, it is a "running" bamboo, which means it spreads easily by underground runners or rhizomes, often popping up in unexpected and unwanted places. It is also kept as a house plant, being much better behaved when confined to a pot. More sedate clumping bamboos also send out runners, but these are much shorter and so spread much more slowly. Bamboo is also famous for its "gregarious" flowering habits; plants of some species all flower at the same time and then die, which is a problem for the giant panda, who depends on these bamboo for food, and for gardeners who awake to find their hedge dead.

Frank N. Meyer brought specimens of fishing pole and other bamboos to America from Asia. Born Dutch, Meyer immigrated to America at a young age and hoboed around the country until famed plant explorer David Fairchild picked him to lead expeditions into China to look for new plants. The European defeat of the Boxer Rebellion had opened China to exploration, and a race for new discoveries was on. Meyer made four trips to Asia, spending nearly all of the years from 1905 through 1918 on foot in China, Siberia, and central Asia. Introducing some twenty-five hundred different plants to America, including the Meyer lemon, Meyer spruce, and Meyer bamboo, he survived armed bandits, thuggish soldiers, glaciers, deserts, jungles, and Siberian winters. Deserted outside Tibet and again in central Asia, he made his way alone using only maps and a compass. Truly an extraordinary man, he rambled to escape depression: "I am pessimistic by nature . . . and have not found a road which leads to relaxation. I withdraw from humanity and try to find relaxation with plants." On his last trip, he mysteriously disappeared overboard; no one knows whether he fell, jumped, or was pushed.[24] Meyer bamboo closely resembles fishing pole bamboo, and it is entirely possible that your fishing pole is a descendent of stock that Meyer discovered. To know whether your cane pole is possibly Meyer's, take a gander of it in cross section: American cane tends to be more smoothly circular whereas the Asian bamboo often has one side flattened.

But, more to the point, go fishing. Sure, you're an alien, your cane pole's an alien, the worm you'll use is an alien, the fish you'll catch is an alien, and the pond it's in is unnatural. But that's the American way. We're all strangers in a strange land.

Notes

As American as Apple Pie

1. U.S. Congress, Office of Technology Assessment, *Harmful Non-Indigenous Species in the United States*, OTA-F-565 (Washington, D.C.: U.S. Congress, Office of Technology Assessment, 1993), 53.

Out of Africa

1. L. Holm, J. V. Pancho, J. P. Herberger, and D. L. Plucknett, *A Geographical Atlas of World Weeds*, in handout from Hybrid Bermudagrass Spriggers Workshop meeting, ed. G. W. Burton (Tifton, Ga: Rural Development Center, 1992).

2. M. E. Francis, *The Book of Grasses* (Garden City, N.Y.: Doubleday, 1912).

3. G. W. Burton, "Bermudagrass," in *Forages*, 2d ed., ed. H. D. Hughes, M. E. Heath, and D. Metcalfe (Ames: Iowa State College Press, 1951), 270, cited in Carl H. Hovermale and Greg Cuomo, *Bermudagrass Variety Evaluations in South Mississippi*, Bulletin 1059 (Starkville, Miss.: Office of Agricultural Communications, Mississippi State University), http://msucares.com/pubs/bulletins/b1059.htm (accessed March 11, 2003). Spalding's diary supposedly dates Ellis's introduction to 1751, although Ellis wasn't made royal governor of Georgia until 1757.

4. Duncan, quoted in Janet I. Rodekohr, "The Beauty of Tough Turf," *University of Georgia Research Magazine* 29 (Summer 2000).

5. Charles V. Piper, *Forage Plants and Their Culture* (New York: Macmillan, 1914), 244.

6. Lyman Carrier, *The Beginnings of Agriculture in America* (New York: McGraw-Hill, 1923), 251.

7. Mitich, "Colonel Johnson's Grass: Johnson."

8. Victor R. Boswell, "Our Vegetable Travelers," *National Geographic* 96 (August 1949): 194.

9. David Rhodes, outline course material for Horticulture 410, "Okra–HORT410–Vegetable Crops," Purdue University, http://www.hort.purdue.edu/rhodcv/hort410/okra/okra.htm; Agricultural Marketing Service, "USDA Revises Grading Standards for Frozen Okra," news release, September 27, 1999, http://www.ams.usda.gov/news/252c.htm (accessed February 26, 2004).

10. Eric P. Prostko, Enrique Rosales-Robles, and James M. Chandler, "Wild Okra Control with Bromoxynil and Pyrithiobac," *Journal of Cotton Science* 2 (1998): 100–103, 100.

11. David Livingstone, *Missionary Travels and Researches in South Africa* (Project Gutenberg, 1997), chap. 2, http://ibiblio.org/gutenberg/etext97/mtrav10.txt (accessed March 10, 2003).

12. Native Seeds, catalog listing, http://www.nativeseeds.org (information for Watermelon; accessed March 10, 2003); U.S. Department of Agriculture, National Resources Conservation Service, Plants Database, http://plants.usda.gov (information for *Citrullus lanatus*; accessed March 10, 2003).

13. Purdue University Center for New Crops and Plant Products, New Crops Resource Online Program, "Sesame" (factsheet, http://www.hort.purdue.edu/newcrop/med-aro/factsheets/SESAME.html; accessed March 10, 2003).

14. Francis Porcher, *Resources of the Southern Fields and Forests, Medical, Economical, and Agricultural. Being also a Medical Botany of the Confederate States; with Practical Information on the Useful Properties of the Trees, Plants, and Shrubs* (Charleston, S.C.: Evans and Cogswell, 1863), 194–95.

15. Lewis Gray and Esther Thompson, *History of Agriculture in the Southern United States to 1860*, vol. 1 (Washington, D.C.: Carnegie Institute of Washington, 1933), 194.

16. U.S. Department of Agriculture, "Crop Profile for Sesame in United States," April 2000, online at http://cipm.ncsu.edu/cropprofiles/docs/ussesame.html#N_3_ (accessed March 10, 2003).

17. Raleigh H. Merritt, *From Captivity to Fame; or, Life of George Washington Carver* (Boston: Meador, 1929), 162; Herbert Myrick, *The Book of Corn* (New York: Orange Judd, 1903), 168; Matt. 13: 24–30.

18. Carrier, *The Beginnings of Agriculture*, 250.

19. USDA, NRCS, Plants Database (information for *Vigna unguiculata*; accessed March 11, 2003).

20. L. H. Bailey, *Cyclopedia of American Agriculture: A Popular Survey of Agricultural Conditions, Practices and Ideals in the United States and Canada*, vol. 2 (New York: Macmillan, 1909), 266.

21. Texas Department of Transportation, "The History of the Black-Eyed Pea" (excerpts from *Texas Highways Magazine*, July 1994), http://www.athenstx.org/History.htm (accessed March 11, 2003).

22. International Institute of Tropical Agriculture, "Cowpea," http://www.iita.org/crop/cowpea.htm (accessed March 11, 2003).

23. University of California Sustainable Agriculture Research and Education Program Online Cover Crop Database, http://www.sarep.ucdavis.edu/cgi-bin/CCrop.exe (information for cowpea; accessed March 11, 2003).

24. James A. Duke, *Handbook of Energy Crops* (West Lafayette, Ind.: Center for New Crops and Plants Products, Purdue University, 1983), e-book only, http://www.hort.pur-

due.edu/newcrop/duke_energy/dukeindex.html (information for *Vigna unguiculata* (L.) Walp. ssp. *Unguiculata*; accessed March 11, 2003); Boswell, "Our Vegetable Travelers."

25. K. O. Rachie and R. T. Wurster, "The Potential of Pigeon Pea (*Cajanus cajan* Millsp) as a Horticultural Crop in East Africa," *Acta Horticulturae* (ISHS) 21 (1971): 172–78, http://www.actahort.org/books/21/21_28.htm (accessed March 11, 2003).

26. Karen Hess, *The Carolina Rice Kitchen* (Columbia: University of South Carolina Press, 1992), 99.

27. Duke, *Handbook of Energy Crops*, n.p.

28. "Traditional Food: What Zimbabweans Eat," *Zimbabwe Magazine* (February 2000), http://www.zimbabwebiz.com/zimbiz/magazine/02–2000/feb01.htm (accessed March 11, 2003).

A Green Nightmare

1. Figures taken from Garden Club of America, "The New American Lawn," http://www.gcamerica.org/pamphlets/lawnbrochure.html; *Smaller American Lawns Today*, "Environmental Impacts of Intensive Lawn Maintenance," http://camel.conncoll.edu/ccrec/greennet/arbo/salt/salt.html (accessed March 11, 2003).

2. *Gardenvisit.com Garden Guide*, "Virginian Garden Design in America," http://www.gardenvisit.com/got/18/2.htm; British Broadcasting Corporation, "Edward Beard Budding," http://www.bbc.co.uk/history/historic_figures/budding_edwin_beard.shtml (accessed March 11, 2003).

3. Paul Hashagen, "Firefighting in Colonial America," *Firehouse* (September 1998), http://www.firehouse.com/magazine/american/colonial2.html (accessed March 11, 2003).

4. Quoted from *Rural Essays* (New York: R. Worthington, 1856), 152.

5. Sarah Faiks, Jarrett Kest, Amanda Szot, Molly Vendura, "Revisiting Riverside: A Frederick Law Olmsted Community," (master's thesis, University of Michigan, 2001), http://www.snre.umich.edu/ecomgt/pubs/riverside.htm (accessed March 10, 2003); Frank J. Scott, *The Art of Beautifying Suburban Home Grounds* (New York: D. Appleton, 1870), 108, 60–61.

6. Scott, *The Art of Beautifying*, 107, 110.

7. Ibid., 107.

8. Scott's grass list in *The Art of Beautifying*, 110.

9. Lyman Carrier, *The Beginnings of Agriculture in America* (New York: McGraw-Hill, 1923), 241.

10. John James Ingalls, "In Praise of Blue Grass," *Kansas Magazine* (1872), reprinted in *Grass*, Yearbook of Agriculture series (Washington, D.C.: U.S. Government Printing Office, 1948).

11. Strickland, quoted in Charles V. Piper, *Forage Plants and Their Culture* (New York: Macmillan, 1914), 412.

12. Henry W. Longfellow, "The White-Man's Foot," in *The Song of Hiawatha: Complete Poetical Works* (Boston: Houghton-Mifflin, 1920), 162; Jefferson and Crevecoeur quotes taken from Alfred W. Crosby, "Ecological Imperialism: The Overseas Migration

of Western Europeans as a Biological Phenomenon," *Texas Quarterly* 21 (Spring 1978): 103–17; plantain from Grieve, *A Modern Herbal* (New York: Hafner Publishing, 1971), 2: 643–44; and Alexander C. Martin, *Weeds: A Golden Guide* (New York: Golden Press / Racine, Wis.: Western, 1987), 111–12.

13. Williams letter cited in Carrier, *The Beginnings of Agriculture*, 241; Piper, *Forage Plants and Their Culture*, 171, claims it is a native.

14. Porcher, *Resources*, 562; Scott, *The Art of Beautifying*, 110; James Buckman, *Science and Practice in Farm Cultivation* (London: Robert Hardwicke, 1865), 69.

15. Michigan Department of Agriculture, "Food Safety Advisory: Mexican Vanilla Extract May Be Lethal," December 11, 1997, news release online at http://www.mda. state.mi.us/newsarchive/archive/1997/1297/121197b.html (accessed March 11, 2003); R. B. Hillman, outline course material for Poisonous Plants, VtMed 647, "Moldy Sweet-clover Poisoning," Cornell University (September 2002), http://web.vet.cornell.edu/ CVM/HANDOUTS/plants/SweetClover.html (accessed March 11, 2003).

16. American Garden Club, quoted in *American-lawns*, "The History of Lawns in America," http://www.american-lawns.com/lawns/lawn_history.html (accessed March 10, 2003).

17. *American-lawns*, "The History of Lawns in America."

18. U.S. Department of Agriculture, National Resources Conservation Service, Plants Database, http://plants.usda.gov (information for *Festuca* L. *fescue*; accessed April 15, 2003).

19. West Virginia University Extension Service, "Factsheet: The Tall Fescue Endophyte Story," http://www.caf.wvu.edu/~forage/fescue_endophtye/Story.htm (accessed April 13, 2003); Randy Weckman, "A Plant Pathologist Takes on Tall Fescue's Endophyte," *Magazine*, University of Kentucky College of Agriculture (Winter/Spring 2003), http://www.ca.uky.edu/agc/magazine/2003/WinterSpring2003/Articles/htmlfiles/plant_pathologist.htm; D. Hannaway and others, *Tall Fescue* (Festuca arundinacea *Schreb.*) Pacific Northwest Extension PNW 504 (Corvallis, Org.: Oregon State University, 1999), http://www.css.orst.edu/News/Publicat/Hannaway/TallFes/complete.html (accessed April 15, 2003).

20. That Jesus' adulterous weeds were, in fact, *Lolium temulentum* is merely a modern supposition; their actual identification is unknown. But *L. temulentum* is a notorious contaminant of Middle Eastern wheat.

21. Porcher, *Resources*, 564.

22. M. Grieve, "Darnel, Bearded," in *A Modern Herbal* (New York: Dover, 1971).

23. Martin Adjei, "Controlling Mole Crickets on Bahiagrass Pasture with Nematodes," Article of the Month series, University of Florida, Institute of Food and Agricultural Science, June 2000, http://sfbfp.ifas.ufl.edu/A6–00.html (accessed April 17, 2003); Floridaturf.com, "Bahiagrass," http://www.floridaturf.com/index.html (accessed April 16, 2003).

24. J. D. Sauer, "Revision of *Stenotaphrum* (Gramineae: Paniceae) with Attention to Its Historical Geography," *Brittonia* 24 (1972): 202–22, quoted in Philip Busey, "St.

Augustine Grass," in *Turfgrass Biology, Genetics, and Breeding*, ed. M. D. Casler and R. D. Duncan (Hoboken, N.J.: John Wiley and Sons, 2003).

25. Busey, "St. Augustine Grass."

26. *Plant Explorers*, "Frank N. Meyer," http://www.plantexplorers.com/Explorers/Biographies/Meyer/index.html (accessed April 17, 2003); Sandra L. Anagnostakis, "An Historical Reference for Chestnut Introductions into North America," Connecticut Agricultural Experiment Station (factsheet PP001 [1/03], http://www.caes.state.ct.us/FactSheetFiles/PlantPathology/fspp001f.htm; accessed April 17, 2003).

27. Richard L. Duble, "Zoysiagrass," Texas Agricultural Extension Service, http://aggie-horticulture.tamu.edu/PLANTanswers/turf/publications/zoysia.html (accessed April 18, 2003); Gilbert Landry, *Lawns in Georgia*, Bulletin 773, Cooperative Extension Service, University of Georgia.

28. Floridaturf.com, "History of Turf Production: The Early Years," http://www.floridaturf.com/sodearly.htm (accessed April 17, 2003); "Scientist to Survey Grass Roots," *Augusta Chronicle*, August 23, 1999, http://www.augustachronicle.com/stories/082399/tec_LG0404–2.000.shtml (accessed April 21, 2003).

29. Ritters Florist and Nurseries, catalog listing, http://www.4ritter.com/Ornamental grasses.htm (information for China love grass; accessed April 21, 2003).

A Sow's Ear from a Silk Purse

1. Charles Sargent, "Moraceae," in *Silva of North America*, vol. 5 (New York, 1947), v, viin1, 76.

2. William Strachey, quoted in Sargent, *Silva of North America*, 81.

3. Sargeant, *Silva of North America*, 81.

4. Ibid., 76.

5. Historic New Harmony, http://www.ulib.iupui.edu/kade/newharmony/home.html; Marilyn Smith, "The Northampton Silk Project," online history project, Smith College, 2002, http://www.smith.edu/hsc/silk/ (accessed February 12, 2004).

6. Kent Historical Society, "John Brown: Citizen of Kent," http://www.geocities.com/Heartland/Park/9580/brown.html (accessed February 12, 2004).

7. Thomas Jefferson, "Query V.I.," in *Notes on the State of Virginia*, ed. William Peden (Chapel Hill: University of North Carolina Press, 1955), 42.

8. Marc Leepson, "Stealing Monticello," in *Saving Monticello: The Levy Family's Epic Quest to Rescue the House That Jefferson Built* (New York: Simon and Schuster, 2002).

9. M. M. Graff, *The Men Who Made Central Park* (New York: Greensword Foundation, 1982).

10. S. A. Spongberg, *A Reunion of Trees* (Cambridge, Mass.: Harvard University Press, 1990).

11. "The Ailanthus, or 'Tree of Heaven,'" *New York Times*, December 27, 1852.

12. Henry James, *Washington Square*, in *Novels: 1881–1886* (New York: Library of America, 1985), 15–16.

13. Andrew Jackson Downing, "Shade-Trees in Cities," in *Rural Essays* (New York: R. Worthington, 1856), 311.

14. Isaac Newton, Introduction, in U.S. Department of Agriculture, 1862 Report of the Commissioner of Agriculture (Washington, D.C.: Government Printing Office, 1863).

15. Betty Smith, Preface, *A Tree Grows in Brooklyn* (Philadelphia: Blakiston, 1943).

16. "The Ailanthus, or 'Tree of Heaven,'" *New York Times*, December 27, 1852.

17. Trouvelot, quoted in Sue Hubbell, *Broadsides from the Other Orders* (New York: Random House, 1993), 179.

18. Ibid., 180.

19. Sandy Liebhold, "Gypsy Moth in North America," U.S. Department of Agriculture Forest Service, Northeastern Research Station (1998), http://www.fs.fed.us/ne/morgantown/4557/gmoth/ (accessed February 18, 2004); and M. McManus and others, *Gypsy Moth*, Forest Insect and Disease Leaflet 162 (U.S. Department of Agriculture Forest Service, 1980).

20. The 1920 contamination reported by Environmental Education for Kids (EEK!), "Alien Invasion: Gypsy Moth Time Line in North America," http://www.dnr.state.wi.us/org/caer/ce/eek/earth/invade.htm; and 1993 contamination summarized by *Gypsy Moth in Virginia*, "Asian Gypsy Moth Project," http://www.gypsymoth.ento.vt.edu/asian.html (accessed March 4, 2004).

21. *Gypsy Moth in Virginia*, http://www.gypsymoth.ento.vt.edu/vagm/ (accessed February 20, 2004).

22. C. R. Weeden and others, eds., *Biological Control: A Guide to Natural Enemies in North America* (Ithaca, N.Y.: Cornell University, 2002), e-book only, http://www.nysaes.cornell.edu/ent/biocontrol/ (accessed November 29, 2004).

23. Ibid.

24. Ibid.

25. Joseph S. Elkington, Dylan Parry, and George Boettner, "Introduced Tachinids Explain Decline of Invasive Browntail Moth" (paper presented at the Entomological Society of America 2001 annual meeting, San Diego), abstract, http://esa.confex.com/esa/2001/techprogram/paper_2712.htm (accessed February 12, 2004).

26. *Gypsy Moth in Virginia* Web site.

27. Ibid.

Psychedelic Gardens

1. Researchers point to ergot as the possible cause of such diverse events as the mass possession of the nuns of Loudon; the Salem, Massachusetts, witch craze; Peter the Great's 1722 defeat at Constantinople; the more manic moments of the French Revolution; and the 1951 poisoning of hundreds of French who ate tainted bread.

2. Valloir chose St. Anthony because the third-century Egyptian saint's bones wound up in nearby Dauphine following their disinterment, first in Egypt to escape the Saracens, then in Constantinople as Crusader booty. Anthony's temptations were famous in Europe, attracting the brushes of Bosch, Bruegel, Dali, and Ernst, among others.

3. Albert Hofmann, "A Challenging Question and My Answer," in *The Road to Eleusis: Unveiling the Secrets of the Mysteries*, ed. R. Gordon Wasson, A. Hofmann, and Carl A. P. Ruck (New York: Harcourt, Brace, Jovanovich, 1980), 9. Hofmann notes that Hosack was well connected enough to have accompanied Alexander Hamilton on the morning of his duel with Aaron Burr. Stearns was himself a prominent doctor. In addition to controlling postpartum hemorrhages, ergot also controls migraines.

4. Albert Hofmann, *LSD: My Problem Child* (New York: McGraw-Hill, 1980).

5. Francisco Hernandez, *Rerum Medicarum Novae Hispaniae Thesaurus seu Plantarum, Animalium Mineralium Mexicanorum Historia* (Rome, 1651), quoted in Richard E. Schultes, "A Contribution to Our Knowledge of *Rivea corymbosa*, the Narcotic Ololiuqui of the Aztecs," Botanical Museum, Harvard University, 1941, and quoted in Hofmann, *LSD*.

6. Hofmann, *LSD*.

7. The scientific names remain confusing, but *Rivea corymbosa* and *Turbina corymbosa* are the same species, which Linnaeus originally named *Convolvulus corymbosa* and was once upon a time classed as *Ipomoea corymbosa*. According to many morning glory experts, *Ipomoea tricolor* and *I. violacea* are also identical. See R. Gordon Wasson, "The Hallucinogenic Fungi of Mexico: An Inquiry into the Origins of the Religious Idea among Primitive Peoples," *Botanical Museum Leaflets* 19, no. 7 (1961): 152–53, and R. Gordon Wasson, "Notes on the Present Status of *Ololiuhqui* and the Other Hallucinogens of Mexico," *Botanical Museum Leaflets* 20, no. 6 (1963): 161–212.

8. See both U.S. Department of Agriculture, National Resources Conservation Service, Plants Database, http://plants.usda.gov (information for *Ipomoea tricolor*), and U.S. Department of Agriculture, Agricultural Research Service, National Genetic Resources Program, Germplasm Resources Information Network (GRIN), http://www.ars-grin.gov/cgi-bin/npgs/html/index.pl (information for *Ipomoea tricolor*; accessed December 9, 2003).

9. See, for example, information on *Ipomoea tricolor* history at Morning Glory Corner, "The *Ipomoea tricolor* Story," http://www.exoticplants.org.uk/Ipomoea_tricolor.html (accessed December 8, 2003).

10. Charles Savage, Willis W. Harman, and James Fadiman, "Morning Glories: The Naturally Occurring Psychedelics, Related to LSD," in *Altered States of Consciousness: A Book of Readings*, ed. Charles Tart (New York: John Wiley, 1969).

11. L. Frank Baum, *The Wonderful Wizard of Oz* (New York: Dover, 1963), 93.

12. Alfred W. McCoy, *The Politics of Heroin in Southeast Asia* (New York: Laurence Hill, 1972).

13. Hosea Ballou Morse, *The Trade and Administration of China* (London and New York: Longmans, Green, 1913), 355; and David Edward Owen, *British Opium Policy in China and India* (New Haven, Conn.: Yale University Press, 1934), 80, cited in McCoy, *Politics of Heroin*, 80–89.

14. The Delano story comes from Geoffrey C. Ward, "A Fair, Honorable, and Legitimate Trade," *American Heritage* 37, no. 5 (1986): 49–64; the other fortune hunters from Jacques M. Downs, *The Golden Ghetto: The American Commercial Community at*

Canton and the Shaping of American China Policy, 1784–1844 (Bethlehem: Lehigh University Press, 1997); Indian opium figures come from Earley V. Wilcox, *Tropical Agriculture* (London: D. Appleton, 1916), 218.

15. David L. Cowen and Donald F. Kent, "Medical and Pharmaceutical Practice in 1854," *Pharmacy in History* 39, no. 3 (1997): 91–100.

16. Samuel Taylor Coleridge, "Kubla Khan," in *The Norton Anthology of English Literature*, 7th ed., vol. 2, ed. M. H. Abrams (New York: W. W. Norton, 2000), 439–40.

17. Thomas De Quincey, *Confessions of an English Opium Eater and Selected Essays*, ed. David Masson (New York: A. C. Burt, 1856), 157, 186.

18. Wilcox, *Tropical Agriculture*, 218.

19. F. E. Oliver, *The Use and Abuse of Opium*, Massachusetts State Board of Health, 3rd Annual Report (Boston: Wright and Potter, 1872), 162–77.

20. Gerald Starkey, "The Use and Abuse of Opiates and Amphetamines," in *Drug Dependence and Abuse Resource Book*, ed. Patrick Healy and James Manak (Chicago: National District Attorneys Association, 1971), 481–84, provides the graphic description, while David Courtwright, "Opiate Addiction as a Consequence of the Civil War," *Civil War History* 24, no. 1 (1978): 105–6, guesstimates the use of hypodermics; both cited in Jerry Mandel, "The Mythical Roots of U.S. Drug Policy: Soldier's Disease and Addicts in the Civil War," Schaeffer Library of Drug Policy, http://www.druglibrary.org/schaffer/History/soldis.htm (accessed December 10, 2003).

21. International Society of Nephrology, "Bibliography of Papers on the History of Nephrology," part 5.1, http://www.isn-online.org (accessed November 29, 2004).

22. Ryan J. Huxtable and Stephan K. W. Schwarz, "The Isolation of Morphine—First Principles in Science and Ethics," *Molecular Interventions* 1 (2001): 189–91. People being people, Sertürner's priority has been challenged by two Frenchmen, whose cause, however, has not yet won majority.

23. Flora of North America Editorial Committee, eds., "*Papaver somniferum*," in *Flora of North America North of Mexico* (New York: Oxford University Press, 1993).

24. King James Bible, Ex. 30:23–25, Sg. 4:14, Jer. 6:20, Ezek. 27:19. While most Bibles translate the Hebrew word *kaneh* as calamus, some argue that the Hebrew refers to lemongrass, *Cymbopogon citrates*. Both are aromatic trade items, and either plant could be correct. C. Plinius Secundus, *The Historie of the World*, bk. 12, trans. by Philemon Holland (1601), 356–79. Robert Beverley, *History of Virginia* (Richmond, 1855).

25. Gerard, quoted in Chelsie Vandaveer, "How Was the Biblical Plant Used?" (2002), *Killerplants.com*, http://www.killerplants.com/herbal-folklore/20020513.asp; and M. Grieve, "Sedge, Sweet," *A Modern Herbal* (New York: Dover, 1971).

26. Charles Boewe, "Constantine Samuel Rafinesque," in *The Kentucky Encyclopedia* (Lexington: University Press of Kentucky, 1992).

27. Confederate States of America, *Standard Supply Table of the Indigenous Remedies for Field Service and the Sick in General Hospitals* (elec. ed., Chapel Hill: University of North Carolina, 2000), http://docsouth.unc.edu/imls/remedies/remedies.html (accessed November 6, 2003).

28. The quote comes from a sample ephedra warning letter that objects to the presence of ephedra in a drug, U.S. Food and Drug Administration, Department of Health and Human Services, "Warning Letter," http://www.fda.gov/bbs/topics/NEWS/ephedra/warningsample.html (accessed November 6, 2003).

29. *Herballove.com*, "Calamus," http://www.herbolove.com/library/herbal/calamus.asp (accessed November 6, 2003).

30. "Our Apathy to Gardens Astounds English Expert," *New York Times*, November 9, 1913.

31. Beverley, *The History of Virginia*, 139. Bacon's Rebellion occurred in 1706. The "coolness" of jimsonweed alludes to the now-discarded doctrine of the four humours, which had the properties of being wet, dry, hot, or cold.

32. Kirsten Bonde, "The Genus Datura: From Research Subject to Powerful Hallucinogen," *Ethnobotanical Leaflets* (Winter 1998), http://www.siu.edu/~ebl/leaflets/datura.htm (accessed November 7, 2003).

33. Charles Thompson, appendix to Thomas Jefferson, *Notes on the State of Virginia*, ed. William Peden (Chapel Hill: University of North Carolina Press, 1982), 199. Philadelphian Thompson (1729–1824) served twenty-five years as secretary to the Continental Congress, designed the Great Seal of the United States, safeguarded the Declaration of Independence throughout the Revolution, and advocated the rights of Indians and women and the abolition of slavery. Dr. Bond is Thomas Bond (1712–1784), a native of Philadelphia who founded, with Benjamin Franklin's help, the Pennsylvania Hospital in 1751 and, although sixty years old, organized the medical department of the newly formed Continental Army.

34. Thomas Jefferson, "Letter to Dr. Samuel Brown, July 14, 1813," in *The Writings of Thomas Jefferson*, vol. 13, ed. Albert E. Bergh (Washington, D.C.: Thomas Jefferson Memorial Association, 1907).

35. Joseph Dalton Hooker, *Himalayan Journals, or Notes of a Naturalist* (Project Gutenberg, 2004), chap. 3, http://www.ibiblio.org/gutenberg/cdproject/cd/etext04/hmjnc11h/chap3.html (accessed November 9, 2003).

36. Hooker, *Himalayan Journals*; Mark Twain, *Following the Equator* (New York: Harper and Brothers, 1899); Kevin Rushby, *Children of Kali* (New York: Walker, 2002); and review of *Children of Kali* in the *Guardian*, January 18, 2003, http://books.guardian.co.uk/review/story/0,12084,876098,00.html (accessed November 9, 2003).

37. Jules Verne, *Around the World in Eighty Days*, in *The Omnibus Jules Verne* (New York: Blue Ribbon, 1931), 938.

38. Eugene Sue, "The Ambuscade," in *The Wandering Jew* (Project Gutenberg, 2002), bk. 2, chap. 22, http://ibiblio.org/gutenberg/etext02/es02v11.txt (accessed November 9, 2003); *Guardian*, review of *Children of Kali*.

39. *Guardian*, review of *Children of Kali*.

40. Lyster H. Dewey, "Hemp," in *Yearbook of the United States Department of Agriculture* (Washington, D.C.: Government Printing Office, 1913), 283–346.

41. Oregon NORML, "Hemp for Victory," http://www.pdxnorml.org/Hemp_for_Victory_1942.html (accessed November 29, 2004).

42. C. A. Dodge, *A Report on the Culture of Hemp and Jute in the United States*, U.S. Department of Agriculture Office of Fiber Investigations, Report No. 8 (1896), 21.

43. Porcher, *Resources*, 273–74.

44. J. P. Remington, George B. Wood, and others, eds., *The Dispensatory of the United States of America* (Philadelphia: Lippincott, 1918).

45. Marco Polo, *The Travels of Marco Polo* (New York: Grosset and Dunlap, 1942), 48.

46. See, for example, articles published online at National Organization for the Reform of Marijuana Laws (NORML) Web site, http://www.norml.org.

Bad Air and Worse Science

1. Robert S. Desowitz, *The Malaria Capers* (New York: W. W. Norton, 1991), 128–65.

2. Centers for Disease Control, "Malaria: General Information," http://www.cdc.gov/travel/malinfo.htm (accessed February 26, 2004).

3. "Home and Foreign Gossip," *Harper's Weekly* (January 30, 1875): 95.

4. Etymology and Walpole's quote from *Oxford English Dictionary* (OED), s.v. "Malaria" (New York: Oxford University Press, 1989).

5. Desowitz, *Malaria Capers*, 200–201.

6. Ibid., 202–6.

7. William S. Pierpoint, "Edward Stone and Edmund Stone: Confused Identities Resolved," *Notes and Records of the Royal Society of London* 51, no. 2 (1997): 211–17.

8. Mary Bellis, "History of Aspirin," About.com, http://inventors.about.com/library/inventors/blaspirin.htm (accessed February 12, 2004).

9. Charles B. Coale, "History of the Weeping Willow," in *The Life and Adventures of Wilburn Waters* (Johnson City, Tenn.: Overmountain Press, 1994).

10. M. Grieve, "Eucalyptus," in *A Modern Herbal* (New York: Dover, 1971); Leigh Rayment, "Antoine Raymond Joseph de Bruni D'Entrecasteaux," *Discoverers Web*, http://www.win.tue.nl/~engels/discovery/entrecast.html; Jane Resture, "The Voyages of d'Entrecasteaux," *Oceania* Web site, http://www.janesoceania.com/oceania_dentrecasteaux/ (accessed February 19, 2004). According to the OED, the name *eucalyptus* come from Greek for well-covered, referring to the flowers' being protected by a cover prior to opening.

11. Ian Tyrell, *True Gardens of the Gods* (Berkeley: University of California Press, 1999), 26–30; and Robert L. Santos, "The Early Years," in *The Eucalyptus of California: Seeds of Good or Seeds of Evil* (Denair, Calif.: Ally-Cass, 1997).

12. "Eucalyptus a Febrifuge," *Harper's New Monthly Magazine* 44 (December 1871): 630.

13. A. J. H. Crespi, "Eucalyptus, Pine, and Camphor Forests," *Littell's Living Age* 183 (1889): 115.

14. "The Eucalyptus in the Roman Campagna," *Littell's Living Age* (April–June 1881): 376.

15. Santos, "The Early Years."

16. Ibid.

17. Ibid.

18. Ibid.

19. Parker Ranch Web site, http://www.parkerranch.com; John Duchemin, "The Troubled Trust of Parker Ranch," *Pacific Business News* (September 22, 2000), http://pacific.bizjournals.com/pacific/stories/2000/09/25/story1.html; "Hawaii: Actions against Eucalyptus Expansion," *World Rainforest Movement Bulletin* (May 2000), http://www.wrm.org.uy/bulletin/34/Hawaii.html (accessed February 19, 2004).

20. Charles F. Millspaugh, *American Medicinal Plants: An Illustrated and Descriptive Guide to the American Plants Used as Homoeopathic Remedies: Their History, Preparation, Chemistry and Physiological Effects* (New York: Boericke and Tafel, 1887), 35.

21. "Our Upas Trees," *New York Times*, July 2, 1855; "A Friend of the Ailanthus," *New York Times*, July 10, 1855; "Ailanthus Again," *New York Times*, July 13, 1855; and Millspaugh, *American Medicinal Plants*.

22. Dr. Foersch, article in *London Magazine* (December 1783): 512–17, quoted in H. Yule, "Upas," *Hobson-Jobson Dictionary* (London, 1886); Richard Gustafson, "The Upas Tree: Pushkin and Erasmus Darwin," *PMLA* (March 1960): 102–3.

23. James Richardson, "Curiosities of Plant Life," *Scribner's Monthly* (April 1872): 655.

24. J. A. Duke, "Promising Phytomedicinals," in *Advances in New Crops*, ed. J. Janick and J. E. Simon (Portland, Ore.: Timber Press, 1990), 491–98.

25. Harvey Felter and John Lloyd, *King's American Dispensatory* (Sanby, Ore.: Eclectic Medical Productions, 1898).

26. J. E. Simon and others, "*Artemisia annua* L., A Promising Aromatic and Medicinal," in *Advances in New Crops*, ed. J. Janick and J. E. Simon (Portland, Ore.: Timber Press, 1990), 522–26.

Bioterror

1. William Trent, "Journal," *Pen Pictures of Early Western Pennsylvania*, ed. John W. Harpster (Pittsburgh: University of Pittsburgh Press, 1938), 103–4.

2. The story, the quotes, and various attributions of blame are easily found. E. Stearn and A. Stearn, "Smallpox Immunization of the Amerindian," *Bulletin of the History of Medicine* 13 (1939): 601–13. Also cited in Elizabeth A. Fenn, *Pox Americana: The Great Smallpox Epidemic of 1775* (New York: Hill and Wang, 2001), 88.

3. *The Cholera Epidemic of 1873 in the United States*, U.S. Executive Document Number 95 (Washington, D.C.: Government Printing Office, 1875), quoted in R. G. Robertson, *Rotting Face* (Caldwell, Idaho: Caxton, 2001), 300.

4. Quoted in Geoffrey Plank, *An Unsettled Conquest: The British Campaign against the Peoples of Acadia* (Philadelphia: University of Pennsylvania Press, 2000); quoted in Daniel N. Paul, *We Were Not the Savages* (Black Point, N.S.: Fernwood Books, 2001).

5. Fenn, *Pox Americana*, 131–32.

6. Philip J. Pauly, "Fighting the Hessian Fly," *Environmental History* 7, no. 3 (2002): 485–507, www.lib.duke.edu/forest/Pauly.pdf (accessed February 27, 2004).

7. William T. Sherman, "Vicksburg," in *The Memoirs of General W. T. Sherman*, vol. 1 (Project Gutenberg, 2004), http://ibiblio.org/gutenberg/etext01/1shrm12.txt (accessed October 16, 2003).

8. Jeffrey K. Smart, "History of Chemical and Biological Warfare: An American Perspective," in Office of the Surgeon General, Department of the Army, 1997, Virtual Navy Hospital, *Textbook of Military Medicine: Medical Aspects of Chemical and Biological Warfare*, http://www.vnh.org/MedAspChemBioWar/chapters/chapter_2.htm#PRE (accessed October 23, 2003).

9. U.S. Army General Order No. 100, quoted in A. M. Prentiss, *Chemicals in War: A Treatise on Chemical Warfare* (New York: McGraw-Hill, 1937); quoted in Smart, "History of Chemical and Biological Warfare."

10. Jeffrey Lockwood, "Entomological Warfare: History of the Use of Insects as Weapons of War," *Bulletin of the Entomological Society of America* 33 (1987): 76–82; and R. L. Metcalf and R. A. Metcalf, *Destructive and Useful Insects: Their Habits and Control* (New York: McGraw-Hill, 1993), 14.71.

11. "The Yellow Fever Plot," *New York Times*, May 29, 1865.

12. "Ex-Governor Luke P. Blackburn," obituary, *New York Times*, September 15, 1887.

13. "The Yellow Fever Plot," *New York Times*, May 7, 1865 and May 16, 1865.

14. "The Great Fever Plot," *New York Times*, May 26, 1865; and "The Trial of the Assassins," *New York Times*, May 30, 1865.

15. *Famous Trials*, "Summation of the Hon. John Bingham, Special Judge Advocate in the Lincoln Assassination Conspiracy Trial," http://www.law.umkc.edu/faculty/projects/ftrials/lincolnconspiracy/binghamclose.html (accessed October 24, 2003). Hyams seems to have been a double agent, working for the Confederacy in Canada but also reporting to the Union. He revealed Confederate plans to seize a passenger ferry and free Confederate POWs held on Johnsons Island in Lake Erie; although the ship was seized on September 19, 1864, the rescue failed. See Bootnecks Scots in the Civil War, "Bennett G. Burley, CSN: The Philos Parsons Affair," http://www.scots-in-the-civil-war.net/parsons.htm (accessed October 24, 2003).

16. "General News," *New York Times*, May 22, 1865; and "An Unrepentant Rebel," *New York Times*, August 20, 1879.

17. See the relatively objective Mark Wheelis, "First Shots Fired in Biological Warfare," *Nature* 395 (September 17, 1998): 213; the more alarmist H. P. Aldebari, "The Secret History of Anthrax," *WorldNetDaily* (November 6, 2001), http://www.wnd.com/news/printer-friendly.asp?ARTICLE_ID=25220 (accessed February 26, 2004); and the intentionally scarifying Michael Sayers and Albert Kahn, *Sabotage! The Secret War against America* (New York and London: Harpers, 1942). Sayers and Kahn claim, without substantiation, that German spies killed a repentant Dilger.

18. See also "Cowboys: And Their Alien Habits" for description.

19. Henry Landau, *The Enemy Within: The Inside Story of German Sabotage in America* (New York: Putnam, 1937); Jules Witcover, *Sabotage at Black Tom: Imperial Germany's Secret War in America, 1914–1917* (Chapel Hill, N.C.: Algonquin, 1989); Mark Wheelis, "Biological Sabatoge in WWI," in *Biological and Toxin Weapons: Research, Development and Use from the Middle Ages to 1945* (Oxford: Oxford University Press, 1999), 35–62.

20. "London Youth Died of Anthrax," *New York Times*, September 25, 1930.

21. Ed Regis, *The Biology of Doom* (New York: Henry Holt, 1999), 27–31, 70–74, 224, 235–36.

22. Nicholas D. Kristof, "Japan Confronting Gruesome War Atrocity," *New York Times*, March 17, 1995; Peter Williams and David Wallace, *Unit 731: Japan's Secret Biological Warfare in World War II* (London: Routledge, 1989); Sheldon Harris, *Factories of Death: Japanese Biological Warfare 1932–45 and the American Cover-up* (New York: Routledge, 1994), 3–149 . Williams and Wallace discuss at length the charges of American biological warfare in Korea.

23. Arjun Srinivasan and others, "Glanders in a Military Research Microbiologist," *New England Journal of Medicine* 345, no. 4 (2001): 256–58.

24. Quoted in Regis, *Biology of Doom*, 207.

25. Barbara Hatch Rosenberg, "Anthrax Attacks Pushed Open an Ominous Door," *Los Angeles Times*, September 22, 2002. Rosenberg was chair of the Federation of American Scientists Working Group on Biological Weapons.

Cowboys

1. International Museum of the Horse (IMH), "American Mustang," http://www.imh.org/imh/bw/mustang.html#toc (accessed April 22, 2003).

2. IMH, "American Quarter Horse," (accessed April 22, 2003).

3. Quoted in IMH, "American Mustang."

4. Wild Horse and Burro Freedom Alliance, "Wild Horse Annie and Her Campaign to Save Our Wild Horses/Burros," http://www.savewildhorses.org/annie.htm (accessed April 23, 2003).

5. MHR Viandes Meats, "Horse," http://www.mhr-viandes.com/en/docu/fami/che.htm (accessed April 23, 2003).

6. *Save the Horses*, http://www.savethehorses.com/faqs.html (accessed April 23, 2003).

7. Ibid.

8. Alan M. Hoyt, *History of the Texas Longhorns*, online book, Texas Longhorn Reference Library, Texas Longhorn Showcase, http://www.candyscorral.com/library/HoytHistory/history.htm (accessed November 30, 2004).

9. *The Glory Days*, online book, Texas Longhorn Reference Library, Texas Longhorn Showcase, http://www.candyscorral.com/library/HoytHistory/history.htm (accessed November 30, 2004); and Hoyt, *History of the Texas Longhorns*.

10. Dwight G. Bennett, *Driving Cattle, and Piroplasmosis (Tick Fever)*, online book, Texas Longhorn Reference Library, Texas Longhorn Showcase, http://www.candyscorral. com/library/HoytHistory/history.htm (accessed November 30, 2004); and Committee on Foreign Animal Diseases of the U.S. Animal Health Association, "Babesiosis," in *Foreign Animal Diseases* (Richmond, Va.: U.S. Animal Health Association, 1998).

11. Quoted in Black, "Cattle Tick Fever."

12. Friedrich Katscher, "*Salmonella* or *Smithella*," *Nature* 388 (July 24, 1997): 962; and C. E. Dolman and Richard J. Wolfe, *Suppressing the Diseases of Animals and Man: Theodore D. Smith, Microbiologist* (Cambridge, Mass.: Harvard University, Press, 2003).

13. Neal Black, "Cattle Tick Fever," United States Animal Health Association Web site, http://64.233.179.104/search?q=cache:i5uESocb0N0J:www.usaha.org/history/ century.html+%22Neal+Black%22+%22Animal+Health.%22&hl=en&start=3.

14. Committee on Foreign Animal Diseases, "Babesiosis," in *Foreign Animal Diseases*.

15. Jim Davis and Anna Johnson-Winegar, "The Anthrax Terror: DOD's Number-One Biological Threat," *Aerospace Power Journal* (Winter 2000): 15–29, http://www.air power.maxwell.af.mil/airchronicles/apj/apj00/win00/davis.htm (accessed May 1, 2003).

16. Ibid.

17. Pam Belluck, "Anthrax Outbreak of '57 Felled a Mill but Yielded Answers," *New York Times*, October 27, 2001; P. C. Turnball and others, *Guidelines for the Surveillance and Control of Anthrax in Humans and Animals*, 3d ed. (World Health Organization, 1998); and M. Meselson and others, "The Sverdlovsk Anthrax Outbreak of 1979," *Science* 266, no. 5188 (1994): 1202–8.

18. Evelyn Boswell, "Speaker: Anthrax Studies Hold Promise for Better Treatment," *Discovery Newsletter of Research and Scholarship*, Montana State University at Bozeman (March 2002), http://www.montana.edu/~wwwvr/discovery/DiscMar02/featuredstories2. html (accessed May 1, 2003); Ross E. Milloy, "Anthrax Hides along Cattle Trails of the Old West," *New York Times*, October 29, 2001; Rosie Mestel, "Anthrax's Dogged Detective," *Los Angeles Times*, December 17, 2001.

19. Paul de Kruif, *The Microbe Hunters* (New York: Pocket Books, 1964).

20. K. A .H. Mörner, "Presentation Speech" (acceptance speech for Nobel Prize in Physiology or Medicine 1905), *Nobelprize.org*, http://www.nobel.se/medicine/laureates/ 1905/press.html (accessed May 1, 2003).

21. F. J. Turner, *The Significance of the Frontier in American History* (New York: Henry Holt, 1920), 1.

22. J. D. Burton, "*Maclura pomifera*, Osage-Orange," in *Silvics of North America*, vol 2: *Hardwoods*, Agriculture Handbook 654 (Washington, D.C.: Forest Service, U.S. Department of Agriculture, 1990), http://www.na.fs.fed.us/spfo/pubs/silvics_manual/ Volume_2/maclura/pomifera.htm (accessed May 1, 2003).

23. E. P. Powell, *Hedges, Windbreaks, Shelters and Live Fences: A Treatise on the Planting, Growth, and Management of Hedge Plants for Suburban and Country Homes* (New York: Orange Judd, 1911); and James Conrad, "A Brief History of the Bois d'Arc

Tree" (1994), *Roughing Out the Osage Bow*, http://www.osageorange.com/Roughing_out_T.html (accessed May 1, 2003).

24. Ellwood House and Museum, "History of Barbed Wire," http://www.ellwood house.org/barb_wire (accessed May 1, 2003).

25. F. A. Silcox, "To Insure against Drought, a Vast Plan Takes Shape," *New York Times*, July 29, 1934.

26. Bryce Nelson, "F. D. R.'s 'Trees' Periled," *New York Times*, October 2, 1974.

27. For example, Doug Davis, "Country Music Classics," *Cleveland Country Magazine*, http://www.cwmusic.com/CountryClassics.htm (accessed May 22, 2003), claims confused radio listeners led Nolan to change the lyrics, while "The Sons of the Pioneers," *Welcome to My Country Classics Site*, http://hillbillyman69.tripod.com/welcome-tomycountryclassicssite/id34.html, claims they changed the words to encourage the cowboy motif.

28. Quoted in Max E. Stanton, "'All Things Common': A Comparison of Israeli, Hutterite and Latter-day Saint Communalism" (David O. McKay Lecture, Brigham Young University, Hawaii, 1992), http://w3.byuh.edu/academics/ace/Speeches/Mckay/mckayindex.html (accessed May 24, 2003).

29. Francis Porcher, *Resources of the Southern Fields and Forests, Medical, Economical, and Agricultural. Being also a Medical Botany of the Confederate States; with Practical Information on the Useful Properties of the Trees, Plants, and Shrubs* (Charleston, S.C.: Evans and Cogswell, 1863).

30. Chelsea Vandaveer, *Killerplants.com*, "Plants That Changed History: How Were Plants Used to Make Glass" (2002), http://www.killerplants.com/plants-that-changed-history/20020618.asp (accessed May 23, 2003).

31. *Jamestown Rediscovery*, "A Timeline of Events and References Leading up to and through the Founding of Jamestown," http://www.apva.org/history/timeline.html (accessed May 23, 2003).

32. U.S. Department of Agriculture, Natural Resources Conservation Service, Plants Database (information for *Salsola*; accessed May 22, 2003).

33. Quoted in "Governor Sheldon Advised about Thistles," *New York Times*, September 20, 1895. Hansbrough's program and the weed's noxiousness appear in "The Pest of the Two Dakotas," *New York Times*, February 18, 1894, 16.

34. "Thistles Bring $5 a Ton," *New York Times*, December 1, 1934.

35. "Russina Thistle Growing at U.S. Atom Test Site," *New York Times*, January 5, 1962; and "Tumbleweeds Are Burying a Town in South Dakota," *New York Times*, November 10, 1989.

36. D. W. Cudney and others, "Russian Thistle," *Pest Notes*, University of California, Division of Agriculture and Natural Resources, 7486 (December 2000): 1–3, http://www.ipm.ucdavis.edu/PMG/PESTNOTES/pn7486.html (accessed May 23, 2003).

37. Jan Suszkwi, "Scientists in Montpellier Are Exploring the World for Biological Control Agents," *Agricultural Research Magazine* (April 2001): 10–13, http://www.ars.usda.gov/is/AR/archive/apr01/world0401.pdf (accessed May 23, 2003).

38. California Department of Food and Agriculture, *Encycloweedia*, Noxious Weed Index, http://www.cdfa.ca.gov/phpps/ipc/encycloweedia/encycloweedia_hp.htm (information for Russian Thistle or Common Russian Thistle; accessed May 23, 2003).

. . . and Indians

1. American Museum of Natural History, "Humans and Other Catastrophes," summary of 1997 spring symposium, http://www.amnh.org/science/biodiversity/extinction (accessed April 1, 2003).

2. "Origin of the Tallgrass Prairie," text accompanying online promotion for the documentary *America's Lost Landscape: The Tallgrass Prairie*, New Light Media and the University of Northern Iowa (1995–2004), http://www.uni.edu/~lostland/ (accessed November 30, 2004).

3. Quoted in Doug MacCleery, "The Role of American Indians in Shaping the North American Landscape," Forest History Society, http://www.lib.duke.edu/forest/usfscoll/people/Native%20Americans/AmIndian.html (accessed March 20, 2003).

4. Stephen J. Pyne, *Fire in America: A Cultural History of Wildland and Rural Fire* (Princeton, N.J.: Princeton University Press, 1982), 79–80.

5. Calvin Fremling and Barry Drazkowski, *Ecological, Institutional, and Economic History of the Upper Mississippi River* (N.p.: Resource Studies Center, St. Mary's University of Minnesota, 2000).

6. T. W. Neumann, "Human-Wildlife Competition and the Passenger Pigeon: Population Growth from System Destabilization," *Human Ecology* 4 (1985): 389–410.

7. An internationally recognized dog group, the United Kennel Club maintains an online list at http://ukcdogs.com/breeds/breedlist.shtml.

8. Barbara Andrews, "The Chihuahua," *The Dogplace.com*, http://www.thedogplace.com/Reference/Chihuahua/history.htm (accessed March 20, 2003); Lawrence A. Clayton and others, *The De Soto Chronicles: The Expedition of Hernando De Soto to North America in 1539–1543* (Tuscaloosa: University of Alabama Press, 1993).

9. Hans Zinsser, *Rats, Lice, and History* (New York: Little, Brown, 1984).

10. Samuel Hearne and Philip Turner, *The Journals of Samuel Hearne and Philip Turner* (Toronto: Champlain Society, 1934).

11. Douglas F. Fix, "Rickettsia," *Medical Microbiology*, http://www.cehs.siu.edu/fix/medmicro/ricke.htm (accessed March 20, 2003).

12. Suzanne Austin Alchon, "The Great Killers in Precolumbian America: A Hemispheric Perspective," *Latin American Population History Bulletin* 27 (1997). Ross McPhee, a proponent of the hyperdisease theory of American megafauna extinction, speculates that perhaps lice were the vector that carried lethal diseases across Beringia.

13. Kirkpatrick Sale, *The Conquest of Paradise* (New York: Alfred A. Knopf, 1990).

14. F. M. Rick and others, "Crab Louse Infestation in Pre-Columbian America," *Journal of Parasitology* 88, no. 6 (2002): 1266–67.

15. Parasite and Parasitological Resources, Graphic Images of Parasites index, http://www.biosci.ohio-state.edu/~parasite/images.html (information for *Pediculus humanus,* body lice, and *Phthirus pubis,* pubic, or crab, lice; accessed April 1, 2003).

16. Centers for Disease Control, Laboratory Identification for Parasite of Public Health Concern, http://www.dpd.cdc.gov/dpdx/Default.htm (information for head lice; accessed April 1, 2003).

17. Sevier has his hagiographers ("The Story of John Sevier," *Tennessee Online: Tennessee's Online History Magazine,* http://www.vic.com/tnchron/class/JSevier.htm; accessed April 1, 2003), vilifiers (American Indian Women's Movement and Warrior Society, "The Massacre of My People in Kentucky: The Great Cherokee Children Massacre at Ywahoo Falls," http://www.geocities.com/nativeamericanadvocate/PAGE4; accessed November 30, 2004), and middle-of-the-roaders. See also *Patriot Resource,* History: American Revolutionary Era, "John Sevier," http://www.patriotresource.com/ people/sevier.html (accessed April 1, 2003).

18. Brigham Young, quoted in *Stories Related to the Ancestors of John Hoopes* Web site, "The Bear River Massacre," http://www.angelfire.com/ne/hoopesgenealogy/bear rivermassacre.htm (accessed April 1, 2003). For details regarding the battle, see Mae Perry, "The Northwestern Shoshone," in *The History of Utah's American Indians,* ed. Forrest S. Cuch (Salt Lake City: Utah State University Press, 2000).

19. "Death Runs Riot," ep. 4 of *The West,* PBS, September 1996, selected text online at http://www.pbs.org/weta/thewest/program/episodes/four/whois.htm (accessed April 1, 2003).

20. James E. Quinlan (supposed author), *Tom Quick, the Indian Slayer: And the Pioneers of Minisink and Wawarsink* (Monticello, N.Y.: De Voe and Quinlan, 1851), reprinted as *The Original Life and Adventures of Tom Quick, the Indian Slayer* (Deposit, N.Y.: Deposit Journal, 1894).

21. Centers for Disease Control, "*Escherichia coli* O157: H7" (factsheet, http:// www.cdc.gov/ncidod/dbmd/diseaseinfo/escherichiacoli_g.htm; accessed March 21, 2003); and E. J. Baron and others, "Escherichia coli," *Bailey and Scott's Diagnostic Microbiology,* 9th ed. (St. Louis: C. V. Moseby, 1994).

22. Karl Reinhard, "Diagnosing Ancient Diphyllobothriasis from Chinchorro Mummies," http://www.unl.edu/Reinhard/chinch.html (accessed March 21, 2003).

23. Centers for Disease Control, Parasitic Disease Information, "*Ascaris* Infection" (factsheet, http://www.cdc.gov/ncidod/dpd/parasites/ascaris/factsht_ascaris.htm; accessed April 1, 2003). See also Parasites and Parasitological Resources, "Life Cycle of the *Ascaris* spp.," http://www.biosci.ohio-state.edu/~parasite/lifecycles/ascaris_lifecycle.html (accessed March 21, 2003).

24. Parasites and Parasitological Resources, "*Trichuris* spp. (whipworms)," http:// www.biosci.ohio-state.edu/~parasite/trichuris.html (accessed March 21, 2003).

25. Parasites and Parasitological Resources, "Pinworms (*Enterobius vermicularis, Oxyuris* spp.)," http://www.biosci.ohio-state.edu/~parasite/enterobius.html (accessed March 21, 2003).

26. Ibid.

27. *Herbs2000.com*, "Pau d'Arco, *Tabebuia* spp.," http://www.herbs2000.com/herbs_pau_darco.htm (accessed March 21, 2003); and *Nutrimed Labs Newsletter*, "Guess What's Coming for Dinner! (Internal Parasite Infestation)," http://www.nutrimed.com/WORMS.HTM (accessed March 23, 2003).

28. Walter Fertig, "Are Some Weeds Really Native?" *Castillega* 20, no. 1 (2001), http://uwadmnweb.uwyo.edu/WYNDD/WNPS/Newsletters/March2001WNPSnews.pdf (accessed March 21, 2003).

29. Donald W. Lathrap, "Our Father the Cayman, Our Mother the Gourd: Spinden Revisited, or a Unitary Model for the Emergence of Agriculture in the New World," in *Origins of Agriculture*, ed. C. A. Reed (Hague: Mouton, 1977), 713–751, disputed at *A Mesoamerican Archaeology*, http://www.angelfire.com/zine/meso/meso/lagenaria.html (accessed March 30, 2003). See also Charles B. Heiser, *The Gourd Book* (Norman: University of Oklahoma Press, 1979).

30. Chandler S. Robbins, "Non-Native Birds," in *Our Living Resources: A Report to the Nation on the Distribution, Abundance, and Health of U.S. Plants, Animals, and Ecosystems* (Washington, D.C.: U.S. Department of the Interior, 1995). Daniel H. Botkin, "The Naturalness of Biological Invasions," *Western North American Naturalist* 61, no. 3 (2001): 261–66.

31. Lathrap, "Our Father the Cayman." See also Juan Carrera Colín, "Las botellas de asa y pico de Cotocollao: Discusión preliminar en torno a su origen y evolución," *Antropología Ecuatoriana* 4/5 (1986/1987): 51–61.

32. *Agropecuária Brasil Oriental Ltda* Web site, "About Yerbe Mate," http://www.brasiloriental.com.br/sobre1_i.html (accessed March 30, 2003). See also *Wayne's World: An Online Textbook of Natural History*, Index, http://waynesword.palomar.edu/indxwayn.htm (information for Yerba Mate; accessed March 30, 2003).

33. Glen H. Doran and others, *Florida Archaeology: An Overview* (N.p.: Florida Anthropological Society, 1997).

34. Alexander Wilson, "Purple Martin," *American Ornithologist* (London: Whittaker, Meacher, and Arnot, 1832), quoted in Alexander Sprunt Jr., "Purple Martin, *Progne subis*," *United States National Museum Bulletin* 179 (1942): 489–508.

35. James R. Hill III, "Thanks to Native Americans, Purple Martins Underwent a Complete Tradition Shift," *Purple Martin Update* 8, no. 1 (1998): 8–9.

36. Alvar Nuñez Cabeça de Vaca, *The Relation of Alvar Nuñez Cabeça de Vaca*, trans. by T. Buckingham Smith (Albany: H. C. Murphy, 1871).

37. *Coronado's Exploration into the American Southwest*, "The Mysterious Journey of Friar Marcos de Niza," http://www.psi.edu/coronado/journeyofmarcosdeniza.html (accessed April 5, 2003).

An Entangled Bank

1. Charles Darwin, *On the Origin of Species by Means of Natural Selection* (London: J. Murray, 1859).

2. John Stolarczyk, "History of the Carrot," World Carrot Museum, http://website.lineone.net/~stolarczyk/history2.html; and *Vilmorin Clause & Cie* Web site, "Une histoire et des marques prestigieuses," http://www.vilmorin-clause.com/entreprise/histoire.html (accessed October 10, 2003).

3. Ibid.

4. Ibid.

5. John Riddle, *Contraception and Abortion from the Ancient World to the Renaissance* (Cambridge, Mass.: Harvard University Press, 1992), 59.

6. Riddle, *Contraception and Abortion*, 28–29.

7. AMG Laboratories, "Finally, It's Here. Miss. Sufferers Take Heart. Beta-Carotene," http://www.amgnetwork.com/ms/beta-car.htm (accessed September 29, 2003).

8. BBC News Online, "How 'Cat's Eyes' Helped Change the World," July 23, 2002, http://news.bbc.co.uk/1/hi/uk/2146171.stm (accessed September 29, 2003).

9. Letter from Dr. Gordon Conway to Greenpeace, January, 22, 2001, available online at *Ag BioTech InfoNet*, http://www.biotech-info.net/golden.html (accessed October 10, 2003). This Web site has numerous related articles; among the most helpful are Ingo Potrykus, "The 'Golden Rice' Tale," *AgBio World*; Michel Pollen, "The Great Yellow Hype," *New York Times Magazine*, March 4, 2001; and Tina Hesman, "Bioengineered Rice Loses Glow as Vitamin A Source," *Saint Louis Post-Dispatch*, March 4, 2001. Potrykus is the scientist behind golden rice, Pollen an environmentalist, and Hesman is a reporter.

10. William Carlos Williams, "Queene Anne's Lace," in *The Harper American Literature*, compact ed., ed. Donald McQuade and others (New York: Harper and Row, 1987), 1828.

11. Benjamin Slade, "The Nine Herbs Charm," in *The Anglo-Saxon Minor Poems*, ed. E. van Kirk Dobbie (New York: Columbia University Press, 1942), 119–20.

12. Peter Kalm, *Peter Kalm's Travels in North America*, ed. Adolph Benson (New York: Wilson-Erickson, 1937), 1.64.

13. Plant Conservation Alliance, "Alien Plant Invaders of Natural Areas," http://www.nps.gov/plants/alien/common.htm (accessed October 14, 2003).

14. Glasshouse Works (Stewart, Ohio), online catalog, http://www.glasshouseworks.com/perr-p.html.

15. Nicholas Culpepper, *The English Physitian; or, An Astrologo-Physical Discourse of the Vulgar Herbs of this Nation. Being a Compleat Method of Physick, Whereby a Man May Preserve His Body in Health; or Cure Himself Being Sick for Three Pence Charge, with Such Things Only as Grow in England, They Being Most Fit for English Bodies* (London: Peter Cole, 1652).

16. Culpepper, *A Physicall Directory: A Translation of the London Dispensatory Made by the College of Physicians in London. Being That Book by Which All Apothecaries are Strictly Commanded to Make All Their Physic* (1649). Dylan Warren-Davis, "Nicholas Culpepper—Herbalist of the People," *Traditional Astrologer* 5 (Summer 1994); and Christine Stockwell, "Nicholas Culpepper, the Herbalist," *The Culpepper*

Connection!, http://gen.culpepper.com/places/intl-eng/wakehurst3.htm (accessed October 10, 2003).

17. Warren-Davis, "Nicholas Culpepper."

18. Culpepper, "To the Reader," in *The English Physitian.* See also Stockwell, "Nicholas Culpepper, the Herbalist," and Warren-Davis, "Nicholas Culpepper."

19. *HerbMed,* "*Plantago major,*" http://www.herbmed.org/herbs/Herb12.htm#Category2Herb12; and A. B. Samuelson, "The Traditional Uses, Chemical Constituents and Biological Activities of *Plantago major* L. A Review," *Journal of Ethnopharmacology* 71, nos. 1–2 (2000): 1–21, http://www.ncbi.nlm.nih.gov/entrez/query.fcgi?cmd=Retrieve&db=PubMed&list_uids=10904143&dopt=Abstract&itool=iconabstr (accessed September 30, 2003).

20. *Welcome to the Cig-No Solution* Web site, http://www.ggginc.com/cigno/why.htm; and Clare Baker, International College of Herbal Medicine, Herb of the Month, "*Plantago,*" (May/June 2002), http://herbcollege.com/herbofthemonth.asp?id=41 (accessed October 1, 2003).

21. Body and Fitness, *Health Journal,* "Psyllium," http://www.bodyandfitness.com/Information/Herbal/Research/psyllium.htm; and *Herbs2000* Web site, "Psyllium," http://www.herbs2000.com/herbs/herbs_psyllium.htm (accessed September 30, 2003).

22. V. Hanson and others, "Psyllium," in *Alternative Field Crop Manual,* New Crop Resource Online Program, Purdue University, http://www.hort.purdue.edu/newcrop/afcm/psyllium.html (accessed September 30, 2003).

23. Marcia Dunn, "John Glenn Won't Leave Earth without Metamucil," AP Online, October 27, 1998, http://www.ap.org.

24. U.S. Department of Agriculture, National Resources Conservation Service, Plants Database, http://plants.usda.gov (information for *P. lanceolata, P. major, P. ovata,* and *P. psyllium;* accessed September 30, 2003).

25. Food and Drug Administration, Docket No. 96P-0338, "Food Labeling: Health Claims; Soluble Fiber from Certain Foods and Coronary Heart Disease," *Federal Register* 63, no. 32 (February 1998), http://vm.cfsan.fda.gov/~lrd/fr980218.html (accessed September 30, 2003).

26. D. K. Early, "Amaranth Intercropping Techniques of Andean Quechua Peasants," in *Advances in New Crops,* ed. J. Janick and J. E. Simon (Portland, Ore.: Timber Press, 1990).

27. Paul Gepts and Cristina Mapes, "The Crop of the Day: Amaranth," online handout, http://agronomy.ucdavis.edu/gepts/pb143/crop/amaranth/amaranth.htm (accessed December 1, 2004).

28. Samuel Purchas, *Hakluytus Posthumus, or Purchas His Pilgrimes,* vol. 15 (Glasgow: Maclehose, 1906), 341–44, 412–14.

29. Purchas, *Hakluytus Posthumus,* 442.

30. John Locke, "Of the Beginning of Political Societies," in *Two Treatises of Government,* bk. 2, *Of Civil Government* (London, 1690), sec. 102, chap. 8.

31. Jose de Acosta, *The Naturall and Morall Historie of the East and West Indies,* trans. by Edward Grimston (London: V. Sims, 1604), quoted in *Out of Many: A History of the American People,* 3d ed., vol. 1, ed. J. M. Faragher and others (Boston, 2001).

32. Purchas, *Hakluytus Posthumus,* 341–44.

33. Ibid.

34. Quoted in *"Amaranthus cruentus, Amaranthus hypochondriacus,"* in *Neglected Crops: 1492 from a Different Perspective,* ed. J. E. Hernández Bermejo and J. León (Rome: FAO / United Nations Plant Production and Protection, 1994).

35. Purchas, *Hakluytus Posthumus,* 340, 342–43.

36. Bermejo and León, *"Amaranthus cruentus."*

37. Culpepper, "Amaranthus," in *Culpepper's Complete Herbal* (New York. W. Foulshain, 1932).

38. John Milton, *Paradise Lost,* ed. Merritt Y. Hughes (Garden City, N.Y.: Doubleday, Doran, 1935), 92.

39. Clement of Alexandria, "On the Use of Ointments and Crowns," in *The Anti-Nicene Fathers: Translations of the Writings of the Fathers down to* A.D. 325, trans. Robert Alexander (New York: Christian Literature Company, 1895).

40. M. Eleanor Irwin, "Fair Flowers of Paradise in Clement of Alexandria and Others" (paper presented at the Canadian Society for Patristic Studies, May 24, 1990, Vancouver, B.C.), http://web.odu.edu/webroot/instr/sci/plant.nsf/pages/wreaths (accessed October 11, 2003).

41. D. H. Putnam and others, "Amaranth," in *Alternative Field Crops Manual,* Center for New Crops and Plant Products, Purdue University, January 2000, http://www.hort.purdue.edu/newcrop/afcm/amaranth.html (accessed December 1, 2004); "Grain Amaranth, a Lost Crop of the Americas," Thomas Jefferson Agricultural Institute, http://www.jeffersoninstitute.org/pubs/amaranth.shtml (accessed December 1, 2004).

42. Hans-Martin Buerki, "RE: *Amaranthus retroflexus,*" Thu, 11 Feb 1999 19:34:00 -0800 (PST), Archives, IUCN, The World Conservation Union Web site, http://indaba.iucn.org/archives/aliens-l/wwwmsgs/July98–April99/00000345.htm (accessed October 11, 2003). Buerki cites several authorities for his argument.

House Pests

1. Milton Ellsworth Parker, *Food-Plant Sanitation* (New York: McGraw-Hill, 1948), 171.

2. This and other general information on the American cockroach is taken from Kathyrn A. Barbara, "American Cockroach," *UF/IFAS Featured Creatures,* no. EENY–141 (2000), http://creatures.ifas.ufl.edu/urban/roaches/american_cockroach.htm (accessed January 10, 2004).

3. *Newton's Apple,* Teacher's Guide, "Cockroaches," episode 1008, PBS, http://www.ktca.org/newtons/10/ckroach.html (accessed January 16, 2004).

4. Orkin, Inc., "Cockroaches Linked to Fifty Known Pathogens," press release, April 17, 2003, http://www.orkin.com/pressroom/release2003_0417.asp (accessed January 16, 2004).

5. "Vermin of Democracy Driven Out—Hearst," *New York Times*, October 7, 1906.

6. "A New War—On Vermin," *New York Times*, October 9, 1921.

7. Emmanuel Bourcart and Donald Grant, *Insecticides, Fungicides, and Weedkillers: A Practical Manual on the Diseases of Plants and Their Remedies, for the Use of Manufacturing Chemists, Agriculturists, Arboriculturists and Horticulturists* (London: Scott, Greenwood, 1913), 131–32; Struan Robertson, "Zyklon-B Poison Gas," A History of Jews in Hamburg, http://www.rrz.uni-hamburg.de/rz3a035/ZyklonB.html (accessed January 16, 2004).

8. Steven Valles, "German Cockroach," *UF/IFAS Featured Creatures*, no. EENY-2 (1996), http://creatures.ifas.ufl.edu/urban/roaches/german.htm (accessed January 9, 2004).

9. Kim McCanless, "Oriental Cockroach," *UF/IFAS Featured Creatures*, no. EENY-159 (2000), http://creatures.ifas.ufl.edu/urban/roaches/oriental_cockroach.htm (accessed January 9, 2004).

10. Tom Turpin, "By Any Name, a Cockroach Is Still a Cockroach," Purdue Extension Entomology, November 10, 1994, reissued November 13, 1997, http://www.entm.purdue.edu/entomology/ext/outreach/OSL_files/html/1997/1997-11-13.html (accessed January 16, 2004).

11. See, for example, Barbara Mikkelson and David P. Mikkelson, "La Cucaracha," *Snopes.com Urban Legends Reference*, http://www.snopes.com/horrors/food/tacobell.htm (accessed January 9, 2004).

12. Centers for Disease Control, *Plague Home Page*, http://www.cdc.gov/ncidod/dvbid/plague (accessed January 18, 2004). The Caffa story is well known; see, for example, Melissa Loftus, Alex Sherman, Ashley Quan, and Mieko Griffin, "Path of the Plague," in *The Black Death*, online book, *Insecta Inspecta*, http://www.insecta-inspecta.com/fleas/bdeath/Path.html (accessed February 26, 2004).

13. Daniel Defoe, *A Journal of the Plague Year* (New York: Doubleday, Doran, 1935), 53, 57, 64, 62.

14. Ibid., 76, 209, 123, 204.

15. See Edward Marriott, *Plague* (New York: Metropolitan Books, 2003), for a detailed account of the two men's rivalry.

16. Henry Mayhew, *London Labour and the London Poor*, vol. 3 (London: G. Woodfall, 1851), xx, 8. Mayhew's four volumes are a fascinating compendium of little-known Victorian lore.

17. Mayhew, *London Labour*, vol. 3, 9–20; Beatrix Potter, *The Tale of Samuel Whiskers, or the Roly-Poly Pudding* (London: F. Warne, 1908).

18. Bonnie Tocher Clause, "The Wistar Institute Archives: Rats (Not Mice) and History," *Mendel Newsletter* (February 1998), http://www.amphilsoc.org/library/mendel/1998.htm; Wistar Institute, "History," Wistar Institute Homepage, http://www.wistar.

upenn.edu/about_wistar/history.html (accessed December 2, 2004); Michael Rosenthanl, "Caspar Wistar," American History Project, Palomar College (Summer 2002), http://daphne.palomar.edu/marguello/sum02/hist101/rosendahl280/wistar.htm (accessed January 21, 2004).

19. Brendan A. Maher, "Test Tubes with Tails," *Scientist* 16, no. 3 (2002): 22–23; "Profile: C57BL/6J," *JAX/Notes* no. 438 (July 1989), http://jaxmice.jax.org/library/notes/438b.html (accessed December 2, 2004); Joe Wright, "The Mother of All Lab Mice," *All Things Considered*, National Public Radio, September 18, 2002, http://studentweb.med.harvard.edu/JMW16/html/themotherofalllabmice.html; Michael Stroh, "From Pets to Pests to Tests," *Baltimore Sun*, December 5, 2002, http://pages.slc.edu/~krader/sunarticle.html (accessed January 23, 2004).

20. Lee M. Silver, *Mouse Genetics* (New York: Oxford University Press, 1995).

21. Yunas Bhonoah, "Warfarin—Rat Poison or Wonder Drug," Warfarin Web site, http://www.ch.ic.ac.uk/local/projects/bhonoah/historical.html; and "History of WARF," in *WARF: Fifty Years*, ed. William R. Jordan III., http://www.warf.ws/aboutus/index.jsp?catid=39&subcatid=27.

It Seemed a Good Idea at the Time

1. *Are We There Yet?* Web site, "Shofuso: Pine Breeze Villa," http://www.fieldtrip.com/pa/58785097.htm; Harmon Jolley, "When Kudzu Came to Town," *Chattanoogan.com* (September 1, 2003), http://www.chattanoogan.com/articles/article_40400.asp (accessed February 9, 2004).

2. Richard Mack and Spencer Barrett, *Predicting Invasions of Nonindigenous Plants and Plant Pests* (Washington, D.C.: National Academies Press, 2002), 38.

3. John W. Everest and others, *Kudzu in Alabama: History, Uses, and Control*, pub. no. ANR–0065 (Alabama Cooperative Extension System, 1999), http://www.aces.edu/department/ipm/kudzu.htm; Bonnie Millar, "Kudzu," *Invasive Species and Forest Ecosystem Effects*, Ecology and Social Change, Duke University, http://www.biology.duke.edu/bio217/bmm10/kudzu.htm (accessed February 9, 2004).

4. Gail Clement, "David Grandison Fairchild," *Everglades Biographies*, Reclaiming the Everglades Collection, State University System of Florida, http://everglades.fiu.edu/reclaim/bios/fairchild.html; *DCPages.com*, "Cherry Blossom Festival History," http://dcpages.ari.net/Dccb/cbhist.html (accessed February 9, 2004).

5. Florida Historical Marker Program, "Kudzu Developed Here," http://dhr.dos.state.fl.us/bhp/markers/markers.cfm?ID=washington; Max Shores, "The Amazing Story of Kudzu," online press release, University of Alabama Center for Public Television and Radio, http://www.cptr.ua.edu/kudzu/; David Fairchild, "Reminiscences of Early Plant Introduction Work in South Florida," *Proceedings of the Florida State Horticultural Society* 51 (1938): 11–33.

6. Everest, *Kudzu in Alabama*. Kerry O. Britton and others, "Kudzu," in *Biological Control of Invasive Plants in the Eastern United States*, ed. R. van Driesche and others, U.S. Department of Agriculture Forest Service Publication FHTET-2002–04 (2002),

http://www.invasive.org/eastern/biocontrol/pdf/25.Kudzu.pdf and http://www.garden-banter.co.uk/archive/55/2003/07/2/36237 (accessed February 9, 2004).

7. Everest, *Kudzu in Alabama*, and Shores, "The Amazing Story of Kudzu."

8. Leo Nico and Erynn Maynard, "*Cyprinus carpio*," (factsheet, U.S. Geological Survey, Nonindigenous Aquatic Species Database, http://nas.er.usgs.gov/queries; accessed February 5, 2004).

9. National Aquarium in Washington, D.C., http://www.nationalaquarium.com/involved.html; Al Kowaleski, "Carp in North America: A Brief History," Carp Anglers Group, http://www.carpanglersgroup.com/northamericancarphistory.html (accessed February 5, 2004); Nico and Maynard, "*Cyprinus carpio*" (accessed February 5, 2004).

10. Duke of Argyll, "About Rejected Fishes," *New York Times*, July 25, 1880; Rudolph Hessel, "Carp for Open Waters," *Chicago Field*, quoted in *New York Times*, August 15, 1880.

11. Isaac Walton, *The Compleat Angler* (London: Chatto and Windus, 1875), 140; Eugene Balon, *Domestication of the Carp* Cyprinus carpio (Ontario: Royal Ontario Museum, 1974).

12. "Organization of the American Acclimatization Society," *New York Times*, June 13, 1871.

13. "The Acclimatization Society," *New York Times*, March 21, 1878.

14. "More Foreign Birds for Oregon," *New York Times*, February 12, 1891; "Imported Song Birds Thrive," *New York Times*, December 27, 1895; "Imported Song Birds in Oregon," *New York Times*, January 18, 1897; "Cincinnati's Importation of Singing Birds from Germany," *New York Times*, May 5, 1873; "Importation of Song Birds," *New York Times*, May 8, 1874; Christopher Lever, *They Dined on Eland* (London: Quiller Paena, 1992), briefly discusses both the Cincinnati and Portland societies.

15. Kim Todd, "Words on the Wing," in *Tinkering with Eden: A History of Exotics in America* (New York: W. W. Norton, 2001), 3; "American Acclimatization Society," *New York Times*, November 15, 1877.

16. T. C. Boyle, "A Bird in the Hand," in *T. C. Boyle Stories* (New York: Viking, 1998), 602. My colleague Kurt Ayau told me about Boyle's story.

17. William J. Kern, *European Starling* (factsheet SS–WEC–118, University of Florida/IFAS, 1997, http://edis.ifas.ufl.edu/UW118; www.starlings.net; accessed February 5, 2004).

18. Meredith West and Andrew King, "Mozart's Starling," *American Scientist* (March/April 1990): 106–15.

19. Laurence Sterne, *A Sentimental Journey* (London: Chatto and Windus, 1912), 259–61, 272.

Misplaced Americans

1. Paul Radin, *The Trickster: A Study in American Indian Mythology* (New York: New York Philosophical Library, 1956), discusses the Coyote trickster cycle.

2. Meriwether Lewis and William Clark, *The Journals of the Voyage of Discovery*, quoted in Jeffrey Olson, "Wolves Were the Top Dogs in 1800," *Lewis and Clark: The Plants and Animals* (1999), annual magazine of the *Bismark Tribune*.

3. Quoted by Michelle Garland, "Species Report: Coyote," *Illinois Natural History Survey Report*, no. 366 (Winter 2001), http://www.inhs.uiuc.edu/chf/pub/surveyreports/winter-01/coyote.html (accessed January 5, 2004).

4. Rhode Island Department of Environmental Management, *The Eastern Coyote in Rhode Island*, http://www.state.ri.us/DEM/programs/bnatres/fishwild/pdf/coyotes.pdf (accessed January 5, 2004).

5. Environmental Protection Agency, "Sodium fluoroacetate (1080) Chemical Profile 8/90," *EPA Pesticide Fact Sheet*, no. 174 (October 1988 [updated August 1990]), http://pmep.cce.cornell.edu/profiles/rodent/sodium-fluoro/rod-prof-sod-fluoroacetate.html; *Livestock Protection Collar User Manual*, National Wildlife Research Center, USDA, http://www.aphis.usda.gov/ws/nwrc/research/EPA_products.html (accessed January 5, 2004); and Jessica Speart, "War on the Range," *Wildlife Conservation* (September/October 1992): 60–61.

6. Environmental Protection Agency, "Sodium Cyanide," *R.E.D. Facts* (September 1994), http://www.epa.gov/docs/REDs/factsheets/3086fact.pdf (accessed January 5, 2004).

7. Speart, "War on the Range."

8. Center for Disease Control, "Translocation of Coyote Rabies—Florida, 1994," in *Morbidity and Mortality Weekly Report* 44, no. 31 (1995): 580–581; 587, http://www.cdc.gov/mmwr/preview/mmwrhtml/00038451.htm (accessed January 5, 2004).

9. Mark Twain, *Roughing It*, 2 vols. (New York: Harper and Brothers, 1904), 1:48.

10. Ernest Thompson Seton, "The Coyote's Song" (1913), quoted in Garland, "Species Report: Coyote," (accessed March 3, 2004); and Terry Tempest Williams, "Redemption," in *An Unspoken Hunger: Stories from the Field* (New York: Vintage, 1995).

11. See, for example, the American Museum of Natural History, Bestiary index of extinct North American megafauna, http://www.amnh.org/science/biodiversity/extinction/ResourcesBestiaryFS.html (accessed December 19, 2003).

12. James A. McCann, Lori N. Arkin, and James D. Williams, *Nonindigenous Aquatic and Selected Terrestrial Species of Florida* (Gainesville, Florida, 1996), http://aquat1.ifas.ufl.edu/mccontnt.html (accessed December 19, 2003).

13. Ibid.

14. Larry L. Smith and Robin W. Doughty, *The Amazing Armadillo* (Austin: University of Texas Press, 1984), 67.

15. Ibid., 49–59.

16. Quoted online at *Biodiversity on the Internet*, www.biodiversity.org.uk/ibs/envmath/resources/year3/env324/projectsold/cameron/arch1.htm; Lev. 13: 45–46.

17. W. F. Kirchheimer and E. E. Storrs, "Attempts to Establish the Armadillo (*Dasypus novemcinctus*) as a Model for the Study of Leprosy: Report of Lepromatoid Leprosy in an Experimentally Infected Armadillo," *International Journal of Leprosy* 39 (1971):

693–702. There are dozens of articles on HD in armadillos, including Bruce S. Schroeder and others, "Armadillo Exposure and Hansen's Disease: An Epidemiologic Survey in Southern Texas," *Journal of the American Academy of Dermatology* 43 (2000): 223–8, and J. H. Smith and others, "Leprosy in Wild Armadillos (*Dasypus novemcinctus*) of the Texas Gulf Coast: Epidemiology and Mycobacteriology," *Journal of the Reticuloendothelial Society* 34, no. 2 (1983): 75–88.

18. Richard Henry Dana, *Two Years before the Mast* (New York: Doubleday, 1949), 271–71.

19. Larry Blakely, "Thomas Nuttall," *Who's in a Name? People Commemorated in Eastern Sierra Plant Names*, http://www.csupomona.edu/~larryblakely/whoname/who_nut.htm; James L. Reveal, "Thomas Nuttall," outline course material for History of Systematic Botany, PBIO 250, Norton-Brown Herbarium, University of Maryland, http://www.inform.umd.edu/PBIO/pb250/pltax62.html; Juel M. Trask, "Major Andrew Henry, Fur Trader—Early Western Adventurer," *Southwest Frontier and the Fur Trade*, http://klesinger.com/jbp/ahenry1.html (accessed January 7, 2004).

20. U.S. Department of Agriculture, National Resources Conservation Service, Plants Database, http://plants.usda.gov (information for *Solanum rostratum*; accessed February 26, 2004).

21. "Bugs, Worms, and Beetles," *New York Times*, July 13, 1896.

22. "Paris Green a Drug in the Market," *Minneapolis Tribune*, reprinted in *New York Times*, July 14, 1895. Paris green was the preferred insecticide at the time.

23. "Color Manufacture," *New York Times*, April 30, 1873; Andy Meharg, "The Arsenic Green," *Nature* 423, no. 688 (2003), http://www.nature.com/cgi-bin/doifinder.pl?URL=/doifinder/10.1038/423688a (accessed January 7, 2004).

24. "Millions of Fish and Fowl Dying," *New York Times*, August 9, 1878.

25. "Skirmishing with Beetles," *New York Times*, October 3, 1881; "Danger Lurking in Georgia Potatoes," *Charleston News*, quoted in *New York Times*, May 19, 1884; "Potato Bugs as Pets," *New York Times*, August 11, 1877.

26. Texas Cooperative Extension Program, "Did You Know," *Upper Coast Crop Improvement Newsletter*, vol. 6, no. 4 (2002), http://www.tpma.org/news_letters/_upper_coast/CIN05242002.html (accessed January 9, 2004). Druggists at the time also dispensed poisons and pesticides, explaining why farmers approached DeRyee. The weevil had first been spotted two years earlier at Brownsville, Texas.

27. Del Deterling, "The Boll Weevil: A Century of Pestilence," *Progressive Farmer* (October 1992); and W. P. Flint and C. L. Metcalf, *Insects: Man's Chief Competitors* (Baltimore: Williams and Wilkins, 1932), 129.

28. "War on the Boll Weevil," *New York Times*, January 29, 1903; "Boll Weevil Doesn't Like Castor Beans," *New York Times*, September 7, 1903; "He Claims $50,000 Prize," *New York Times*, October 15, 1903; "Quick Death to Boll Weevil," *New York Times*, April 18, 1904; "Boll Weevils Their Meat," *New York Times*, July 16, 1904; "Plea for the Swallows," *New York Times*, May 6, 1907.

29. Deterling, "The Boll Weevil"; Office of Pesticide Programs, Environmental Protection Agency, "Methyl Parathion Summary: Based on Recent Use Changes," http://www.epa.gov/pesticides/op/methyl_parathion/methylsum.htm; and Daniel Imhoff, "Food for Thought: King Cotton," *Sierra* (May 1999): 34–36.

30. National Cotton Council of America, "Boll Weevil Eradication," http://www.cotton.org/tech/pest/bollweevil/eradication2.cfm; Union of Concerned Scientists Web site, Food and Environment, "Bt Cotton," October 22, 2002, http://www.ucsusa.org/food_and_environment/biotechnology_archive/page.cfm?pageID=360 (accessed January 8, 2004).

31. Shelley Brigman, "Boll Weevil," http://www.geocities.com/skibbie61/weeevil.html (accessed January 8, 2004). Brigman cites Roy Shoffner's *Enterprise–the First 110 Years* (Tallahassee: Rose, 1996) as her major source.

Gone Fishin'

1. U.S. Environmental Protection Agency, Office of Water, "Appendix B: Total Lake, Reservoir, and Pond Acres in the Nation," in *Water Quality Condition in the United States: A Profile from the 1998 National Water Quality Inventory: Report to Congress* (Washington, D.C.: Office of Water, 2000); and Ronald W. Tuttle, "Farm Ponds," in *Encyclopedia of Water Science*, ed. B. A. Stewart and Terry A. Howell (New York: Marcel Dekker, 2003).

2. Kenneth Brower, "Can of Worms," *Atlantic Monthly* (March 1999).

3. *Worm Watch Canada*, http://www.naturewatch.ca/english/wormwatch/index.html (accessed March 9, 2004).

4. Charles Darwin, *The Formation of Vegetable Mould through the Action of Worms* (New York: D. Appleton, 1886), 36–43.

5. Christina Bjergo and others, "Non-native Aquatic Species in the United States and Coastal Waters," in *Our Living Resources* (Washington, D.C.: U.S. Department of the Interior, National Biological Service, 1995); U.S. Geological Survey, Nonindigenous Aquatic Species Database, http://nas.er.usgs.gov/queries (information for *Pygocentrus nattererei*; accessed March 10, 2004).

6. USGS, Nonindigenous Aquatic Species Database (information for *Micropterus dolomieu*).

7. Ibid.

8. Kentucky State University Aquaculture Program, "Largemouth Bass," http://www.ksuaquaculture.org/fish.lmbass.htm (accessed March 10, 2004).

9. U.S. Department of Agriculture, National Agricultural Statistics Service, *Trout Production*, Report, February 27, 2004, http://usda.gov/nass/pubs/reportname.htm (accessed April 8, 2004).

10. USGS, Nonindigenous Aquatic Species Database (information for *Oncorhynchus mykiss*; accessed March 10, 2004).

11. USGS, Nonindigenous Aquatic Species Database (information for *Salmo trutta*; accessed March 9, 2004).

12. "Discussions about Fish," *New York Times*, April 4, 1882.

13. "Brown Trout Acclimatized," *New York Times*, November 20, 1885.

14. Norman Maclean, *A River Runs through It and Other Stories* (Chicago: University of Chicago Press, 1976), 5. Henry David Thoreau, *The Annotated Walden*, ed. Philip Van Doren Stern (New York: Clarkson N. Potter, 1970), 229–30.

15. Thoreau, *The Annotated Walden*, 229–30, 306–7.

16. Maclean, *A River Runs through It*, 2.

17. David Crockett, *The Life of David Crockett* (New York: A. L. Burt, 1902), 347–48.

18. John Lawson, *A New Voyage to Carolina*, ed. Hugh Lefler (Chapel Hill: University of North Carolina Press, 1967), 17.

19. Harriet Beecher Stowe, *The Annotated Uncle Tom's Cabin*, ed. Philip Van Doren Stern (New York: Eriksson, 1964), 207–8.

20. Sojourner Truth, *The Narrative of Sojourner Truth*, ed. Jeffrey Stewart (New York, 1991), 196–97.

21. Reed F. Noss and others, *Endangered Ecosystems of the United States: A Preliminary Assessment of Loss and Degradation*, U.S. Geological Survey, Biological Resources, http://biology.usgs.gov/pubs/ecosys.htm (accessed March 10, 2004).

22. Lawson, *A New Voyage*, 107.

23. Francis Porcher, *Resources of the Southern Fields and Forests, Medical, Economical, and Agricultural. Being also a Medical Botany of the Confederate States; with Practical Information on the Useful Properties of the Trees, Plants, and Shrubs* (Charleston, S.C.: Evans and Cogswell, 1863), 587; U.S. Forest Service, Fire Effect Information System database (information for *Arundinaria gigantea*; accessed March 10, 2004).

24. Isabel Cunningham, *Frank N. Meyer: Plant Hunter in Asia* (Ames: Iowa State University Press, 1984), 13.

Index

Bosisto, Joseph, 73
bottle gourd, 118–23
Bouquet, Henry, 82
Boyle, T. C., 167
Broussonetia papyrifera. See mulberry, paper
Brown, John, 32
Bt, 40–41, 184–85
Bubonic plague. *See* Black Death
Bubulcus ibis. See cattle egret
Burkholderia mallei. See glanders
Burroughs, William S., 148

calamus. *See* sweet flag
California, 33, 74–75
Canadian night crawler, 189
cane, 197–99
Canis domesticus. See dog
Canis latrans. See coyote
Cannabis indica. See marijuana
Cannabis sativa. See marijuana
Carassius auratus. See goldfish
carp, 161–65
Carroll, Lewis, 65
carrot, 124–29
Carson, Rachel, 40
Carver, George Washington, 14
Castile soap, 103–4
Castle, William, 155
Catesby, Mark, 9
catfish, 196
cattle egret, 119
cattle tick, 95–96
cattle, 94–98
centipede grass, 27–28
Charleston grass, 26–27
Cheney, Ward, 31–32
Cherokee, 82, 115
Cherry Blossom Festival, 160
Cheyenne, 115–16
Chickasaw, 120
Chinchona. See quinine
Chipley, Florida, 160
Chivington, John, 115–16

Choctaw, 30, 82, 120
cholera, 82–84
Cibola, 122
Cincinnati Society of Acclimatization, 165
Citrillus lanatus. See watermelon
Clemens, Samuel. *See* Twain, Mark
clover. *See* white clover
Cobb, Jonathan, 31
cockroach, American, 143–45
Cockroach, German, 143, 145–47
cockroach, Oriental, 147–48
Coleridge, Samuel Taylor, 48–49, 136, 140
colonial bent grass. *See* Rhode Island grass
Compound 1080, 172
Compsilura concinnata, 41
Connor, Patrick Edward, 115
constipation, 134
Cooper, Ellwood, 74
Cope, Channing, 161
Cornwallis, Charles, 84
Cornwallis, Edward, 84
Coronado, Francisco Vásquez de, 94
Cortez, Hernando, 30, 92, 113
coumarin, 22–23
cowpea, 13–17
coyote, 170–74
Coyote, Wile E., 172, 173
crab lice, 114
creeping bent grass, 22
Crevecoeur, Hector St. John de, 21
Crockett, Davy, 198
Croton bug, 145–46
Culpepper, Nicholas, 132–33, 139
Cunningham, John, 127
cyanide gas, 146–47
Cynodon dactylon. See Bermuda grass
Cyprinus carpio. See carp

Dana, Henry, 178
darnel, 25
Darwin, Charles, 124, 188